Management for Professionals

More information about this series at
http://www.springer.com/series/10101

Daniel Simon • Christian Schmidt

Editors

Business Architecture Management

Architecting the Business
for Consistency and Alignment

 Springer

Editors
Daniel Simon
Scape Consulting GmbH
Cologne
Germany

Christian Schmidt
Scape Consulting GmbH
Frankfurt/Main
Germany

ISSN 2192-8096 ISSN 2192-810X (electronic)
Management for Professionals
ISBN 978-3-319-14570-9 ISBN 978-3-319-14571-6 (eBook)
DOI 10.1007/978-3-319-14571-6

Library of Congress Control Number: 2015938181

Springer Cham Heidelberg New York Dordrecht London
© Springer International Publishing Switzerland 2015

Printed on acid-free paper

Springer International Publishing AG Switzerland is part of Springer Science+Business Media (www.springer.com)

Foreword

The act of undertaking enterprise architecture has much in common with wine tasting. The critics of enterprise architecture would probably say: "I agree; both activities are expensive, overly analytical, and the participants get caught up in long-winded debates about definitions and subtleties that most people don't care about!"

As you can imagine, this is not my opinion and definitely not the point I'm trying to make here. Rather, the commonalties I see between both activities are that they mean different things to different people, that they are concerned with collective meaning-making, and that they are deeply social in nature.

Deciding if a wine is good is greatly determined by personal preferences. Don't get me wrong, wine connoisseurs may reach a consensus and affirm that a certain wine is well balanced. However, such a consensus says neither very much about the personal preferences of each wine connoisseur nor what wine they would enjoy during a supper with close friends. Similarly, the literature on enterprise architecture offers a large range of definitions and perspectives on the meaning of the term "enterprise architecture" as well as what constitutes its adequate (good) practice. Despite this lack of unanimous agreement, a pragmatic practitioner will notice, in general, that there is agreement that enterprise architecture is about helping enterprises to be more effective and that it is important to understand both the business and technical aspects in order to reach this goal. Like wine tasting, enterprise architecture is about getting together with other people and trying to make sense of our experiences, our reality. Whereas wine tasting is concerned with the sensorial experiences procured by wine consuming, enterprise architecture is concerned with the realities of working and evolving in an enterprise. Moreover, both activities are very social in nature in that both activities require and unfold in the context of people interacting together.

I have been an enterprise architecture practitioner and scholar for a number of years now. I have participated in enterprise architecture-related activities that have been recognized by MIT, Gartner, and Forrester. Through these activities, like many readers of this book, I have often experienced the challenges of doing enterprise architecture and trying to help enterprises be more effective. Often, the literature had little to offer me on how to actually do the work and have effective meaning-making discussions with fellow workers about the enterprise we shared. This was especially true when discussing the nontechnical aspects of the enterprise.

In the field, in my experience, the term "business architecture" is steadily establishing itself as the de facto term when referring to the concerns of making sense and evolving the business aspects of an enterprise. Sadly, in my opinion, despite its importance, it is still very underdeveloped and fragmented. A great deal of the available material overly focuses on modeling and refers very little to the wealth of knowledge that exists on the subjects of enterprises, organizations, and their design: knowledge that lies in the fields of management, sociology, psychology, and many others.

The value of this book lies in the fact that the authors are contributing to the development of business architecture and its practices in a way that is useful for practitioners and academics and also makes use of existing knowledge provided by important organizational scholars such as Demings, Argyris, Schein, Porter, Ansoff, Martin, Kaplan, Norton, Mintzberg, Drucker, and Friedman.

As stated by Schopenhauer: "Thus the task is not so much to see what no one yet has seen, but to think what nobody yet has thought about that which everybody sees." Accordingly, this book offers a refreshing way to think about business architecture in the context of enterprise architecture. This book is one of very few that provides a business-oriented perspective on business architecture, a perspective that contrasts with available literature that is mostly technically oriented. In other words, the book goes beyond depicting business architecture, like many technically oriented perspectives do, as concerned with modeling the non-IT aspects of an enterprise (e.g., processes and organization structure) using standards (e.g., BPMN and ArchiMate). Rather, the book discusses business architecture in a way that is relevant and meaningful for non-IT professionals who must make decisions.

Enjoy

École de technologie supérieure   James Lapalme
Montreal, Canada

Preface

Without doubt, enterprise architecture (EA) management has evolved to become an important discipline in practice throughout the past years. In essence, it advocates being intentional about the architecture of the enterprise and managing its constituents as a coherent whole rather than as isolated parts—in line with what one of the authors in this book calls "things work better when they work together, on purpose." From a conceptual point of view, one aspect area to be managed as such is the business architecture. But are we not often told that EA management at its core is in fact about the information technology (IT)? Obviously, this tends to be propagated or at least practiced as such by some professionals in the field, showing only moderate awareness for the business architecture and associated management practices. However, one may also consider it an unforced restriction of the overall scope in EA management that prevents essentials of the business from being addressed in a way as holistic and systematic as this is usually the case with IT landscapes today.

Reviewing the literature, it becomes apparent that there are only few books on EA management that deal with the business architecture in a comprehensive way and focus on how to use it in practice. In addition, those works that do cover it to some extent usually take up an IT-oriented perspective on that part of the enterprise architecture as well. As indicated, a reason for this might be the fact that "enterprise architecture management" is often equated with "enterprise IT architecture management."

This is also evident in our own work as practitioners in the field. Quite frequently, we hear statements questioning the role of architecture in the business and suggesting the IT to be the "center of the universe" in EA management:

- "Enterprise architecture? That's about the application systems, data, and technologies used to support the business—it gives us a structured description of our IT landscape."
- "Business architecture? You mean the processes? Yes, this is where you should map your application systems to."

- "Strategy and business model? That's none of our business. Of course, it's relevant, but that's not architecture, right?"
- "Well, but how does this affect the IT? Why should we look into this if it does not have any implications on the IT?"
- "Business folks are not interested in architecture. Architectural approaches do not really help there; they only work in the IT."

To experienced architects in the field, this may sound familiar. For us, such claims to some extent set the motivational foundation for this book. Enterprises consist of much more than information technology; considering only this part or viewing the enterprise architecture only from that single perspective will thus not provide a holistic understanding of the enterprise and allow it to be managed in such a way. Furthermore, the enterprise—as some purposive, bold endeavor or under-taking—is by definition a motivational entity with a clear purpose; architecting efforts going beyond the IT will thus have to include this part as well.

The intention of this book therefore is to provide a "breath of fresh air" in this respect. While some might argue that architecting the business does not happen in practice, this book demonstrates the opposite: it provides various examples of real-life business architecture management. This is also supported by experiences from our own practice: throughout different engagements, business architecture has proven to be a crucial instrument not only to facilitate the dialog with the business (from an IT point of view) but also to support strategy making and translation into proper execution.

Even in a lack of such practical insights and success stories, there would still be the question of alternatives to help coherently manage the increasing complexity and dynamics in today's enterprises. From our experience, this question usually remains unanswered. This book, in contrast, provides answers: it details the concept of business architecture, illustrates approaches of how to bring it to reasonable use, and explains the role it may thus play to master the aforementioned challenges. To achieve this, we strived to integrate both experiences from practice and the latest research. Armed with this diverse input, the book is supposed to represent a progressive piece of work in terms of the business aspects of EA management, addressed in a way that is meaningful for non-IT professionals as well.

This book would not have become a reality without the support of some people in our professional environment. First of all, we would like to thank the individual authors who made the effort to write a chapter and shared their personal experiences and/or valuable insights about business architecture management. Second, we would like to thank all colleagues in the architecture management field with whom we have worked on business architecture themes and had fruitful discussions in the past years. These discussions have been a major inspiration for us to edit this book. In addition, we acknowledge the support of James Lapalme, who was willing to contribute a foreword to this book, to review and comment on some of the manuscripts, and to give advice in the final steps of this book's production. Finally, we are grateful to all who remain passionate about bringing architectural thinking into the business and keep pointing out that enterprise architecture management is about more than just "structure and vision" for the IT landscape.

We trust that you will enjoy this book and will find it inspiring. Feel free to contact us with questions and comments concerning contents of this book or architecture management matters in general.

Cologne, Germany   Daniel Simon
Frankfurt, Germany   Christian Schmidt

Contents

Introduction: Demystifying Business Architecture

Daniel Simon

Abstract

Business architecture management is no longer a buzz phrase, it has become reality in many organizations. However, there is still some way ahead to further proliferate the business architecture concept and help grasp its meaning and use. To this end, following the outline of this book's motivation and specific objectives, this chapter introduces a comprehensive business architecture framework, including business motivation, business model, and business execution as the main constituents. This framework represents this book's foundation. Finally, this chapter explains the corresponding structure of this book and briefly introduces the individual contributions.

1.1 Background

Since the late 1980s, enterprise architecture (EA) management has garnered increasing attention in both research and practice. In particular, this is due to the holistic and structured view it takes toward an enterprise's elements and their relationships, as rooted in the understanding of the term *"enterprise architecture,"* as the "fundamental concepts and properties" of the enterprise "in its environment, embodied in its elements, their relationships, and the principles of its design and evolution" (ISO 2013). In other words, it can be considered an abstract and integrated conception of the enterprise that includes different aspect areas (including, e.g., information systems architecture) and that may be captured (and thus documented) for different temporal states (e.g., current, target). Enterprise architecture elements may thus range from goals and strategies via products and business capabilities to applications and technology components, for example.

D. Simon (✉)
Scape Consulting GmbH, Cologne, Germany
e-mail: daniel.simon@scape-consulting.de

© Springer International Publishing Switzerland 2015
D. Simon, C. Schmidt (eds.), *Business Architecture Management*, Management for Professionals, DOI 10.1007/978-3-319-14571-6_1

It has been widely acknowledged that an integral part of the overall enterprise architecture—and thus one main aspect area—is represented by the *business architecture*. According to Gharajedaghi (2011), business architecture can be considered "a general description of a system. It identifies its purpose, vital functions, active elements, and critical processes and defines the nature of the interaction between them." With the relevant system being the enterprise, this is in line with the Business Architecture Guild (2014), considering the business architecture as "*a blueprint of the enterprise that provides a common understanding [. . .] and is used to align strategic objectives and tactical demands.*" As such, it does not begin or end at the bounds of the organization, but may represent portions of a business that have been outsourced, for example.

The business architecture thus represents a multi-faceted area (in terms of the various elements of relevance). As put in simple words by Friedman (1962), ultimately the "business of a business is business." It is thus of crucial importance for designers of a business architecture (whether they call themselves architects or not) to understand the desired future of the enterprise and the way the "business generates value, creates a deliverable package, and exchanges it with money" (i.e., the business model), for example (cf. Gharajedaghi 2011). It may be considered the primary purpose of *business architecture management*, then, "*to identify and communicate the strategic and operational characteristics of the business to multiple audiences.*" In that way, it may ultimately facilitate strategic decision making with respect to, for example, potential mergers, acquisitions, divestitures, and outsourcing opportunities (Wilson 2007).[1]

All too often, however, the business architecture—especially when it comes to the strategic facets—still remains a minor matter in the overall EA context, since much of the focus of attention centers on the information technology (IT) parts (Simon et al. 2013). Actual management of the business architecture still seems in its infancy; to some extent, there still appear to be difficulties among practitioners in grasping business architecture's meaning and use, which obviously hinder its adoption and proliferation. For EA management to become an accepted discipline not only among IT managers but also among business folks, a comprehensive yet straightforward approach to business architecture is essential though.

1.2   Objectives of the Book

Despite the overall progression of the EA management field throughout the past years, business architecture has apparently remained some sort of forgotten constituent; in fact, only limited progress has been made toward fully capturing the business elements of the enterprise architecture and treating these as actual design

---

[1] While not every organization formally recognizes and thus explicitly documents it, one may argue that every business has an architecture. Business architecture management, then, is about being intentional (and strategic) about it.

variables (rather than sole context factors for development of the IT architecture). At the same time, the need for business architecture becomes increasingly prevalent in the different areas of strategic management. For example, systems thinking (cf. Gharajedaghi 2011), which can be considered a basic architectural principle, is recognized as a promising means to facilitate the examination of the cause-and-effect-relationships between different strategic measures (Wang and College 2006). In addition, research reports an insufficient consideration of relations and dependencies between different elements of the business model in today's state of the art as well as an absence of formalized means of graphical representations that allow structured and comparable visualizations of business models (Burkhart et al. 2011)—issues that one may expect to be resolved by making use of an architectural approach.

This book aims to reduce this gap and advance the knowledge in the field of business architecture, stretching from business motivation and model to business execution (as detailed later in this chapter). The book focuses on the use of architectural thinking in these areas, thus aligning different parts to a consistent whole. As such, the book is targeted not only at architecture professionals and researchers but also others working in the strategic business management field, whether they explicitly label their activities as architectural work or not. Specifically, this book serves the following purposes:

- Help grasp the concept of business architecture by offering a comprehensive and systematic framework
- Facilitate the effective management of the business architecture by depicting techniques for bringing business architecture to use and providing guidelines on how to develop core business architecture artifacts
- Contribute to a greater understanding among business professionals of how architectural approaches can support their work
- Illustrate to architects how architectural approaches can be used way beyond the management of the IT landscape
- Help organizations develop their business architecture management practices further by presenting innovative approaches and going beyond what the majority of organizations already does in the business architecture space
- Provide practice-oriented advice on how to establish business architecture management

In line with this book's dedicated focus on the business content of the overall enterprise architecture, there is only a limited discussion of IT architecture aspects. This does not mean the book intends to suggest substituting the IT focus in current architecture management practices with a business focus, but giving due consideration to the integral role of the business architecture in the overall enterprise architecture, including its relevance at points where IT is not even affected or not yet an issue.

1.3 Foundation of the Book: The Business Architecture Framework

This book's understanding of business architecture is based on a three-constituent content framework consisting of *business motivation, business model*, and *business execution* (see Fig. 1.1 for a high-level view), as originally been put forth by Simon et al. (2014). The framework is not meant to prescribe that the three constituent areas necessarily have to be treated as one architectural domain and be labelled as such (that is, this book's intention is not to have some sort of scope war in which it takes a dogmatic position), but to capture and structure the non-IT elements of the enterprise architecture, including those that may not even been directly related to IT at all. Similar to as it is done in the enterprise IT architecture space (with, e.g., application architecture, data architecture, technology architecture), one may also have three dedicated architecture domains here and call these motivation architecture, business architecture (that is, in the purest sense as being represented by the business model), and organizational (or operational) architecture, for example.[2] Also note that the framework is not meant to say that the three constituent areas necessarily have to be (completely) implemented at once (see Chap. 15 for an illustration of a concern-oriented approach); there may be some elements that are essential right from the beginning [one may wonder whether, e.g., strategies are not always required in an architecture model; so calling these extensions (according to, e.g., The Open Group 2011, 2013) is actually misleading], but others may be added step by step later.

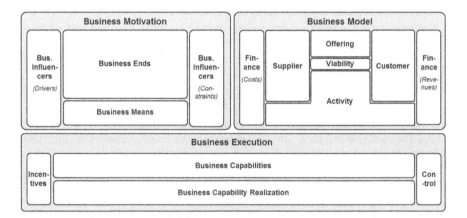

Fig. 1.1 Business architecture framework

---

[2] Areas such as brand architecture, financial architecture, etc. may here be considered cross-cutting themes.

1.3.1 Business Motivation

In general, the business motivation captures the enterprise's strategic direction and explains why it operates in a certain way. One may distinguish between three main types of elements within the business motivation (see Fig. 1.2): business ends, business means, and business influencers (OMG 2010). Fundamental *business ends* are the mission and core values of the enterprise. While the mission represents the fundamental purpose beyond just making money and can be considered a declaration of the reason for being (Drucker 1973) of an enterprise that reveals what it "wants to be and whom it wants to serve" (David 2013), the core values are the essential and enduring tenets of an enterprise, requiring no external justification but having an intrinsic value and importance to those inside the enterprise. Values thus capture the ideals, customs, or institutions an enterprise promotes or agrees with (OMG 2010). Together, mission and core values constitute the core ideology of an enterprise (cf. Collins and Porras 1994, 1996).

The vision represents the overall image (challenging, maybe even unattainable) of what the enterprise wants to become (OMG 2010). It should be noted that, as depicted colorfully in Chap. 14, the scope of the vision should extend beyond the organization itself to include different perspectives within the overall enterprise and thus become meaningful for all relevant stakeholders (including, e.g., partners, investors). It is not a one-time, specific target that can be met and then discarded. In that way, it is supposed to provide a continuous source of motivation (cf. Kantabutra and Avery 2010).

More focused than a vision, goals and objectives then represent certain results desired with respect to the state or condition of the enterprise (or parts thereof). Objectives are more specific than goals, thus being time-targeted and measurable, for example. As such, objectives quantify goals and may be linked with key

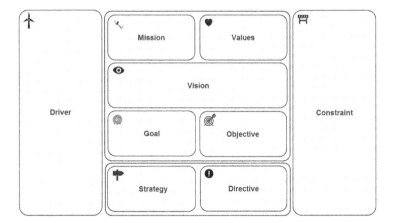

Fig. 1.2 Business motivation content

performance indicators; they can be considered targets that the enterprise seeks to meet to achieve its goals (cf. OMG 2010).

Business means represent the instruments employed to achieve the various ends. At the core of these means is the strategy—a general course of action (potentially be detailed by tactics) that sets direction and channels efforts towards goals/objectives (and thus provides focus on what is important and what is not) (cf. OMG 2010).[3] One may distinguish between corporate strategy for general market definition, competitive strategy for specific market navigation and leapfrogging respective competitors, and functional strategy here (cf. Simon et al. 2014). In addition to that, directives may be used to constrain or liberate behavior, whether it relates to how defined courses of action should be carried out (OMG 2010) or, in general, to provide a framework or, say, guide rails for decision making. Directives may come in the form of principles and maybe even policies (as long as the latter is still not directly enforceable), for example.

The employment of business means and already the definition of ends are affected by *business influencers*, as either drivers or constraints of strategic choice. These can be internal or external to the enterprise, the latter of which may be categorized according to the well-known PEST scheme (political, economic, social, and technological), for example (cf. Peng and Nunes 2007). An assessment of these influencers may result in a classification into strengths and weaknesses (both internal) as well as opportunities and threats (both external) (OMG 2010).

1.3.2   Business Model

Strategies add up to a certain business model (or even a portfolio of business models for larger and highly diversified enterprises). As some sort of conceptual blueprint of the strategy, the business model "expresses the fundamental business logic and therefore represents the entire system of creating and delivering value to customers, capturing this value by earning profits from these activities and sustaining this value capture" (Simon et al. 2014). As such, the business model can be considered to consist of six main aspects: (1) offering, (2) customer, (3) supplier, (4) activity, (5) finance, and (6) sustainability/viability, each of which captures a number of concepts that together make up the business model (see Fig. 1.3).

---

[3] This understanding of strategy is closer to and thus focuses on what Mintzberg (1987) calls "strategy as plan" (as to, e.g., the position in the environment) rather than "strategy as perspective" (Mintzberg 1987), as the latter may encompass several motivational aspects (e.g., mission, values) that would then all fall under the concept "strategy" and could not be distinguished from one another. In simple words, strategy (in this book's framework) is thus about "determining how we are going to win in the period ahead" (Mind Tools 2014), in line with the "policy core" (Mintzberg 1987) defined by concepts such as mission and values. It should be noted, though, that the act of "strategy making" (and likewise a resulting strategy document) does not only deal with the concept "strategy" but also incorporates, e.g., goals and objectives (as outlined in Chap. 2).

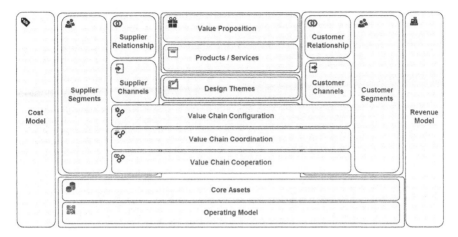

Fig. 1.3 Business model content

Offering The *value proposition*, as a "promise of value to be delivered" (Kettleborough 2012) to the customer, describes "the unique mix of product and service attributes, customer relations, and corporate image that a company offers" (Kaplan and Norton 2000). In essence, the value proposition reflects "the reason why customers turn to one company over another" (Osterwalder and Pigneur 2010). It is based on selected *products* and/or *services* that cater to the needs of specific customer segments, either as gain creators or as pain relievers (cf. Business Model Foundry 2013). In fact, there are different value disciplines that might be incorporated into one's value proposition to the customer. Most prominently, these are product leadership, operational excellence, and customer intimacy (cf. Treacy and Wiersema 1993) (see Chap. 4 for further details); the choice for one discipline will likely determine the operating model to some extent as well (see below).

Customer/Supplier As indicated, a value proposition relates to the needs of specific *customer segments*. These are the groups of people and/or organizations with, e.g., common needs and behaviors, that the enterprise aims to reach and serve (cf. Osterwalder and Pigneur 2010). Segmentation may be based on different aspects, such as geographies, product characteristics, time, and demographics.

Such segments are reached via *customer channels*, for both communication and distribution/sales. They represent the enterprise's interface with the targeted customer segments. Due to their crucial role in the customer experience, these touch points should be given due consideration in business model design. In a similar vein, to facilitate customer growth and retention, the used types of *customer relationships* represent an important part of the business model. These can range from a self-service model to personal assistance and collaboration/co-creation (e.g., via customer workshops), for example (cf. Osterwalder and Pigneur 2010). Essentially, analogical concepts are to be considered at the supply side of the business model, including *supplier segments*, *supplier channels*, and *supplier relationships*.

Activity The *value chain configuration* sets out the main stages of the business' value chain and determines at what of these stages one is involved to what extent. One may decide to have customers carrying out key value chain activities themselves, for example, acknowledging the increasing relevance of approaches such as customer co-creation and open innovation. Related closely to the value chain's overall configuration is the concept of *value chain cooperation*. This may include the use of strategic partnerships with respect to certain parts of the value chain.

Value chain coordination, finally, addresses the question of when and by whom decisions as to product, distribution, price, and so on are made within the value chain and by whom or what the corresponding activities are triggered. There are specific mechanisms for coordination. Postponement, for example, means retaining the product in a neutral status as long as possible and thus postpone differentiation of form and identity to the latest possible point, i.e., nearer to the time of purchase, where demand is likely to be more predictable ("manufacturing postponement"), and/or maintaining a full-line of anticipatory inventory at one or few strategic locations ("logistics postponement"). In contrast, speculation means that changes in form and the movement of goods to forward inventories should be made at the earliest possible time (Bucklin 1965; Pagh and Cooper 1998).

Core assets comprise the tangible and intangible input factors for value creation. There are different types of assets that are key in terms of enabling a certain value proposition to the customer. In particular, one may distinguish core competencies, intellectual assets (incl. know-how, networks, reputation), and physical resources (cf. Wirtz 2011; Osterwalder and Pigneur 2010).

According to Ross et al. (2006), the *operating model* can be understood as an abstract representation of the enterprise's level of business process standardization and integration and, in future terms, may thus be considered as "a general vision of how a company will enable and execute strategies." One may distinguish between different stereotypes of operating models, e.g., diversification (low standardization, low integration), coordination (low standardization, high integration), replication (high standardization, low integration), and unification (high standardization, high integration). In a broader sense, beyond the description of how the enterprise operates across different business units/fields, one may also view the operating model as a representation of significant patterns of business operations to also include, for example, staffing aspects (e.g., contract or permanent), the division of responsibilities within the enterprise, or fundamental ways of working such as lean manufacturing and open innovation. Based on numerous examples of real-life operating models that significantly contribute to the process of value capture (e.g., Apple; see Chap. 4), we argue that the operating model should actually be seen as a fundamental part of the business model (note that the realization or, say, actual content in terms of business processes, organizational units etc. is captured at the business execution level though).

Sustainability/Viability A fundamental concept to business models to sustain value capture and any competitive advantage given a certain business model is what we call "*design themes*." They represent common threads that somehow orchestrate and connect the different elements of the business model (cf. Zott and Amit 2009) or, more generally, dictate their configuration in order to ensure the business model's sustainability/viability. Examples are branding, patenting, cross selling/complementarities, and customer lock-in.

Finance The *revenue model* presents the main streams of revenue, including the associated sales volumes and the mechanisms used in terms of pricing (e.g., fixed-list prices, volume-dependent prices, subscription fees, licensing). On the other hand, the *cost model* identifies the main sources of costs incurred to operate the business model along with the costs' structures or, say, main characteristics (e.g., fixed costs, variable costs). For cost-driven enterprises this part of the business model is essential, as their positioning in the market is based strongly on cost structures (cf. Osterwalder and Pigneur 2010).

1.3.3 Business Execution

Operating a business model requires appropriate structures, utilities, individuals, and so on. These are captured in the business execution constituent of the framework (see Fig. 1.4), thus comprising those elements necessary to execute the business model. At the core of these elements are the business capabilities. A *business capability* is an ability or capacity of the business to perform a particular kind of work and achieve a specific purpose (cf. Ulrich and Rosen 2011). More specifically, it is an ability to execute certain activities (or, say, a pattern of activities) and produce desired outcomes (e.g., product, service) by deploying specific resources and expertise and processing information through a defined series of steps in a dedicated organizational and cultural environment (cf. Simon et al. 2014). Business capabilities encapsulate the elements used to actually realize the outcome and thus abstract from their realization or, say, configuration (cf., e.g.,

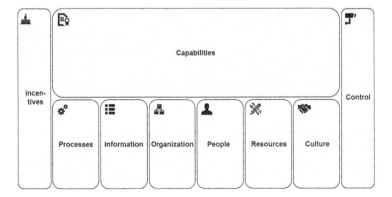

Fig. 1.4 Business execution content

UK Ministry of Defence 2010, defining a capability configuration as a set of "resources"—including their interactions—that when brought together provide a capability); they represent what the business is able to do (or, in future terms, what it will need to be able to do), not how this is done. So, as Wilson (2007) explains, a "key benefit that capability modeling provides over business process modeling is that it focuses on those parts of the business architecture that are the most stable."

As indicated, there are different elements that play a role in *business capability realization*: business processes, information entities, organizational structures, people, resources, and culture. To start off, a business process represents a series of activities or tasks to produce a defined set of products or services or, in general, to accomplish a specific objective [note that a higher-level process of a rather end-to-end character may be considered a "value stream" (Ulrich and Rosen 2011)]. The activities captured within a business process operate on specific information objects. One may also use the term "business object" to represent the informational elements that are relevant in the business (still independent from any IT realization though). As such, they are the fundamental objects of business activity, for which information are gathered, processed, and exchanged (e.g., order, contract, customer).

The organizational structure, then, captures the (executing) units of business activity (divisions/departments, legal entities, locations/sites), along with relevant roles, job positions, and committees. These are assumed or composed of specific individuals, which with their skills make up the people dimension of capability realization. In addition to the (human) expertise captured in the people dimension, there is another important element of capability realization to account for the tangible assets such as (raw) material, equipment, and so on, which are used in certain business processes. This is what the resource concept represents.

The final element of capability realization is culture. In general, the culture of a group can be considered a "pattern of shared basic assumptions that the group learned as it solved its problems of external adaptation and internal integration, that has worked well enough to be considered valid and, therefore, to be taught to new members as the correct way to perceive, think, and feel in relation to those problems" (Schein 1997). For sure, culture already begins in the business motivation, in which values as a representation of preferences for one way of acting over another may be found (see above). As will be explained in Chap. 7, however, culture can be described further (i.e., the "living" constituents of culture, as part of business execution) in terms of evidence (i.e., things that are directly observable such as, e.g., meeting structures, furnishings), acted values (which may be different from stated values), and assumptions (i.e., unspoken rules and beliefs that the values are based on).

These are driven by systems, rules, and structures, both formal and informal, that reward (or punish) behavior (thus to be considered as "levers"), which eventually leads us to the governance facets of business execution. The first one is controls, which refer to compliance to desired behavior, on the one hand, and overall performance, on the other hand. The second one is incentives; here, one may distinguish positive incentives for motivational purposes from deterrents or, say,

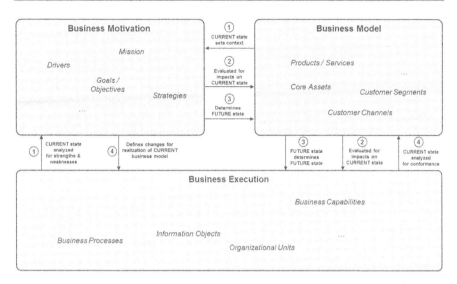

Fig. 1.5 Relationships between the business architecture constituents

safeguards to discourage opportunistic tendencies and enforce desired behavior. These are essential for ensuring the adequate and effective application of the business capabilities and their underlying realization.

1.3.4   Relationships Between the Business Architecture Constituents

The constituent parts of the business architecture, that is, business motivation, business model, and business execution, should not be considered independent from each other. In contrast, managing one part requires at least some consideration of the other parts (see Fig. 1.5):

1. The current state of the business model,[4] including, for example, the offered products and the targeted customer segments, sets the context for (re-) developing the business motivation; it may actually be analyzed in terms of how it works today with respect to customer retention and the logic of cash flow generation (e.g., earn before spend), for example. In addition, the current state of business execution (most likely at the business capability level) may be analyzed for strengths and weaknesses to inform business motivation development.
2. Once strategy options are identified based on that input, they may be evaluated for any impacts on the business model, and in turn, on business execution in its

---

[4] Again, for larger and highly diversified enterprises this may be an entire portfolio of business models, in which diverse (past and current) strategies are reflected.

current state (in terms of what is affected); this is to assess feasibility and, in case of a set of strategy options, to test whether these are mutually supportive and internally consistent (cf. Simon et al. 2014).

3. Once strategic choices are made, this "new" business motivation is translated into a future state of the business model, which, in turn, determines the future state of business execution. This is the case when an organization lives up to its business model, but has identified opportunities for improvement or for even adding a completely new business model [which may initially be tested with "customer development" (cf. Cooper and Vlaskovits 2010), for example].

4. It may, however, occur that an organization does not adequately live up to its business model (in terms of, e.g., costs)—a possible finding from analyzing the current state of business execution for conformance with the business model. In that case, strategies may need to be identified that define changes in the business execution for a proper realization of the current business model, which itself would remain unchanged. In addition, there may be further strategies that do not necessarily affect the business model but, being of a rather "internal" character, may only and immediately impact the execution level (in terms of, e.g., control systems, leadership, incentives, organizational structures, changes to improve employee satisfaction) to optimize and sustain the realization of the business model.

1.4 Outline of the Book

Based on the framework used as a common reference by the different chapters, the book covers a wide spectrum of content in the business architecture arena and considers diverse input for that purpose. In terms of content, there are different aspects that speak to this book's comprehensive character:

- First, business architecture management as described in this book does not take place only at the level of business operations, but also incorporates the strategic/motivational and business model part, as embodied in the introduced business architecture framework.
- Second, in terms of the organizational settings dealt with in the individual chapters, this book is not restricted to cases of large corporations but also addresses business architecture management in small-to-medium enterprises (see Chap. 14).
- Finally, from a geographical point of view, this book includes cases from diverse regions of the world, including Europe as well as North and Middle America.

Similarly, there is a variety of input that makes this book a multi-faceted and particularly rich contribution:

- First, the book contains works of authors from different countries over the world, including, in particular, Germany, the Netherlands, Switzerland, the United Kingdom, and the United States.

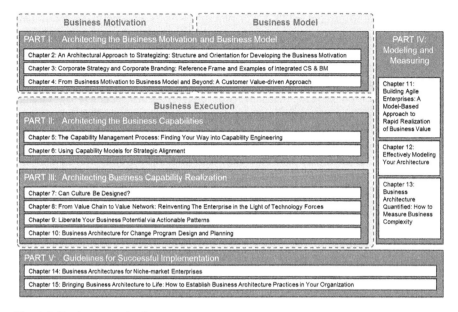

Fig. 1.6 Book structure/navigator

- Second, contributions from both scientists/researchers and practitioners allow for having cutting-edge and established practices alike represented in the book.
- Finally, based on the individual authors' background and focus of activity, there is input from different fields close to business architecture management incorporated in this book, including, for example, brand management, business process management, and cultural change management.

The structure of the book follows the presented business architecture framework, from which—being complemented by some cross-cutting themes (e.g., modeling)—a navigator for this book derives (see Fig. 1.6). Although the chapters of this book are thus in some sort of logical order and fit into each other, they can be read independently from each other. Each chapter is self-contained and uses cross-references where required or reasonable.[5]

In line with our framework, the book is divided into the following parts:

1. Architecting the Business Motivation & Business Model
2. Architecting the Business Capabilities
3. Architecting Business Capability Realization
4. Modeling and Measuring the Business Architecture
5. Guidelines for Successful Implementation

---

[5] Note that, given that this book is an anthology, the individual chapters may to some extent also include personal opinions or views that are not necessarily shared by all other authors in this book.

The navigator illustrated in Fig. 1.6 displays these parts along with the individual chapters that they comprise. Chapters that range across different dimensions of the framework have been located in the book according to the content they deal with most prominently.

Following this introductory chapter, Chap. 2 sets out with a discussion of business motivation development and the benefits to be accrued by taking an architectural approach (as conceptualized content-wise by the framework introduced earlier). Based on a fictitious case of an insurance company, it thus illustrates the use of architectural thinking in strategy making to help avoid conceptual flaws, pre-limited thinking, the selection of presumably ineffective strategies, and severe errors in communication.

Chapter 3 then deals with an element that can be made a significant part of one's business model, but that has not received adequate attention in the architecture context thus far—the corporate brand. In particular, it discusses how to integrate brand management with strategic management and presents a general approach with which to translate strategy into execution from a corporate branding point of view.

Chapter 4 targets the business model concept in a more comprehensive way. Departing from a discussion of the value disciplines that might be followed by an enterprise, it illustrates how the business model provides structure and may thus help making considerate strategic choices and translating these into adequate operational structures. As to the latter part, a significant role is ascribed to the operating model.

Chapter 5 turns to another essential element of the architecture of the business, facilitating the connection of business strategy and model with business operations—the business capabilities. Specifically, it develops a straightforward process for managing capabilities—from preparation via the design of a capability catalog and the specification of capability details to catalog governance.

Chapter 6 then elaborates on the actual use of capabilities in business architecture management. In particular, it describes some scenarios and techniques for applying capabilities. In addition, it sheds light on the so-called "dynamic capabilities" concept and on how this relates to the business model as an integral part of the business architecture.

Chapter 7 recognizes that for effective capability realization it is essential to thoroughly deal with an element that has been significantly underexplored in the business architecture context thus far—a company's culture. In particular, it presents a solid, straightforward approach to capture cultural aspects and design culture for consistency and optimal support of the business strategy.

Chapter 8 depicts the role business architecture may play in the light of prevalent challenges and upcoming changes in the financial service industry (i.e., a closer integration with partners, especially with new players entering the field and offering attractive services via the Internet). Specifically, it argues that in the future it will be indispensable to have business processes managed at an end-to-end level and to make use of common industry standards that enable a functioning flow of information over enterprise boundaries.

Chapter 9 also focuses on the processes and structures part of capability realization. It presents a variety of typical business working practices as formalized and actionable patterns—in support of a certain business model configuration or, in general, in relation to specific business concerns.

Chapter 10 provides a systematic description of how to make effective use of an integrated model of business capabilities, on the one hand, and business objects and processes as core elements of capability realization, on the other hand, for the purpose of change program design and planning. As such, it explains a sort of business architecture application that has a highly innovative character and may enable program management to be approached in a different way than most often practiced today.

Chapter 11 continues by taking an overall perspective on the business architecture and, using a model-based approach from business motivation to execution, shedding light on how to tackle a challenge of increasing relevance in today's enterprises—the development of an appropriate level of agility. It moves along a straightforward way of working for becoming more agile, that is, assessing the current agility of the organization, determining the agility drivers of the organization, assessing how agile the organization needs to be, and, ultimately, defining a course of action to achieve this.

Chapter 12 then provides further advice on how to effectively model the business architecture. It discusses different challenges, patterns, and success factors in that context—predominantly based on several years' experiences of architecture modeling using ArchiMate (The Open Group 2013).

Chapter 13 moves on to another topic of increasing significance in today's enterprises—the management of complexity. It presents a generic approach for conceptualizing and measuring architectural complexity and—systematically walking through this book's business architecture framework—it identifies specific measures for quantifying business architecture in terms of complexity.

Chapter 14 discusses the applicability of business architecture management techniques for the needs of small-to-medium enterprises. Based on a colorful description of a real-life case study with a small restaurant chain in Central America, it demonstrates that using the business architecture as an instrument to pull different fragments together is not only advisable to large enterprises.

Finally, Chap. 15 finishes the book with a number of general guidelines for successful implementation of business architecture management. In particular, these include the setup of the function as a stakeholder-oriented and collaborative practice. It also discusses the organizational anchoring of business architecture management and the evolution that the practice may take within the enterprise over time.

References

Bucklin LP (1965) Postponement, speculation and the structure of distribution channels. J Mark Res 2(1):26–31

Burkhart T, Krumeich J, Werth D, Loos P (2011) Analyzing the business model concept—a comprehensive classification of literature. In: Proceedings of the 32nd international conference on information systems, Shanghai, China, 4–7 Dec 2011

Business Architecture Guild (2014) A guide to the business architecture body of knowledge (BIZBOK™ guide) version 4.0. http://c.ymcdn.com/sites/www.businessarchitectureguild. org/resource/resmgr/BIZBOKV4IntroductiIn.pdf. Accessed 27 Oct 2014

Business Model Foundry (2013) The value proposition canvas. http://www. businessmodelgeneration.com/canvas/vpc. Accessed 22 Sept 2014

Collins JC, Porras JI (1994) Built to last: successful habits of visionary companies. HarperBusiness, New York

Collins JC, Porras JI (1996) Building your company's vision. Harv Bus Rev 74(5):65–77

Cooper B, Vlaskovits P (2010) The entrepreneur's guide to customer development – a "cheat sheet" to the four steps to the epiphany (Self-published)

David FR (2013) Strategic management concepts: a competitive advantage approach. Prentice Hall, Upper Saddle River, NJ

Drucker P (1973) Management: tasks, responsibilities, practices. Harper & Row, New York

Friedman M (1962) Capitalism and freedom. University of Chicago Press, Chicago

Gharajedaghi J (2011) Systems thinking: managing chaos and complexity – a platform for designing business architecture. Morgan Kaufmann, Burlington, MA

ISO (2013) Frequently asked questions: ISO/IEC/IEEE 42010. http://www.iso-architecture.org/ ieee-1471/faq.html. Accessed 27 Oct 2014

Kantabutra S, Avery GC (2010) The power of vision: statements that resonate. J Bus Strategy 31 (1):37–45

Kaplan RS, Norton DP (2000) Having trouble with your strategy? Then map it. Harv Bus Rev 78 (5):167–176

Kettleborough J (2012) Seeing eye to eye: how people professionals can achieve lasting alignment and success within their business. AuthorHouse, Bloomington, IN

Mind Tools (2014) What is strategy? The three levels of strategy. http://www.mindtools.com/ pages/article/what-is-strategy.htm

Mintzberg H (1987) The strategy concept I: five Ps for strategy. Calif Manage Rev 30(1):11–24

OMG (2010) The business motivation model, version 1.1. Object Management Group, Needham, MA

Osterwalder A, Pigneur Y (2010) Business model generation—a handbook for visionaries, game changers, and challengers. Wiley, New Jersey

Pagh JD, Cooper MC (1998) Supply chain postponement and speculation strategies: how to choose the right strategy. J Bus Logist 19(2):13–33

Peng GCA, Nunes MB (2007) Using PEST analysis as a tool for refining and focusing contexts for information systems research. In: Proceedings of the 6th European conference on research methodology for business and management studies, Lisbon, Portugal, 9–10 July 2007, pp 229–236

Ross JW, Weill P, Robertson DC (2006) Enterprise architecture as strategy. Harvard Business School Press, Boston

Schein EH (1997) Organizational culture and leadership. Jossey-Bass, San Francisco

Simon D, Fischbach K, Schoder D (2013) An exploration of enterprise architecture research. Commun Assoc Inf Syst 32(1):1–72

Simon D, Fischbach K, Schoder D (2014) Enterprise architecture management and its role in corporate strategic management. Inf Syst e-Bus Manag 12(1):5–42

The Open Group (2011) TOGAF® version 9.1. Van Haren, Zaltbommel

The Open Group (2013) ArchiMate® 2.1 specification. Van Haren, Zaltbommel

Treacy M, Wiersema F (1993) Customer intimacy and other value disciplines. Harv Bus Rev 71 (1):84–93

UK Ministry of Defence (2010) The MOD architecture framework version 1.2. https://www.gov.uk/mod-architecture-framework. Accessed 22 Sept 2014

Ulrich W, Rosen M (2011) The business capability map: the "Rosetta stone" of business/IT alignment. The Enterprise Architecture Advisory Service Executive Report 14(2), Cutter Consortium, Arlington, TX

Wang JC, College HW (2006) Corporate strategic management and business re-engineering effort analyzed by the balanced scorecard model. J Am Acad Bus 10(1):102–109

Wilson C (2007) Transforming business architecture: creating a common language between business and IT. Align J (January/February):62–67

Wirtz BW (2011) Business model management: design – instruments – success factors. Gabler, Wiesbaden

Zott C, Amit R (2009) Designing your future business model: an activity system perspective. Working Paper 781. IESE Business School—University of Navarra, Madrid

Part I

Architecting the Business Motivation and Business Model

An Architectural Approach to Strategizing: Structure and Orientation for Developing the Business Motivation

2

Daniel Simon

Abstract

It has been widely acknowledged that effective strategizing in today's competitive environment has become a challenging task and thus requires a deliberate approach. This has also driven calls for a greater cross-fertilization of the field with other disciplines. In particular, good practices from architecture management may be considered a promising means to provide strategists with a reasonable structure and orientation for developing the business motivation (including, e.g., goals, strategies, and principles). Against this background, this chapter illustrates the use of architectural thinking in strategy development. Based on a fictitious case study, it explains how the use of an architectural approach that provides a clear structure can help achieve higher consistency, effectiveness, completeness, and comprehensibility.

2.1 Introduction

In today's competitive business world, effective strategic management has become a challenging endeavor for strategists and executives. Many may actually find it scary to commit to a new strategy, being confronted with a future one can only guess at and making decisions that explicitly cut off possibilities and options (cf. Martin 2014). In addition, there are several issues that need to be reasonably coped with when a new strategic direction is due to be developed and successfully implemented. Among others, relevant questions in that context are:

- How are effective strategies identified?
- How can overall consistency of a set of strategies be ensured?

D. Simon (✉)
Scape Consulting GmbH, Cologne, Germany
e-mail: daniel.simon@scape-consulting.de

© Springer International Publishing Switzerland 2015
D. Simon, C. Schmidt (eds.), *Business Architecture Management*, Management for Professionals, DOI 10.1007/978-3-319-14571-6_2

- How can it be ensured that the main strategic issues are completely addressed?
- How can it be ensured that different strategy options can be identified (or, in other words, that specific options are not excluded upfront)?
- How can the main messages of a strategy be explained and motivated?
- How can needs for strategic changes be located?

To cope with these questions, a systematic approach to strategy making is inevitable. At the core of this is a thorough conceptualization of the business motivation (capturing the strategic direction and thus constituting the way of doing business; see Chap. 1) with

- well-defined concepts (e.g., goals, strategies, principles, etc.), and
- well-defined relationships between these concepts (e.g., strategy supports the achievement of a goal),

which can provide orientation to strategists and conceptually guide them through main strategic management tasks. In essence, a corresponding business motivation canvas (distinguishing business ends, means, and influencers; see Fig. 1.2 in Chap. 1) allows for injecting strategic management with an appropriate level of architectural thinking. It is not about escaping the fear of the unknown and the necessity to make hard choices, it is about using a structure that helps increase the odds of success (cf. Martin 2014).

To illustrate the use of architectural thinking in strategy making, this chapter draws on the fictitious case of an insurance company that has originally been developed and described to illustrate the use of ArchiMate, a common language for architecture modeling (The Open Group 2013). The following sections thus describe stages of the strategy development process of the fictitious insurer ArchiSurance. In this chapter, the original ArchiSurance example (cf. Jonkers et al. 2012) is extended by integrating own real-life experiences from different enterprises with respect to facets of strategy making (i.e., although this case extension is fictitious as well, it refers to incidents that have occurred equally or at least similarly in practice).

So let's assume that, once a new strategy had been deemed necessary, ArchiSurance set up a corresponding project called "Unite & Move On." A project team with members of all business divisions was defined, headed by the director of strategy and business development. Interviews and workshops were scheduled to gain the required senior management input for the strategic choices to be made.

> ArchiSurance is the result of a merger of three previously independent insurance companies:
>
> - Home & Away, specializing in homeowners' insurance and travel insurance
> - PRO-FIT, specializing in car insurance

(continued)

- Legally Yours, specializing in legal expense insurance

It was formed to take advantage of numerous synergies between the three organizations, which now represent the main divisions of ArchiSurance. While the three pre-merger companies sold different insurance products, they shared several similarities in their business models. All three sold directly to consumers and small businesses, predominantly through the web, email, telephone, and postal mail channels. They were based in modern office complexes in major metropolitan areas. Each had strong reputations for integrity, service quality, and financial stability.

The lead investors of the three companies began merger talks after they noticed that lower-cost competitors were entering their markets, that there were new opportunities in high-growth regions, and that each company required significant new investments to remain competitive. They realized that only a larger enterprise could simultaneously control its costs, maintain its customer satisfaction, invest in new products and technologies, and successfully enter emerging markets.

ArchiSurance offers all the insurance products of the three pre-merger companies, and intends to frequently adjust its offerings in response to changing market conditions. Like its three predecessors, ArchiSurance predominantly sells its products directly to its customers.

2.2   Deliberate Classification of Strategic Constituents

In preparation of the scheduled interviews and workshops, the project team started off by conducting an initial SWOT analysis (i.e., identifying strengths, weaknesses, opportunities, and threats), which was planned to provide an adequate context for discussion. The SWOT analysis assimilated the outcomes of several customer workshops that had previously been carried out to identify the most prevalent pains and expected gains of the customers [as per the "Value Proposition Canvas" depicted by Business Model Foundry (2013)]. Without too much further conceptual structure the team then basically went into these discussions.

As a result, right early in the project, the introduction of self-services for ArchiSurance's customers was put on the table, following numerous mentions by senior management stakeholders from all divisions in the initial interviews and workshops in the course of the development of the new strategy. Self-services here include the possible change of personal data (e.g., address) and the generation of policy overviews, for example. However, whether this is an end in itself or whether it actually serves an overarching purpose like cost reduction or an increase in customer satisfaction should be carefully evaluated. As self-services are a topic that had been around for some time in all pre-merger companies, believed to be introduced in the near future, the stakeholders tended to treat it as a given target and classified it as a goal, not considering the actual purpose behind it any more. The discussions thus went straight to some sort of solution. Alternatives were not really considered, but would had been difficult to come up with anyway, given that the actual goal behind it was unclear.

Once the project team realized that they missed to capture the actual goals and were not about to properly consider different strategic options to realize these goals, they slightly changed their approach and started up the next workshops with a brief conceptual introduction, including a thorough differentiation between business means and business ends. This high-level conceptualization of the business motivation, exemplified on a corresponding poster, became the basis for all remaining workshops. The interviewers kept asking "why?" in case means were mentioned before the underlying goal was specified. By doing this, the project team managed to classify needs and suggestions mentioned by the stakeholders in an appropriate way. The basis for this was their motivational framework with well-defined concepts, including a *differentiation between means and ends*.

2.3 Development of a Consistent and Modular System of Goals/Objectives

Once the stakeholder needs and concerns were captured, the project team grouped them systematically to derive overall goals. The team then set these goals in relation with one another, basically indicating whether a goal supports others or, in contrast, obviously conflicts with other goals and thus has a negative impact on their realization. For example, the team found out through its discussions that the goal "control costs," at least for the first time, has a potential conflict with the goal "increase customer satisfaction," as the latter likely required significant investments in technology that allowed faster process times, better data quality, and new service offerings. This conflict could then be made explicit to senior management for prioritization and decision making.

Another issue the team faced was that by aggregating the stakeholder needs and concerns in its goal definition process it initially arrived at a goal called "improve product portfolio manageability and consistency." Obviously, this represents a very "rich" goal that may incorporate several target-related aspects (e.g., simplicity, costs, agility). The fact that the essence of the goal was not immediately visible— potentially hidden in any further descriptions once completely documented at a later point—made it difficult to systematically identify appropriate means in succeeding work sessions. However, once the core aspects of the goal were recalled and explained to each participant, numerous means could actually be identified that were meant to help realize that goal and effectively channel efforts towards it (OMG 2010). Exemplary principles were reuse, standardization, centralization, modularity, ease of use, and automation (cf. The Open Group 2011), whereas a reduction of the product portfolio, the simplification of product descriptions, and an increased offering of (cross-divisional) product combinations were identified as potential strategies for goal achievement.[1] Now, at first glance, it did not really become clear to others that had not participated in the workshops why a certain means was assigned to the "rich" end and what the specific contribution of the means is respectively. The project team, in turn, concluded that this may be a general issue that would complicate communication and thus understanding of the set goals and the reasons for the corresponding means. Therefore, the goal was *split into its integral parts*: "reduce product complexity," "increase product synergies," "reduce portfolio administration costs," and "increase time-to-market" (in terms of both new and changed products). Other identified goals were double-checked for sufficient *modularity* as well and then structured according to the dimensions of the "Balanced Scorecard" (Kaplan and Norton 2001).

In a next step, these overall goals—expressed in relatively broad terms—were broken down or, say, cascaded (cf. ISACA 2012) to specific, measurable objectives (meeting the SMART criteria, i.e., being specific, measurable, attainable, realistic, and time-bounded). These objectives were thus associated with precise targets. In consequence, the definition of objectives went hand in hand with the initial, high-level design of a target architecture at the business capability level. That is, based on the defined goals, relevant business capabilities received specific target values, e.g., in terms of costs, size, or delivery times. Other objectives were of a more general character (i.e., they applied to several capabilities at once), such as the improvement of ArchiSurance's net promoter score (measuring customer satisfaction). This focus on outcomes allowed for the identification of appropriate strategic actions in the next step.

2.4 Development of a Comprehensive and Suitable Set of Strategies for Goal Achievement

The project team continued with the *identification of appropriate means* for realizing the defined goals and objectives. ArchiSurance's overall *business model* in place provided the context for the discussion [in line with what Simon et al. (2014) outline; see below for further details with respect to the role of the business model in strategy development]. For example, the intended strategy of launching third-party administration services (e.g., claims settlement) to other insurers raised the question of consistency given the fact that business processes were to still be operated in a diversified way to some extent across ArchiSurance's three main divisions while, on the other hand, third-party administration was likely

---

[1] Note that these strategies are formulated in a "gap-like" way to emphasize the new aspects. They may well be part of a "larger" (e.g., the overall product strategy) or more generic strategy (e.g., product leadership). They are not yet meant to represent strategic programs or even projects though (cf. Yelin 2005). In contrast, they should be considered less specific than an action plan (that includes decisions with respect to, for example, the "who" and "when"). In line with the strategy definition provided in Chap. 1, they represent the "conception preceding action" (Mintzberg 1987).

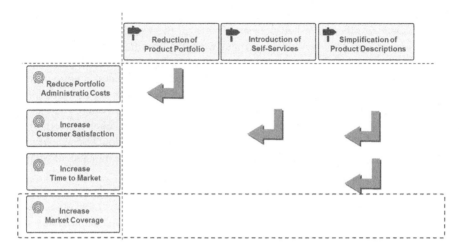

Fig. 2.1 Cross-reference map of goals and strategies

to require some degree of immediate standardization. As a result, a shared back-office for the three main divisions, which had originally been planned to be implemented at a later point of time, was added as another strategic move and even assigned with a high priority. With the shared back-office, working to higher capacity due to its new service offering, ArchiSurance was hoping to prevent mass redundancies. This alternative action had been ruled out considering that one of the main assets present in ArchiSurance's business model was reputation.

Finally, an overview was created with the goals and objectives and the supporting strategies that had been identified (cf., e.g., Simon et al. 2014), thus providing *visual traceability* in terms of which courses of action were intended to deliver what outcomes and how these related back to the overall goals set out to achieve (see simplified representation in Fig. 2.1, with goals at the X-axis and strategies at the Y-axis). By doing this, it was made apparent that the goal "increase market coverage" was not addressed at all by the developed strategic options. Obviously, discussions had revolved around measures tackling the integration and consolidation challenges following the recent merger, while the pursued internationalization—one of the main original drivers behind the merger—did not find adequate consideration. In other words, the team was able to identify strategy white spots. These white spots were then eliminated and replaced by appropriate strategies. Here, the increase of cooperations in neighboring countries and the establishment of own sites in one low-cost country (as a pilot) were found an appropriate approach—at least as a first step of ArchiSurance's internationalization. For this low-cost country, the team developed some sort of "blue ocean strategy" for health insurances with which to unlock new demand and thus create uncontested market space (cf. Kim and Mauborgne 2005). It came up with this specific strategy against the backdrop of what Wilson (2007) points out nicely: "Companies in every industry and around the world are pursuing blue ocean strategies and re-defining the competitive landscape overnight. Companies left behind to fight it out in crowded red oceans can only look forward to decreasing." So the strategy targeted the many young uninsured that could not afford the high premiums to be paid for health insurance. Therefore, they should be offered insurance with low annual premiums, but with limited coverage in terms of annual benefits. Additional coverage should be available on demand for a considerable surcharge premium.

On the other hand, the cross-reference overview of strategies and goals (Fig. 2.1) allowed for a final check of whether, after all, strategies may have entered the agenda that are not sufficiently grounded in the overall system of goals and objectives. Not only would this have meant that the motivation for such a strategy was unclear, and thus difficult to explain to ArchiSurance's staff, but this would have also implied that strategies had been identified that are not really the "right" ones in terms of the desired ends as they do not serve any of the defined strategic purposes. Indeed, the project team found two strategic choices that were not related to any goal at all. Talks with the chief executive officer, who had brought these strategies onto the agenda, did not lead to their removal though. Despite the fact that they were not really rooted in the strategic goals, to which all leading stakeholders (including the chief executive officer) had agreed before, the chief executive officer insisted on their survival. At least did the discussion lead to the formulation of an additional goal; although it was some sort of artificial it made the motivation for the corresponding strategies explainable.

Together with main players of the steering committee of the "Unite & Move On" project, the project manager finally double checked all identified strategies (i.e., also those that were already assigned to a goal) in terms of their goal contribution. Although this only led to minor adjustments (in editorial terms), it had a positive impact on the commitment of the involved stakeholders and served well for the purpose of quality assurance. Afterwards, the strategic choices found approval in the steering committee and both goals/objectives and strategies were signed off in the executive board.

2.5   Identification of Needs for Strategic Change/Amendments

To be able to track whether the selected strategies are successfully implemented and finally completed and whether the determined goals are met, the project team moved on by developing appropriate metrics for measurement. Here, the deliberate classification of the strategic constituents (see above) helped ensure that successful strategy implementation was not to be equated with goal achievement and that *dedicated metrics* were thus developed *for both goals and strategies*. Along with the relationships between the formulated goals and strategies at hand this represented the basis for the implementation and application of a coherent measurement system, with which progress can be measured on a continual basis, reasons for lagging behind target can be located, and ineffective choices (e.g., strategy is implemented successfully, but there is no or only moderate impact on the related goal) can be detected.

In other words—or in COBIT terms (ISACA 2012)—the metrics for measuring the application of means then serve as "lead indicators," while the metrics for measuring the achievement of goals and objectives are rather "lag indicators" in that context. Measuring the introduced number of self-services, for example, can help evaluate whether ArchiSurance progresses towards higher customer satisfaction and may thus initially indicate to be on the right track. Due to whatever reason, however, the choice for self-services may eventually not lead to increased customer satisfaction, which may be measured by the net promoter score as a "lag indicator." Appropriate (potentially corrective) actions can then be taken immediately. The basis for this is the thorough *separation of means and ends* along with their expected cause-and-effect relationships explicitly documented.

2.6   Comprehensible Communication of Strategic Choices

In addition to the setup of a coherent measurement system, the project team was tasked with the preparation of communication measures and instruments. Here, the project team decided to create, among other things, a "one-pager" with the main elements of ArchiSurance's new strategic positioning. Not only did it present ArchiSurance's overall business motivation in terms of ends and corresponding means, but in a simplified way it did also outline the relationships between these strategic elements and could thus be used both to explain the existence of individual elements and to navigate through the motivation as a whole:

This picture (see simplified representation in Fig. 2.2) became an important instrument for the succeeding communication of ArchiSurance's new strategic positioning. It allowed the communication to be delivered in form of a *consistent, understandable, and capturing story*: from drivers and constraints via goals and objectives to strategies. Even further, it actually represented the new overall ArchiSurance "story" itself, which explained its purpose, aspiration, and orientation, to which structures and people should align (cf. Graves 2012).

An important aspect in visualization and communication of this story, however, was the level of detail used for that purpose. To make people not only understand the story in general but also think about what the story means for oneself individually and how it can be adopted in the daily work, the elements that made up the story were not broken down into all their details. Deliberately, some room was left for self-interpretation. This was complemented by few overarching themes of the new story, one of which was "simplicity," formulated to activate people and make them an active part of the story's implementation. Special emphasis was put on the theme "simplicity," for which it was clear that different associations and perceptions would exist. Due to its importance for the further coalescence of the "new" ArchiSurance, an active engagement of each individual was believed to play an essential role for successful strategy implementation.

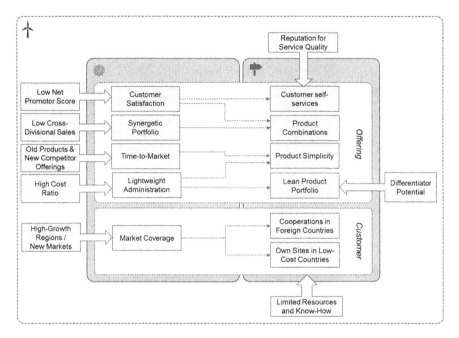

Fig. 2.2 Business motivation one-pager

2.7   Reflection and Discussion

Based on the ArchiSurance case, this chapter has depicted the use of good practices from architecture management in strategy making and thus illustrated how an architectural approach to developing the business motivation can help achieve higher consistency, effectiveness, completeness, and comprehensibility. A key to this is the understanding that the business motivation itself has some kind of architecture, and thus belongs to the overall enterprise architecture, not only for achieving transparency in terms of the elements by which the design of business operations and IT is motivated.

In summary, with a thorough conceptualization in a "motivation canvas," such an architectural approach provides a structure that can help avoid conceptual flaws (such as mistaking strategies for goals), pre-limited thinking (such as promoting specific means without prior clarity about the goal to be achieved thereby and thus shutting out other valid options), the selection of presumably ineffective strategies, and severe errors in communication. In this structure, which is not meant to be of a too much formal character (cf. Simon et al. 2014; also see Chap. 15), the creativity required for strategy making (Mintzberg et al. 2005) can likely be initiated and leveraged effectively; at the same time, such a structure ensures deliberate and rational strategizing and avoids the pitfalls that are present when there is no one doing a proper job of joining the different dots in the motivation sphere—someone that could be called a "strategy architect" (this is about the role, not the label; in other words, this does not mean that everyone who applies architectural thinking needs to be rebranded as an architect). Different strategic techniques (e.g., SWOT analysis, goal decomposition, ERRC grid) can thus be applied in a combined way and properly integrated using an overall model of the business motivation.

In addition to the practices depicted in the preceding sections, there may have been further opportunities though to apply architectural thinking and incorporate additional business architecture pieces that could have further supported ArchiSurance's strategy development process:

1. It may have been reasonable to distinguish between different levels of strategies, such as *corporate and competitive strategies* (cf. Simon et al. 2014). While the corporate strategy basically determines with which products and/or services to operate in which markets (the "where-to-play" decision), the competitive strategy details how to operate in these markets and stand one's ground against competitors by creating a compelling value proposition (the "how-to-win" decision) (cf. Martin 2014). A thorough differentiation of these concepts may have provided an even better structure for the identification of appropriate strategies. For example, based on the intended moves at the corporate strategic level (e.g., the launch of third-party administration services), one may have deliberately watched out for competitive strategies suitable to mitigate risks (i.e., assessed constraints) related to these strategic choices (which here is the entering of a new market).

2. Right at the start, the *business model*—with the structure it provides for some of the main objects of strategy statements—could have been analyzed in terms of any potential elements that may not have been fully realized yet or to which the organization—possibly already the pre-merger organizations—did not really live up (which is more than the implicit use for SWOT analysis and goal identification, for which it provided the boundaries). The business model's scalability, time gaps between earning and spending, and several other design aspects could have been addressed as well. This identification of possible hot spots could have further informed the strategy development process and may have led to additional reasonable strategies.[2] As indicated, these different strategic options could have then been analyzed in terms of consistency and any impacts using the business model as well, as a framework that allows an integrated view of strategic actions, or, more precisely, their particular outcomes (i.e., including their relationships) (see Chap. 4 for

---

[2] Note that such deficiencies may not necessarily be addressed at the strategic level, but may also be possible to be resolved at the lower levels of the business architecture without a strategy defined for this purpose.

an example).[3] As the senior management of ArchiSurance's three divisions tended to focus on their individual strategies in the initial workshops, without any concern for or maybe even to the detriment of other divisions, the necessity to deal with potentially conflicting strategies should not be a surprise. For larger enterprises, for which one may think of a portfolio of business models that is being run, this is of particular relevance. In fact, linking strategies entails not only resolving any conflicts, but rather creating synergies across different business units (e.g., at the activity or product/service levels). Ultimately, since the business model also provides some sort of uniform language to describe how the enterprise is going to work (in form of a single-page view) based on the decisions made in the strategy development process, it could have also been used to further support the communication of the strategic choices (cf. El Sawy and Pereira 2013).

3. The SWOT analysis could have gone into more detail to include a systematic *analysis of* ArchiSurance's *capabilities* and thus avoid creating strategies that are ill-connected to the actual opportunities, needs, and concerns that arise from current business execution (of which capabilities represent an abstraction). In fact, such an investigation may have allowed for visualizing hot spots within the capability landscape (e.g., capabilities with disproportionally high costs) that should be addressed by appropriate strategies (cf. Simon et al. 2014), thus serving as a proper baseline for strategizing (cf. Ulrich and Rosen 2011). Later, once strategic choices have been made and mapped onto the future business model, the designed target architecture at the business capability level should have also been properly detailed. Here, clear responsibilities for business capabilities are crucial to determine which capabilities may have to change and to then meet the corresponding target.

Beyond that, the project team may have also benefited from a closer involvement of someone usually acting at the operational level (e.g., solution architect), who may have brought in valuable practical experiences and thus helped the strategists to "work with their heads in the cloud but with their feet on the ground" in the strategy development process. Such an individual may have also supported the team in challenging and optimizing goal and strategy statements [and keep them simple according to Martin (2014)] and thereby increasing the level of understanding for "ordinary" employees; here, care should be taken that finding the final wording does not become science though (such that it hinders required progress). It is thus crucial to keep in mind that strategy is not about perfection (cf. Martin 2014).

Ultimately, for strategizing and business modeling the joint sessions with the senior management could have taken the form of "future workshops" [the original German term is "Zukunftswerkstatt," coined by Jungk and Müllert (1981)]—a kind of moderated group work supposed to provide a forum in which the future can be

---

[3] Based on that, one may have also come up with a first evaluation of possible effects/impacts on the lower-level architecture (e.g., processes) (cf. Radeke and Legner 2012; Simon et al. 2014).

shaped creatively, with alternative scenarios being considered. At the core of this technique is a fantasy phase, in which some sort of "perfect world" is assumed that avoids restricted thinking and encourages ideas to be expressed no matter of whether they are actually realistic. The evaluation is purposefully separated from the preceding phase of fantasizing.

That being said, the distinction between the concepts of deliberate (i.e., intentional) and emergent strategy (as responses to a number of unanticipated events) [as drawn by Mintzberg et al. (2005)], the latter of which questions the manager's ability to predict the future and create appropriate plans accordingly, should not be misused to become an excuse for avoiding difficult strategic choices or even making no strategic choices at all until the future becomes sufficiently clear. As Martin (2014) points out, if the future is too unpredictable to make reasonable strategic choices, how would one believe that it will become significantly less so? In addition, how would one recognize the point when predictability has increased to a level that allows for making strategic choices?

Further, in relation to the role of architecture management in the strategizing process, there may still be people who do not want to "buy" the idea of using architectural thinking and practices therein as they do not see the required appetite among strategists and executives. Similar statements were made (among others) about the Internet before its rise to success though. To quote Zachman (1997), who, while referring to enterprise architecture, asserted that "in the 21st Century, it will be the determining factor, the factor that separates the winners from the losers, the successful and the failures, the acquiring from the acquired, the survivors from the others," one should better not leave this unconsidered and wait until already being outdistanced.

References

Business Model Foundry (2013) The value proposition canvas. http://www.businessmodelgeneration.com/canvas/vpc. Accessed 22 Sept 2014

El Sawy OA, Pereira F (2013) Digital business models: review and synthesis. In: El Sawy OA, Pereira F (eds) Business modelling in the dynamic digital space: an ecosystem approach. Springer, Berlin, pp 13–20

Graves T (2012) The enterprise as story: the role of narrative in enterprise architecture. Tetradian Books, Colchester

ISACA (2012) COBIT 5 – a business framework for the governance and management of enterprise IT. http://www.isaca.org/COBIT/Pages/default.aspx. Accessed 22 Sept 2014

Jonkers H, Band I, Quartel D (2012) ArchiSurance case study. The Open Group, San Francisco, CA

Jungk R, Müllert NR (1981) Zukunftswerkstätten. Wilhelm Goldmann, Hamburg

Kaplan RS, Norton DP (2001) The strategy-focused organization: how balanced scorecard companies thrive in the new business environment. Harvard School Business Press, Boston

Kim WC, Mauborgne R (2005) Blue ocean strategy: how to create uncontested market space and make the competition irrelevant. Harvard Business School Press, Boston

Martin RL (2014) The big lie of strategic planning. Harv Bus Rev 92(1/2):79–84

Mintzberg H (1987) The strategy concept I: five Ps for strategy. Calif Manage Rev 30(1):11–24

Mintzberg H, Ahlstrand B, Lampel J (2005) Strategy safari—a guided tour through the wilds of strategic management. The Free Press, New York

OMG (2010) The business motivation model, version 1.1. Object Management Group, Needham, MA

Radeke F, Legner C (2012) Embedding EAM into strategic planning. In: Ahlemann F, Stettiner E, Messerschmidt M, Legner C (eds) Strategic enterprise architecture management – challenges, best practices, and future developments. Springer, Berlin, pp 111–139

Simon D, Fischbach K, Schoder D (2014) Enterprise architecture management and its role in corporate strategic management. Inf Syst e-Bus Manag 12(1):5–42

The Open Group (2011) TOGAF® version 9.1. Van Haren, Zaltbommel

The Open Group (2013) ArchiMate® 2.1 specification. Van Haren, Zaltbommel

Ulrich W, Rosen M (2011) The business capability map: the "rosetta stone" of business/IT alignment. The enterprise architecture advisory service executive report 14(2), Cutter Consortium, Arlington, TX

Wilson C (2007) Transforming business architecture: creating a common language between business and IT. Align J (January/February):62–67

Yelin KC (2005) Linking strategy and project portfolio management. In: Levine HA (ed) Project portfolio management: a practical guide to selecting projects, managing portfolios, and maximizing benefits. Jossey-Bass, New Jersey

Zachman J (1997) Enterprise architecture: the issue of the century. Database Program Des 10 (3):44–53

Corporate Strategy and Corporate Branding: Reference Frame and Examples of Integrated Corporate Strategic & Brand Management (CS&BM)

3

Holger J. Schmidt

Abstract

Strategy and brand are central constructs in the field of business management research and practice. But while strategic management has been in place for a long time, the holistic view on brand management has only stirred up some discussion in recent years. In this context, special attention is paid to the corporate brand, as this kind of brand has gained more significance in real life. In the process of corporate branding, it is crucially important that corporate strategy and brand strategy fall in line, as the brand is in this respect not a tool operated by the marketers but instead should be absorbed entirely within the identity of the corporation. So far, both constructs, i.e., strategy and brand, have been largely regarded as separate fields (and the latter even less been made a subject of an enterprise's business architecture), which entails varying views of how corporate strategy and corporate brand mutually affect each other, eventually leading to the question: which is dominated by which? This article is aimed at establishing a core frame of reference of integrated "Corporate Strategic & Brand Management" (CS&BM) and gives explanations by demonstrating specific design perspectives. In line with architectural thinking, particular attention is paid to the interaction of corporate and brand identity, the strategic positioning as well as how to manage positioning at the brand touch points.

3.1 Introduction

Ever since empiric research has shown that enterprises that have incorporated brand orientation are more successful than those that have not (e.g., Madden et al. 2006; Harter et al. 2005; Joas and Offerhaus 2001; Biel 2001; Court et al. 1999), scientists

H.J. Schmidt (✉)
Koblenz University of Applied Sciences, Koblenz, Germany
e-mail: hjschmidt@hs-koblenz.de

© Springer International Publishing Switzerland 2015   35
D. Simon, C. Schmidt (eds.), *Business Architecture Management*, Management for Professionals, DOI 10.1007/978-3-319-14571-6_3

and experts from various subject areas have been addressing the issues of strategic and operative brand management. The subject has caused rivers of ink to flow and there has been a lot of research work while only part of it was implemented. So far there is wide agreement that there is much more to the term brand than its mere operational meaning: an emotional advertising campaign, a fancy corporate design, or a new catchy claim often stimulate the desire for a brand—but this is restricted to certain industries and even then in many cases only with a short-term impact. Yet, the way how successful brand management can be effectively designed and how it can be integrated with enterprise architecture management (as per Simon et al. 2014) and strategic business management in general still needs further clarification (Esch 2012). On the one hand, this is due to the vague understanding of the term itself, as elements like brand identity, brand image, or even positioning from the perspective of different fields of research are still subject to varied interpretations and not demarcated clearly enough from related basic concepts of strategic management (e.g., models of corporate identity as proposed by Birkigt et al. 1998; Baumgarth 2008; Adjouri 2004). On the other hand, marketing itself is to blame: the brand as such has been characterized as a purely operational tool far too often and has been attributed to product policy (e.g., Walsh et al. 2013; Kotler and Armstrong 2010; Homburg and Krohmer 2009) within the systematics of the marketing-mix (product, price, distribution, communication).

Particularly the absence of an integrated approach for the development of company strategies and the management of a company brand seems astonishing as by means of identity-based approaches of brand management (e.g., Aaker 1996; Meffert and Burmann 1996; also refer to Sect. 3.2.1) concepts have been made available that could serve as a base for it. The intention of this chapter is therefore to contribute to the development of such an integrated approach. However, this requires an initial glance at the development of brand comprehension in the course of time (e.g., shown in detail in Baumgarth 2008; Meffert and Burmann 2005). Bearing this in mind, the two perspectives of strategy-oriented brand management and brand-oriented strategy development will consequently be taken to develop a frame of reference in terms of an integrated management of "corporate strategy" and "corporate brand" (CS&B-management). Finally, there is debate about selected and significant design perspectives of integrated CS&B-management, illustrating which role the brand can play as part of change processes.

This chapter focuses on enterprises that—like Deutsche Bank, Siemens, Lufthansa, IBM, or Google—promote a corporate or umbrella brand. However, many of the statements are also relevant for enterprises that—like for example Procter & Gamble, Unilever, or Mars—operate with strong product brands in line with a multi-brand strategy. Nevertheless, these findings require further fine-tuning in this context to ensure a smooth transfer.

3.2 Corporate Strategy (CS) and Corporate Brand Management (CBM): Core Components of a Reference Frame

3.2.1 Brand Management Development

Brands came to life in the middle of the nineteenth century and initially served as symbols of ownership and later also as proof of origin. The latter was becoming increasingly important, as the geographical and emotional distance between manufacturer and customer was growing in the course of the progressing industrialization. More and more the brand's role evolved into a pledge for the merchant's good standing. Later on, during the economic growth in the first half of the twentieth century the number of branded products that was on offer had increased and consequently business sciences started investigating the newly experienced brand as such. Analyzing successful brands in those times led to an approach to brand management that focused on the typical characteristics of brands (Tropp 2011; Meffert and Burmann 2005; Schmidt 2007): products that featured certain attributes like, for example, a high level of consumer awareness and widespread availability, uniform pricing, mass advertising, and promotional packaging were called a trademark or trademarked goods. In this context there was an instrumental view of how brand management was seen: rules for pricing, advertising, packaging, and so on were laid down and their adherence was supposed to guarantee success. In the buyers' markets of the 1980s, brands evolved into a form of marketing concept that allowed manufacturers to distinguish themselves from others. In this context, it seemed necessary for brand management for the first time not only to consider communication policy but also to take account for product development, price, and distribution policy across functions. At the same time, brand managers were focusing on image as a core parameter. However, in the days of the information society of the 1990s it became clear that an isolated view of the image is not sufficient for successful brand management. Changes in morals held by society like, for example, the rising ecologic and social awareness as well as new media and communication channels and subsequent requirement changes imposed on businesses were the reason that the direct interaction between customer and business became more important (see, e.g., the society-driven concept of marketing called "Gesellschaftsorientiertes Marketing" proposed by Raffée and Wiedmann 1989). Subsequently, the "corporate brand" took on greater significance (Esch et al. 2006). On the part of brand management they realized for the first time that a brand must be firmly rooted in the enterprise to be able to radiate its success to the outside world.

The identity-based approach of brand management built on this fundamental idea, which came to being in the 1990s (Aaker 1996; Meffert and Burmann 1996; Kapferer 1992; Brandmeyer and Schmidt 1999) and rapidly spread across science and industry, is today considered the most efficient management model in terms of brands (Burmann et al. 2012). Along the lines of this understanding, success and relevance of brands are primarily reduced to their identity, the development and definition of which requires a strong internal perspective which means that, accordingly, no longer only customers but all stakeholders of a brand, e.g., staff, customers, suppliers, and society play a key role in brand management. Therefore, brand-related activities need to be arranged across functional and organizational borderlines (Meffert 2004), e.g., by including employees of all departments (not only from Marketing) or even external suppliers in the brand management process. With this in mind, brand management is seen as an integrative component of corporate management in which not only marketing activities but, e.g., also the development of staff conduct in accordance with the brand plays a central role (Meffert and Burmann 2005).

If one keeps with the idea of identity-based brand management, the dividing walls of the classical trisection, namely definition of objectives, strategy development, and implementation, will be razed. First of all, the brand influences the goal definition: its specific identity rules out certain objectives right from the start. So from an economic point of view, the premium brand Porsche, which stands for attributes like perfection, innovation, exclusivity and performance, can't possibly pursue the objective of maximizing its sales volume. If Porsche developed and distributed vehicles for the mass market, its brand identity would be hurt in the long run. Second, the brand determines the strategy. If Porsche stands for premium products, engineering skills and timeless design, it wouldn't seem an advisable marketing strategy to operate with multi-brand dealerships that are free to make their own decision at their discretion. Instead, setting up its own dealership network should be obvious. And third the brand Porsche has to find itself in a coherent way in all implementation instruments (e.g., advertisements, processes, incentives), if it does not want to run the risk of diluting its distinctive corporate identity. Hence, the brand has an impact on the entire enterprise and makes sure that all parts are cross-linked, thus making it an essential element from an overall architecture point of view. If this is the case, we call it a brand-oriented enterprise (cf. Baumgarth et al. 2011) in which, as will be explained below, the brand becomes a fundamental part of the business model.

In brand-oriented enterprises the brand has an impact on, casually spoken, everything and everyone. But if the brand is everything, what exactly is it? And how does it interact with corporate strategic management? These questions will be investigated in the following sections.

3.2.2 Corporate Strategy (CS) and Corporate Brand Management (CBM): Going from an Isolated View to an Integrated Understanding

As seen from the perspective of *strategy-oriented brand management*, identity-based and comprehensive models of brand management seem obvious to exemplify the interfaces between strategic management and brand management. Among the large number of approaches (e.g., Haedrich et al. 2003), the model from Hatch and Schultz (2001a, 2008) as well as the model of identity-based brand management according to Meffert and Burmann (1996; developed further by Burmann et al. 2012) outlined at the beginning, are discussed.

The model from Hatch and Schultz (2001a) has been developed and tested for corporate brands (Binckebacck and Baumgarth 2011) and assumes a brand is based on the three elements strategic vision, corporate culture, and image. The strategic vision includes the targets and strategic decisions made by top management while the corporate culture includes the moral values shared by all staff. The image is based on the expectations held by external stakeholders. According to this model, a strong brand identity results from the fact that these three elements coincide to a considerable extent (Baumgarth and Binckebanck 2013). Hence the brand is the result of strategic vision, culture, and image. It is placed at the end of the process not at its beginning. The successful brand manager builds on corporate strategy and is encouraged to bring in line the company conduct that becomes visible at brand touchpoints (e.g., communication, processes, staff conduct) with customer needs to make sure there are no or only minor shortfalls. If this is attained, you will end up with a strong brand; architectural thinking in terms of reasonably connecting the strategic vision, corporate culture, and image to form a strong brand identity and translating this identity into business operations can be considered the basis for this result.

Likewise, the model of identity-based brand management shows some significant points of intersection to strategic management. The focus on sales markets often observed in former brand management approaches and the corresponding communication policy tools are abandoned and the brand image experienced in the market is no longer the sole center of analyses and measures. In fact, the view held by the brand itself, its identity, is on an equal footing as its external view, its image. The former dominating orientation to the outside world "outside-in" is complemented by an inward view "inside-out" (Burmann et al. 2012). To set itself apart from the competition and to gain competitive edge in the long run a company needs to knot together both perspectives (Burmann et al. 2012). The brand, defined as a bundle of benefits with strong features, emerges as a logical consequence at the intersection of brand identity and brand image (Burmann et al. 2012).

The language used in the identity-oriented approach will already give away how it has been affected by strategic management. The call for an "outside-in"-view arises from the theoretical approach of market orientation which describes how competitive advantages can be developed and secured in the long run. Market orientation is reflected in a market-based view (Porter 2000, 2008; Keuper 2010; Burmann et al. 2012), according to which at first the right market has to be selected followed by the setup of a superior position within that selected market (Burmann 2002). The "inside-out" view, which is vitally important for identity-based brand management on the other hand, is due to the resource-based and competence-based view of strategic management which makes company resources and competences accountable to explain competitive edge. Also, comprehending that neither a pure market-oriented nor a resource- respectively competence-oriented view may prove promising, but that much rather linking the different perspectives may be recommended has been promoted in the field of strategic management for a long time (Zentes et al. 2006). Furthermore, it should also be noted that identity-based brand management is not only closely knit with strategic management by language but also with regard to contents. An example that supports this idea is the structure of brand identity, which is defined as a self-perception of internal target groups (Burmann et al. 2012). It mainly consists of six elements: the origin (where do we come from?), the competences (what are we capable of?) the values (what do we believe in?), the personality (how do we communicate?), the accomplishments (what do we bring to the market?) as well as finally the vision (where are we headed?). With the exception of personality, all mentioned elements of brand identity are equally up for discussion in strategic management. The origin plays a major role in the "dynamic capabilities" approach; accordingly, finding new problem solutions is influenced by existing resources and competences (Teece et al. 1997). Competences are an integral part of the already discussed "competence-based view." Values and vision play a central role in society-driven marketing according to Raffée and Wiedmann, which considers itself a driving force for strategic management (e.g., Wiedmann 2004; Raffée and Wiedmann 1989; Wiedmann and Kreutzer 1989). The question what a company brings to the market is finally a starting point for a number of models of strategic marketing management and has already been raised in Ansoff's Product/Market Matrix (1965), for example [also see, e.g., the "Business Model Canvas" (Osterwalder and Pigneur 2010)].

From the viewpoint of *brand-oriented strategic management*, brand management can be assigned to different levels of corporate management, depending on the perspective. According to Ulrich (1981), corporate management needs to distinguish between normative, strategic and operative management. In normative management, the management philosophy is laid down specifying attitude, conviction, and values, according to which the organization should be run. Raffée and Wiedmann (1989) also include the definition of a global objective system as well as the corresponding strategic course. Strategic management, however, determines the medium-term targets and the corporate capabilities, while operative management is about organizing and controlling ongoing affairs (Ulrich 1981; Kreutzer et al. 1989). Based on this three-way split, the fundamental decision to operate with strong brands can be interpreted as a normative decision that determines the consequential employment of further basic marketing strategies like, e.g., market segmentation. The determination of a brand's identity may—as one may also add the decision about the overall brand architecture—be assigned to strategic management, as the transformation of a brand's identity in a corresponding image is to be seen as a medium-term target and presupposes the performance potential of an organization. The implementation of a brand's identity especially in terms of product and communication policy (e.g., packaging design, corporate design, and promotional appearance) and likewise price and distribution policy is a component of operative management.

Above all, seen from the viewpoint of modern strategic management, brands appear to be characterized as a fundamental part of the business model that should mirror the corporate strategy. The brand is often understood as some kind of value proposition of the enterprise which satisfies the needs that are crucial for the buying pattern of the envisaged target group in the respective market with a clear demarcation to the competition (Burmann et al. 2012). With reference to the conception of business architecture as introduced by Simon et al. (2014) as well as in the introductory chapter of this book (Chap. 1), this value proposition (with the brand identity being the related core asset) is derived from the business motivation, which includes the corporate strategy as a core component. The value proposition, on the other hand, will have to be translated into corresponding business execution, as represented by, e.g., processes, structures, and even a brand-related culture. Hence, branding, as the underlying approach to maintain a competitive edge, may be considered a business model design theme.

Based on the previous discussion, we would like to offer the following reference frame of a "Corporate Strategy & Brand Management" approach (CS&BM; see Fig. 3.1). The framework proposes two different levels of corporate strategic and brand management. On the side of corporate strategic management, the first level is called strategic program planning and refers to all decisions about basic strategies (e.g., market field strategies, market stimulation, etc.; see Sect. 3.3.2) and

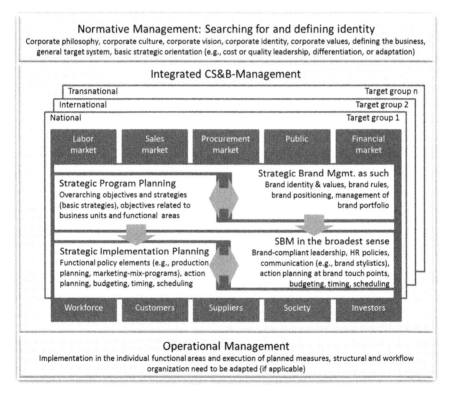

Fig. 3.1 Reference frame of an integrated CS&B-management approach

overarching goals as well as decisions about those goals concerning business sectors or functional areas. It must be closely connected with what we call strategic brand management as such. This first level of strategic brand management contains all decisions about the brand identity and brand values, brand rules, brand positioning, and the management of the brand portfolio. According to our reference frame, the second level of corporate strategic management is called strategic implementation planning. This level includes all decisions about functional policies (e.g., production planning, marketing-mix-programs), action planning, budgeting, timing, and scheduling. Again, management decisions at the second level must be closely linked with all decisions of what we call strategic brand management in the broadest sense and what includes measures of brand-compliant leadership (e.g., leadership guidelines with relation to the brand), brand-related human resource management tools (e.g., trainings about brand-related behavior), brand-related communication activities (e.g., brand stylistics), action planning at brand touch points, and again the budgeting, timing, and scheduling of those activities.

It goes without saying that the described integrated approach to corporate strategic and brand management receives presetting and guidelines from normative management. For instance, decisions about the basic strategic assumptions of the company (e.g., quality or cost leadership, differentiation or adaptation) are taken on a normative level. The integrated corporate strategic and brand management itself provides input to operational management where the implementation in the individual functional areas and the execution of planned measures are set up. In all of that, different markets, different stakeholders, and possibly different geographical areas need to be considered.

This reference frame outlined in Fig. 3.1 is assumed as a contribution to the discussion which needs to be further shaped and fine-tuned. It goes without saying that it cannot display all correlations and interdependencies between strategic management and strategic brand management in the context of corporate branding. Certain, important aspects of the reference frame will be described in the following section by means of selected design perspectives.

3.3 Selected Design Perspectives of the Integrated Approach to CS&B-Management

CS&B-management can only be successful if it does not adopt a biased and focused perspective (e.g., as perceived from the perspective of the sales market) but rather is able to reach all stakeholders of an organization equally. Of course, there may be industries where internal target groups (staff) or procurement markets (suppliers) are less important than in other industries. Nevertheless, it would appear necessary to take a broad view, to bypass any opposition and to keep interfering signals on a low level. Against this backdrop, three central fields of responsibility are displayed in the following and the impacts of the respective activities are examined further.

3.3.1 Definition of Corporate and Brand Identity as Gateway for CS&B-Management

There is no doubt that a corporation's culture shapes how they interact with their stakeholders in a fundamental way. Casually speaking you might be able to define culture with the following statement: "It's about how we do the things around here." In contrast to corporate philosophy which only—frequently in the form of written mission statements—describes the basic values determining the business-related thinking and acting (see Chap. 1), the corporate culture includes the behavioral and object-related level of what is going on in a company and, therefore, also the ascertainment of values (Kreutzer et al. 1989) (see Chap. 7 for further details on culture). Stakeholders will therefore never experience the philosophy of an organization but are faced with the culture that either goes along with the philosophy or else is different. If essential characteristics of the experienced culture are perceived as stable over time and at the same time there is no deviation between target and actual position, then this is what we call corporate identity. Wiedmann defines the term corporate identity as follows: "Corporate Identity (CI) is the specific 'personality of an enterprise' meaning the values, targets, ways of thinking and acting, behavioral routines, capabilities and skills, institutional regulations, and appearances that are typical or deemed typical of a corporation in their entirety" [Wiedmann 2004, p. 1415 (own translation); on the discussion of the term identity as part of corporate identity approaches see Birkigt et al. (1998); a comprehensive literature overview on different definitions of the term identity can be found in Pérez and Rodríguez del Bosque (2014)].

The general concept of a brand comes into play by all means whenever the enterprise—within the scope of its general competitive strategy—pursues a quality leadership and differentiation strategy (Homburg and Krohmer 2009). Then it becomes necessary to identify those elements in the corporate identity that are not only typical of the enterprise and deemed genuine by stakeholders, but likewise are or could be of high relevance to customers and have not yet been captured by the competition to distinguish their brand in the market. It seems logical that without distinctive characteristics that are relevant from a customer's viewpoint to distinguish the enterprise from others with a similar product range, it is likely to be difficult to create that special fascination that is typical for strong brands. On the other hand, it must be mentioned that distinctive characteristics must not only be sought on the functional level but also on the symbolic level. However, this does not mean that at this stage one should already think about diving into the emotional world of advertising. The symbolic characteristics that go along with a corporate brand are much more likely to be found in areas like innovation, process reliability, quality, or trust. In addition, those areas of the corporate identity that are tainted with negative connotations should be left aside. At the end of the day, the objective of brand management is to enhance the positive perception that is based on outstanding accomplishments (Gietl 2013).

The formulation of brand identity is done internally and must hence be considered a concept of statements (Burmann et al. 2012). This concept of statements comes close to reality but does not map it entirely for at least two reasons. First, the perceptions of external target groups can only be accounted for indirectly as judged by the internal target groups (Hatch and Schultz 2008). Second, a target component can link brand identity with corporate vision (Hatch and Schultz 2001b). Hence, the brand identity reflects a brand's characteristic elements for which it stands internally and should stand facing any external parties. However, it must be noted that it does not constitute an ideal. Taking into consideration the specific company situation an initial ideal concept of brand identity should be projected in this process. Following the comparison with the actual situation, though, this ideal concept has to be streamlined to a feasible target concept (Wiedmann and Schmidt 1997). Formally, *brand identity* can be defined as follows: "Brand identity includes those spatio-temporal features of a brand that sustainably shape a brand's character according to the internal target groups' view" (Burmann et al. 2012, p. 30 [own translation]). Conversely, *brand image* must be understood as an acceptance-based concept with which the implementation level of the brand identity by the enterprise can be mirrored.

An organization from the logistics industry can be named as an example of this process where a comprehensive brand project was carried out a few years ago. In order to initially capture the corporate identity, external consultants were called in who compiled and visualized the elements of corporate identity by using different survey methods (shifting through files of guidelines, analyzing internal and external communication material, conducting customer telephone surveys, staff group discussions, individual interviews with executives, workshops with suppliers, etc.). Based on this, a cross-functional steering committee that was operating across hierarchies categorized the most important but still numerous elements of corporate identity according to conciseness (is this really typically characteristic for us?), relevance (is this relevant for our internal and external target groups?), and distinctive power (does this distinguish ourselves from our competition?). As a result, the corporate identity could be boiled down further. The identity of the corporate brand derived from the corporate identity consisted of a central core (brand core) and five values that the brand was supposed to represent internally and in future also externally. What was special about this method was that the brand identity mainly reflected the outstanding achievements communicated in the past and, therefore, met with widespread approval in the course of the implementation.

3.3.2 Development of Strategic Positioning as Core Assignment of CS&B-Management

The term positioning is often understood as a specific highlighting of accomplishments in order to distinguish a business clearly and positively from other businesses, services or products (De Pelsmacker et al. 2013; Bruhn 2010). But in such a perspective of differentiation the viewpoint of customer benefit is somewhat neglected: organizations develop *brand positioning* to strengthen the bundle of characteristics that customers associate or should associate with a company in certain areas with the expectation that this added value is important for the customer (Mudambi and Chitturi 2010). Keller (1993; with reference to Aaker 1982; Ries and Trout 1979; Wind 1982) back then defined the term positioning as sustainable competitive edge or also "'unique selling proposition' that gives consumers a compelling reason for buying that particular brand." Also Burmann et al. (2012, p. 73; also compare the framework provided in Chap. 1) embrace a similar stance, putting brand positioning on the same level as brand value proposition. "It compacts the components of brand identity to very few, brief statements that translate into a pledge promising the satisfaction of needs offered by this brand that is easy to understand by the external target group" (own translation). Hence, as positioning is based on brand identity as well as derived from it, the need for authenticity, relevance, and distinction is also relevant for the positioning.

A well-known supplier in the solar industry that manufactured solar cells and related top-quality products, planned and built solar farms, and worked on new energy concepts, underwent a brand positioning process some time ago. For this purpose the brand identity was taken as a home base which had been compiled and documented in a previous project. As part of the brand identity process those characteristics were filtered out that not only suited the company as well as distinguished themselves from the competition and were relevant to customers but also—from the viewpoint of the decision makers—had the potential to inspire and fascinate current and future customers. This decision was based on in-depth interviews with industry experts and key accounts as well as large-scale studies on market development, industry trends and megatrends. The outcome of the discussions was to characterize the enterprise no longer as a manufacturer of solar modules but as a leading solar enterprise with system expertise which was to become a fundamental aspect of the value proposition to be communicated to the customer.

In terms of an integrated CS&B-management process the closely meshed coordination of positioning with the basic marketing strategies needs to be ensured. This includes, according to Becker (2000; also described by Scharf et al. 2012), the market field strategies (specification of the product/market combinations, "Ansoff matrix"), the market stimulation strategies (price-volume strategy or preferential strategy), the market area strategy (determination and expansion of sales territory) as well as market parceling strategies (mass marketing or market segmentation). So the question whether an enterprise is doing business on the regional, national or international markets or even considers itself a global enterprise (market area strategies) should have a major impact on the wording of the positioning. Secondly, it should be of particular importance at this point, amongst many other questions, to address the question whether the enterprise can position its corporate brand facing the various stakeholders and target groups at different locations or if a uniform positioning for all market segments should be preferred (market parceling strategy).

The above mentioned solar business, for example, thought about the following: would it be beneficial to associate its positioning as a system supplier with a specific designation of origin that should strengthen the perception of competence and innovation amongst customers? This led to the discussion whether this demarcation of origin was well understood in the markets of the individual countries or at least conveyed similar contents. At the end of the day, the business decided to go for a uniform positioning including a demarcation of origin in all serviced markets.

3.3.3 Implementation of Brand Identity Towards the Inside: The Particular Challenge of CS&B-Management

In the course of integrated CS&B-management it becomes obvious that a brand can only unleash its full potential when it is actually lived within the enterprise (Esch 2012). In the past, the dominating position of communication policy to implement brand identity and positioning was often underlined (Bruhn 2001). Practical experience reveals, however, that brand management projects—especially in the context of corporate brands—have often failed since inadequate tools which only focus on external communication are used in the brand implementation phase. This is particularly astonishing as there is a variety of well-known tools that are aimed at bringing staff behavior, brand identity and positioning in line (Schmidt 2011; Schmidt and Kilian 2012). Corporate brands like, for example, Apple, UPS, or Disney, which are striving for distinct positioning, have long realized that many known tools from the field of HR and organization development that are aimed at altering staff behavior (e.g., leadership trainings, personal appraisals, or bonus policies) can also function as brand management tools. This is not only attributed to the visibility of the identity-oriented brand management approach which is seen more often in practice but likewise due to the disappointment experienced by the limited effectiveness of pure communication policy based activities (Rutschmann 2011; Koch 2010). More and more people seem to come to the conclusion that—in association with corporate brands—only a mix of different tools can help align staff conduct with the brand.

Against the backdrop of intensifying customer networks, it becomes more important for the success of corporate brands how the latter interact with their stakeholders. Disruptions in the relationship of customer and brand caused by negative experiences are no longer a private matter but will be rapidly spread in social networks, blogs, rating portals and any other appropriate forums and so made known to a broad public quickly and easily. Here the contact between a supplier's workforce—being representatives of the brand—and customers is of particular importance (Tomczak et al. 2005; Wentzel 2008). At the so-called brand touchpoints, e.g., at customer service desks, in sales conversations or, at trade shows, it will be revealed whether the brand can keep its benefit promise (Perrey and Meyer 2011; Kilian 2012) or not. Any negative experience customers may encounter will rapidly have a negative impact on brand perception. Positive experiences, on the other hand, can strengthen the brand perception in the long run. Since employees in more and more industries do their bit to raise their customers' brand awareness and to a greater extent than previously, consideration must also be given to the fact that staff conduct needs to be managed systematically in accordance with the corporate brand.

The call for the implementation of an instrument mix leads to the conclusion that brand management in association with corporate brands needs to be lined up much broader than in association with product brands. HR policy tools like brand-compliant selection of staff, integration of newly recruited staff or training brand-oriented behavior are also part of the toolkit of a brand manager as are appropriate management or incentive systems (Sackmann 2010). The approach of "internal branding" provides the tools that will enable and motivate employees to promote the brand through their behavior in order to keep the brand's promise. The concept of internal branding includes all measures (e.g., communication, training, workshops) that are aimed at involving staff in the process of branding, informing them about their own brand, filling them with enthusiasm about the brand and finally to govern their behavior for the benefit of the brand (Schmidt and Kilian 2012) (see, e.g., Chap. 4 for a specific example).

So brand management of corporate brands is not to be left entirely to the marketing and sales departments but must penetrate the enterprise in its entirety, which involves the development of the brand in alignment with the (communicated) brand promise and (actual) brand experience at the company's touchpoints with its target groups. Of course, those customers that use a product or a service in the so-called "moments of truth" play a major role in the brand-building process, since a stable and long-term sustainable brand-customer-relationship can only be established through the consistent and continuous transfer of all components of a brand at all brand touchpoints (Burmann and Wenske 2006). But in principle, anybody that is exposed to a brand at the brand touchpoint can be a key multiplier in the overall branding process. And just like one bad musician playing out of tune can spoil the sound of a great orchestra, a badly managed brand touchpoint can portray the overall brand in a rather unflattering light. Since corporate brands usually have a lot of brand touchpoints, it is precisely for them of utmost importance to bring the touchpoints between enterprise and target groups in line with the brand (Schmidt 2006). In addition, a systematic and brand-oriented touchpoint management helps make the workforce aware of the brand strategy in its entirety to generate quick results that have a long-term impact.

This means that it is initially essential to analyze the customer journey through the corporate environment (Schüller 2012), which includes the detection and prioritization of all brand touchpoints. The criteria for such a prioritization should be the significance from the viewpoint of customers and target groups, contact frequency and intensity. In a second step prioritized brand touchpoints should be brought in line with the brand identity during an audit. Can the customer or potential customer actually feel the brand at the touchpoints? Does the brand touchpoint "behave" in a genuine, attractive, and distinctive way towards its target groups? Answering these questions is simple only when the definition of brand identity is based on few, concise characteristics and likewise, clear and plain rules have been developed with which the brand compliance of any measure can be easily assessed. An "on brand" touchpoint should therefore meet the majority of brand rules. Ideas for improvement should be compiled for those brand touchpoints that are not "on brand" in a third step and thus included in an implementation plan. Finally, implementation must be managed and monitored.

Let's take the example of the insurance company that a few years ago strengthened internal brand management by training brand ambassadors that were to explain the developed brand identity and positioning in their local entities. As part of these workshops, employees were encouraged to compare identity and positioning of the brand with the actual situation at the brand touchpoints locally and, should there be any shortfalls, to submit proposals how to bring about a change. These proposals were in return received by the brand ambassadors, boiled down into core projects and in terms of a holistic program management absorbed in the overall action plan of the enterprise (roadmapping) followed by budgeting, timing and specific scheduling processes. A large brand event was held, that involved all employees and where all agreed projects and initial findings were presented. Additionally, the event was the platform for entertainment acts, creativity workshops and visualizations in order to emotionalize staff for the brand and fill them with enthusiasm.

3.4   Conclusion

The old way of thinking, the brand is considered an operational tool that needs to be defined downstream from strategy development is obsolete. Strategy and brand are mutually dependent—at least in the context of strong corporate brands—and consequently a holistic approach needs to be adopted in their respective development. In addition to the examples outlined in this chapter, more ideas on the basis of the outlined CS&B-management approach are welcome that shape the integrated strategy and brand development process. The proposed examples may, however, suffice to raise awareness of research and industry of the need for a stronger involvement of strategic and brand management, as can be supported by the use of an overall business architecture framework.

References

Aaker DA (1982) Positioning your product. Bus Horiz 25(3):56–62
Aaker DA (1996) Building strong brands. The Free Press, New York
Adjouri N (2004) Alles was sie über Marken wissen müssen. Springer Gabler, Wiesbaden
Ansoff H (1965) Corporate strategy. McGraw-Hill, New York
Baumgarth C (2008) Markenpolitik: Markenwirkungen – Markenführung – Markencontrolling, 3rd edn. Gabler, Wiesbaden
Baumgarth C, Binckebanck L (2013) CSR-Markenmanagement – Markenmodell und Best-Practice-Fälle am Beispiel der Bau- und Immobilienwirtschaft. In: Working papers of the institute of management Berlin at the Berlin School of Economics and Law (62)
Baumgarth C, Merrilees B, Urde M (2011) Kunden- oder Markenorientierung – Zwei Seiten einer Medaille oder alternative Routen? Mark Rev St Gallen 28(1):8–13

Becker J (2000) Marketing-Strategien. Systematische Kursbestimmung in schwierigen Märkten – Leitfaden mit Checklisten und Analysen. Vahlen, Munich

Biel AL (2001) Grundlagen zum Markenwertaufbau. In: Esch F-R (ed) Moderne Markenführung, 3rd edn. Gabler, Wiesbaden, pp 61–90

Binckebacck L, Baumgarth C (2011) CSR-Marke. Unveröffentlichtes Paper (eingereicht und präsentiert auf der Konferenz DERMARKENTAG2011), Berlin

Birkigt K, Stadler MM, Funck HJ (1998) Corporate identity. Moderne Industrie, Landsberg/Lech

Brandmeyer K, Schmidt M (1999) Der "Genetische Code der Marke" als Management-Werkzeug. In: Brandmeyer K, Deichsel A (eds) Jahrbuch Markentechnik 2000/2001. Deutscher Fachverlag, Frankfurt, pp 271–289

Bruhn M (2001) Die zunehmende Bedeutung von Dienstleistungsmarken. In: Köhler R, Majer W, Wiezorek H (eds) Erfolgsfaktor Marke: Neue Strategien des Markenmanagements. Vahlen, Munich, pp 213–225

Bruhn M (2010) Marketing – Grundlagen für Studium und Praxis, 10th edn. Gabler, Wiesbaden

Burmann C (2002) Strategische Flexibilität und Strategiewechsel als Determinanten des Unternehmenswertes. Deutscher Universitäts, Wiesbaden

Burmann C, Wenske V (2006) Multi-Channel-Management bei Premiummarken. Mark Rev St Gallen 23(4):11–15

Burmann C, Halaszivich T, Hemmann F (2012) Identitätsbasierte Markenführung: Grundlagen – Strategie – Umsetzung – Controlling. Springer Gabler, Wiesbaden

Court DC, Leiter MG, Loch MA (1999) Brand leverage. McKinsey Q 17(2):100–110

De Pelsmacker P, Geuens M, Van den Bergh J (2013) Marketing communications. A European perspective, 5th edn. Pearson, Harlow

Esch FR (2012) Strategie und Technik der Markenführung, 7th edn. Vahlen, Munich

Esch FR, Tomczak T, Kernstock J, Langner T (eds) (2006) Corporate brand management: Marken als Anker strategischer Führung von Unternehmen, 2nd edn. Gabler, Wiesbaden

Gietl J (2013) Value branding: Vom hochwertigen Produkt zur wertvollen Marke. Haufe, Freiburg

Haedrich G, Tomczak T, Kaetzke P (2003) Strategische Markenführung, 3rd edn. UTB, Stuttgart

Harter G, Koster A, Peterson M, Stomberg M (2005) Managing brands for value creation. http://www.boozallen.com/media/file/Managing_Brands_for_Value_Creation.pdf. Accessed 14 Feb 2014

Hatch MJ, Schultz M (2001a) Are the strategic stars aligned for your corporate brand? Harv Bus Rev 79(2):128–134

Hatch MJ, Schultz M (2001b) Den Firmennamen zur Marke machen. Harv Bus Manager 23 (4):36–43

Hatch MJ, Schultz M (2008) Taking brand initiative. Wiley, San Francisco

Homburg C, Krohmer H (2009) Marketingmanagement: Strategie – Instrumente – Umsetzung – Unternehmensführung, 3rd edn. Gabler, Wiesbaden

Joas A, Offerhaus P (2001) Brand equity: Wie die Marke den Unternehmenswert steigern kann. Spektrum (1):9

Kapferer JN (1992) Die Marke: Kapital des Unternehmens. Landsberg/Lech, Mi-Wirtschaftsbuch

Keller KL (1993) Conceptualizing, measuring, and managing customer-based brand equity. J Mark 57(1):1–22

Keuper F (2010) Die Implosion des Market-based View. In: Keuper F, Hogenschurz B (eds) Professionelles sales & service management. Vorsprung durch konsequente Kundenorientierung, 2nd edn. Gabler, Wiesbaden, pp 3–45

Kilian K (2012) Vom Point of Sale zum Point of Experience. Markenartikel 1–2(2012):100–102

Koch K-D (2010) Was Marken unwiderstehlich macht – 101 Wege zur Begehrlichkeit, 2nd edn. Orell Fuessli, Zürich

Kotler P, Armstrong G (2010) Principles of Marketing, 13th edn. Prentice Hall, Upper Saddle River, NJ

Kreutzer R, Jugel S, Wiedmann K-P (1989) Unternehmensphilosophie und Corporate Identity. Working paper, University of Mannheim, Mannheim

Madden TJ, Fehle F, Fournier SM (2006) Brands matter: an empirical investigation of brand-building activities and the creation of shareholder value. J Acad Mark Sci 34(2):224–235

Meffert H (2004) Identitätsorientierter Ansatz der Markenführung – eine entscheidungsorientierte Perspektive. In: Bruhn M (ed) Handbuch Markenführung, 2nd edn. Gabler, Wiesbaden, pp 293–320

Meffert H, Burmann C (1996) Identitätsorientierte Markenführung. Working paper, Wissenschaftliche Gesellschaft für Marketing und Unternehmensführung, Münster

Meffert H, Burmann C (2005) Wandel in der Markenführung – vom instrumentellen zum identitätsorientierten Markenverständnis. In: Meffert H, Burmann C, Koers M (eds) Markenmanagement. Identitätsorientierte Markenführung und praktische Umsetzung, 2nd edn. Gabler, Wiesbaden, pp 19–36

Mudambi SM, Chitturi P (2010) Optionen der B-to-B-Markenpositionierung. In: Baumgarth C (ed) B-to-B-Markenführung: Grundlagen – Konzepte – Best Practice. Gabler, Wiesbaden, pp 181–198

Osterwalder A, Pigneur Y (2010) Business model generation—a handbook for visionaries, game changers, and challengers. Wiley, New Jersey

Pérez A, Rodríguez del Bosque I (2014) Organizational identity revisited: toward a comprehensive understanding of identity in business. Corp Reput Rev 17(1):3–27

Perrey J, Meyer T (2011) Mega-Macht Marke: Erfolg messen, machen, managen, 3rd edn. Redline, Munich

Porter ME (2000) Wettbewerbsstrategie – Methoden zur Analyse von Branchen und Konkurrenten, 11th edn. Campus, Frankfurt

Porter ME (2008) Wettbewerbsvorteile: spitzenleistungen erreichen und behaupten, 6th edn. Campus, Frankfurt

Raffée H, Wiedmann KP (1989) Wertewandel und gesellschaftsorientiertes Marketing – Die Bewährungsprobe strategischer Unternehmensführung. In: Raffée H, Wiedmann K-P (eds) Strategisches marketing, 2nd edn. Poeschel, Stuttgart, pp 552–611

Ries A, Trout J (1979) Positioning: the battle for your mind. McGraw-Hill, New York

Rutschmann M (2011) Abschied von Branding. Gabler, Wiesbaden

Sackmann SA (2010) Markenorientierte Führung und Personalmanagement. In: Krobath K, Schmidt HJ (eds) Innen beginnen. Von der internen Kommunikation zum Internal Branding. Gabler, Wiesbaden, pp 47–59

Scharf A, Schubert B, Hehn P (2012) Marketing – Einführung in Theorie und Praxis, 5th edn. Schäffer-Poeschel, Stuttgart

Schmidt HJ (2006) Marken mit Struktur statt Bauchgefühl führen. io new management - Zeitschrift für Unternehmenswissenschaften und Führungspraxis (7–8):10–14

Schmidt HJ (2007) Grundlagen der innengerichteten Markenführung. In: Schmidt HJ (ed) Internal branding. Wie Sie Ihre Mitarbeiter zu Markenbotschaftern machen. Gabler, Wiesbaden, pp 13–110

Schmidt HJ (2011) Begriffe und Instrumente des Internal Branding. Media-TREFF (Sonderausgabe Markenkongress B2B 2011):34–37

Schmidt HJ, Kilian K (2012) Internal Branding, Employer Branding & Co.: Der Mitarbeiter im Markenfokus. Transfer Werbeforschung und Praxis 58(1):28–33

Schüller AM (2012) Marketer, begrabt die vier P! Horizont 31:19

Simon D, Fischbach K, Schoder D (2014) Enterprise architecture management and its role in corporate strategic management. Inf Syst e-Bus Manag 12(1):5–42

Teece DJ, Pisano G, Shuen A (1997) Dynamic capabilities and strategic management. Strateg Manag J 18(7):509–533

Tomczak T, Herrmann A, Brexendorf TO, Kernstock J (2005) Behavioral Branding – Markenprofilierung durch persönliche Kommunikation. Thexis 22(4):28–31

Tropp J (2011) Moderne Marketing-Kommunikation: System – Prozess – Management. VS Verlag, Wiesbaden

Ulrich H (1981) Die Bedeutung der Management-Philosophie für die Unternehmensführung. In: Ulrich H (ed) Management-Philosophie für die Zukunft. Gesellschaftlicher Wertewandel als Herausforderung an das Management. Haupt, Bern, pp 11–23

Walsh G, Deseniss A, Kilian T (2013) Marketing – Eine Einführung auf der Grundlage von Case Studies, 2nd edn. Springer Gabler, Wiesbaden

Wentzel D (2008) The impact of employee behavior on brand impression: theoretical and experimental analyses. Hundt Druck, Köln

Wiedmann K-P (2004) Markenführung und Corporate Identity. In: Bruhn M (ed) Handbuch Markenführung. Kompendium zum erfolgreichen Markenmanagement. Strategien — Instrumente — Erfahrungen. Gabler, Wiesbaden, pp 1413–1439

Wiedmann K-P, Kreutzer R (1989) Strategische Marketingplanung – Ein Überblick. In: Raffée H, Wiedmann K-P (eds) Strategisches marketing, 2nd edn. Poeschel, Stuttgart, pp 61–141

Wiedmann K-P, Schmidt HJ (1997) Markenmanagement erklärungsbedürftiger Produkte – Bezugsrahmen und erste Ergebnisse eines Forschungsprojekts. University of Hannover, Hannover

Wind Y (1982) Product policy: concepts, models, and strategy. Addison-Wesley, Reading

Zentes J, Swoboda B, Schramm-Klein H (2006) Internationales marketing. Vahlen, Munich

From Business Motivation to Business Model and Beyond: A Customer Value-Driven Approach

4

Jörg Heiß

Abstract

Business architecture offers a comprehensive view of the business of an enterprise. This chapter explores how to reasonably link the different constituents of the business architecture, primarily at the level of business motivation and business model, while considering effects on the business execution. In particular, this chapter illustrates three main tools/approaches to help gain insights into an enterprise's business motivation and business model (including the operating model): the "Value Disciplines," the "Business Model Canvas," and the 2-by-2 matrix of the operating model in terms of integration/standardization. It is demonstrated that these should not be considered and thus applied isolated from each other. Decisions with respect to the value strategy should be reflected in the business model, for example. Apple is used as an exemplary case to illustrate the application of the three tools. Specifically, it is shown how Apple's (assumed) business motivation is reflected in the business model choices, and how these are in turn implemented at the business execution layer.

4.1 Introduction

What should enterprise architecture (EA) management deliver for a company? You may consider strategy, processes, and systems in focus of EA management activities; this is widely acknowledged. Nevertheless, these parts will exist in an enterprise without fostering a discipline like EA management. Questions like "how is strategy implemented?" may remain unanswered though. Obviously, there are several challenges in aligning strategy, business operations, and the information

J. Heiß (✉)
Hannover Rückversicherung SE, Hannover, Germany
e-mail: joerg.heiss@hannover-re.com

© Springer International Publishing Switzerland 2015   53
D. Simon, C. Schmidt (eds.), *Business Architecture Management*, Management for Professionals, DOI 10.1007/978-3-319-14571-6_4

technology (IT); linking these different levels and developing a consistent model of
an enterprise is therefore a crucial part of EA management.

However, EA management functions that are just there and thrown into the pool
of multiple interests will probably drown. Why is that? EA management can be
misunderstood as a modern approach of building an enterprise or an IT landscape
(as a subset) aligned with strategic targets. But without a holistic view it will be "put
under water" by tactical initiatives, political interests, or short-sighted priorities. In
a best-case scenario it can then only show some value by providing expert skills for
solutions built in projects or through its function as a housekeeper for standards and
principles. So the question remains what is right to make EA management a
success? What are the boundaries for a holistic, consistent EA management
approach?

First, as a matter of fact, EA management will probably not work "bottom-up"
alone. Even if some architecture elements had their origin on an operational level
and then evolved to become part of the business model and strategy, EA management has to look at "top-down" consequences of these elements. This is necessary
to make sure that "bottom-up" developments are part of an overall consistent model
and are reflected well on all levels. At last, all architecture elements should be
related to parts of the strategy. Therefore, it is of high value to analyze the strategy
and identify if there are elements in the architecture that contradict the consistency
from top to bottom.

Second, EA does not implement itself. If an architecture is defined, there have to
be measures to implement it.

Finally, an implemented architecture does not automatically mean that there are
benefits; that is, you have to have measures in place to make sure that the intended
effects are delivered.

All three topics are interesting to look at; in this chapter, the aspect of overall
consistency in the business architecture [including business motivation, business
model, and business execution, as outlined in Simon et al. (2014) and detailed in
Chap. 1] is in focus. Specifically, this chapter explores the linkage between business
motivation and business model and thus targets the following questions:

- How can effects of strategy be analyzed?
- How can strategy be linked to the business model?
- What is the right scope for an operating model[1] and how does it affect business
execution?

To illustrate the use of three tools that help answer these questions and bring the
discussion to a practical level, this chapter refers to one specific, real-life enterprise
throughout all sections; Apple Inc. is known well enough to validate the theory
against a real-life example. It should be kept in mind that it is difficult to discuss the
actual corporate strategy here, since this is not available for the public; however,
there are some obvious key aspects that show how business motivation (factors that

---

[1] The operating model is considered part of the business model (see Chap. 1).

direct an enterprise, including, e.g., values, vision, goals, strategies, and directives), business model (elements of value creation), and business execution (components that implement the business model, such as, e.g., business processes) are interlinked.

4.2   How Does Business Motivation Affect an Enterprise?

Working as an enterprise architect comes with the recurring need to justify architectural decisions. For this purpose, it is very helpful to have accepted architecture principles to rely on. Taking this further, it would actually be most promising to be able to connect any element of the overall architecture with the basics of the enterprise itself, as any substantial principle would have its roots there anyway. To get a holistic view of the fundamental aspects that drive an enterprise, this book's business architecture framework suggests looking into the business motivation, which aggregates all aspects an enterprise's decisions should be founded on.

Most companies do have a strategy document and maybe this also covers the aspects of mission, values, and external drivers, for example. Nevertheless, one should be aware that even if there are explicitly formulated strategy statements it may be necessary to look for implicit add-ons or even contradictory statements from major stakeholders you have to consider.

So the basic question is how to extract the architecture-relevant facts out of the explicitly and/or implicitly given business motivation. Several tools can be used for this purpose; the following subsection describes one of these tools, including its role for the "justification" of the overall architecture. The findings from applying the tool can be used in different contexts:

- Identification of overall strategies or principles
- Creation of a consistent design of the business model
- Support of linking business execution to the business model
- Identification of gaps between the actual business model and the business motivation

4.2.1   Value Disciplines

To build a consistent architecture, it is important to identify what is most important for an enterprise. This should be a key part of its strategy statements. According to Treacy and Wiersema (1993), there are three *value disciplines* an enterprise can pursue (see Table 4.1).[2] All three disciplines need to be developed to a certain level

---

[2] The value disciplines do not necessarily cover all aspects within the business motivation. Nevertheless, they represent one tool to start with, and the results can be combined with findings from additional analyses.

Table 4.1 Value disciplines (Treacy and Wiersema 1993)

Customer intimacy	Summary of value discipline – Do everything to identify the customer's need and make a profound decision of how to fulfil them – Deliver a full range of services – Focus on the long-term profitability of a customer Impact on the architecture – Implement variety of distribution channels (online, on-site, self-service, etc.) – Implement processes to identify and classify the customer, create systems and collect information to support these processes – Develop capability to update product portfolio according to customer's needs
Operational excellence	Summary of value discipline – Leadership in price and convenience for the customer – Manage transactions efficiently – Measure quality and cost of transactions – Concentrate on standard products Impact on the architecture – Reduce overhead costs by focusing production on demand – High level of process automation to improve cost, quality, and performance
Product leadership	Summary of value discipline – Produce continuous stream of state-of-the-art products and services – Concentrate on speed – Pursue new ideas (also from outside the company), do not be afraid to make your own products obsolete – Present the benefits of new products Impact on the architecture – Maintain and improve capabilities to develop and deliver products – Foster creativity – Support fast decision making, avoid bureaucracy – Be able to manage risks of failure

to make the enterprise fit for competition, but there is one to focus on to differentiate.

Only a few companies have succeeded to excel in two of these disciplines, as there are obvious trade-offs. Cost leadership does not fit the offering of a broad, customized product portfolio, while extensive process automation usually does not come with high flexibility. Therefore, one important task for business architects is to identify the company's core value discipline and align the architectural decisions accordingly. For sure this means that from time to time the conflict between upcoming business ideas and their alignment to the existing business has to be managed.

4.2.2   Example: Apple

How does this apply to Apple? At first instance, several people may consider Apple a customer intimate company. If you look into this in more detail, it becomes pretty obvious that Apple is not primarily driven by customer intimacy though. For each product group, Apple basically has a streamlined product portfolio without many variations. Back in 2007 there was only one iPhone. For some time it nearly seemed that Apple adopted a quote from Henry Ford: "You can have an iPhone in every color as long as it is black." Still, in 2013, with several iPhones in the market (5s and 5c in different colors), you would not consider it as a move to customer intimacy. Nokia and Samsung offer smartphones in every size and cover the prize range from low to high end. So if it is not customer intimacy that drives Apple, what is it then?

Looking at the products Apple released for the last decade, it appears that the intention has always been to be the market leader with respect to design, user experience, technology, and product integration. So even if there was no product leadership statement in Apple's strategy, one would most likely identify it as the value discipline by which it is predominantly driven (Fig. 4.1). There is another element from Apple's history that is typical for a "product leader." Obviously, the success of iPhones and iPads dramatically affected the turnover of iPods. Apple was not afraid of replacing one successful product of its own with a new one, as any other company could have come up with a similar device.

How ambitious Apple is to keep its product leadership is recognizable in its latest decisions. Due to the fact that hardware components are available for other players in the industry as well, it becomes increasingly difficult to build an outstanding smartphone, tablet, or notebook. Obviously, Apple noticed that and today concentrates not only on the hardware but sells the whole package with its iLife applications (and other software services) for free on all platforms. By doing

Fig. 4.1 Value discipline for Apple

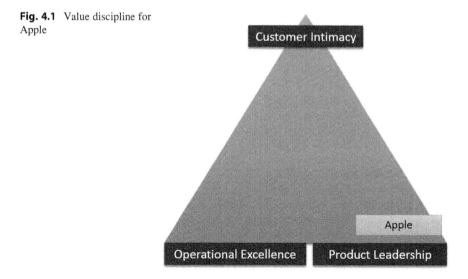

this, it still has an add-on for its products that others cannot copy easily, for the prize of losing around $400 million in software revenue.

Furthermore, there is another important element of product leadership in the smartphone/tablet market—the ecosystem. The user value of a device does not only depend on hardware specifications but also on network effects within the platform. Imagine there would be no WhatsApp available for iPhones. It would not be relevant if you had another "perfect" messenger app, as the value of such apps is related to the number of connected users. This means that in order to maintain product leadership, it is essential to care about the ecosystem. Later in this chapter it is shown which measures Apple has in place for this; for now, such consideration of the ecosystem is meant to indicate that Apple puts product leadership in focus of its activities.

The pure need for being the best was pointed out by Tim Cook (CEO of Apple Inc.) in a recent interview (Grobart 2013): "There's a segment of the market that really wants a product that does a lot for them, and I want to compete like crazy for those customers." Therefore, they are in need to innovate to give customers the extra benefits they can expect for the higher price.

4.2.2.1 Is Apple Excellent in Operations?

Is that all? Perhaps not, as you may find Apple also succeeds in operational excellence. There may be two indications for that:

- First, it managed to develop its supply chain in a way that allows a flexible production with outsourced capacities at very low costs. Although this might be typical for operationally excellent companies in particular, you would probably not consider this a main strategic target for Apple. It is a pure necessity to work with external capacities and technology for building electronic devices.
- Second, with the web-based Apple store as well as the iTunes- and AppStore, it makes use of very convenient, highly efficient solutions to sell products. Although this would also fit for a company driven by operational excellence, for Apple the main driver seems different. It is part of its product leadership approach to have these platforms in place as they are used to support the ecosystem of Apple products.

As pointed out earlier, in every company you will find a certain degree of each discipline, as you can neither leave costs unconsidered nor ignore customer needs and product quality; in fact, the minimum level for each is defined by the competition.

4.2.2.2 Further Strategic Observations on Apple

Focusing on product leadership and caring about the ecosystem is not only important to be attractive for customers. Strategically, it has another value because a well-developed, feature-complete ecosystem is hard to copy for competitors. Consider Microsoft's Windows Phone; although Microsoft tried hard for several years now, Windows Phone is still behind. At the hardware/operating system level it was kind of easy to deliver "nice" products. However, you still do not get all apps and contents that are available for iOS devices, as it is difficult to attract a large community of external developers for the platform.

Furthermore, a strong ecosystem comes with a lock-in effect for users. Once a user has stored his profiles and data in one ecosystem, it costs some effort to move to another one, even if it offers the same features. In fact, Steve Jobs recognized this lock-in as a primary goal of Apple with its cloud services, thus making sure that existing customers choose more Apple products in the future (Chen 2014).

Therefore, you can assume that, from a strategic point of view, Apple also has the iOS ecosystem in focus. Product leadership is connected to that as it means to develop the ecosystem to be best-in-class. Such an ecosystem should be hard to copy and makes it convenient for customers to buy more and more Apple products.

4.3 How to Link Business Motivation to Business Model?

4.3.1 Value of a Business Model

As a business architect you will have the need to break down the given statements from the business motivation into smaller parts that directly affect single architecture building blocks. An overall goal such as "cost saving" may work at the motivational level, but for the "right" architecture you need to define which elements of your architecture at lower levels will be affected by this goal. You can guess that this process is probably not easy. Nevertheless, all relevant stakeholders for your architecture should agree at least on a top level how strategy is translated into a business model. A supporting tool for this purpose is the "*Business Model Canvas*" (Osterwalder and Pigneur 2010).

The basic idea here is very simple. The enterprise has to decide on its position for nine main topics (as explained below).[3] The general value of applying the Business Model Canvas lies on multiple levels:

- *Analyze strategy*: The Canvas helps to visualize the meaning/contents of the strategy in one picture. It can thus be used to discuss the different topics with major stakeholders before designing and implementing the lower-level architecture (e.g., business processes).
- *Design/implement architecture*: During design and implementation of the lower-level architecture, the Canvas gives orientation about the underlying facts of each building block. Especially during the design phase architects need solid information with respect to the elements of the Business Model Canvas. For example, to develop the architecture at the execution level it is important to know which customer segment is addressed. An architecture for the mass

---

[3] The nine building blocks of the Canvas represent major parts of the business model constituent of the architecture framework used in this book (there are some additions in this framework though; see Chap. 1).

market probably looks different than one for a niche market. It may also help to coordinate different projects by defining the main targets for each.

- *Evaluate results*: If the business results do not match the expectations, the Canvas can be used to evaluate which building blocks may have not performed as intended.

The Business Model Canvas is very flexible as well. It can be used to visualize the business model on an enterprise level, just for a single product, or even for single capabilities. As such, it can be employed as a general tool to develop the architecture.

In combination with the ideas of a cause-effect-model, the Business Model Canvas provides an even more systematic picture (King 2012). In this variant, the elements of a Business Model Canvas are ordered in a sequence to group demand, supply, and results for better transparency.

4.3.2 Business Model Canvas for Apple Inc.

To demonstrate the value of using such a Business Model Canvas, this section applies it to Apple Inc. as a whole (not only for a single product or capability). Additionally, it presents some possible alternatives to improve the understanding of the model itself. Note that the Business Model Canvas may be more complex than described here. This example is limited to the chosen scope and does not show the full variations the Business Model Canvas can have.

Figure 4.2 displays the main elements of the Business Model Canvas (ordered by the main three topics Results-Demand-Supply). More details about the different

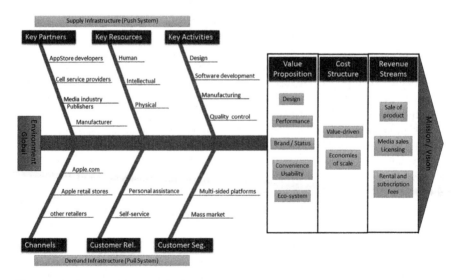

Fig. 4.2 Business model canvas for Apple

parts of the Business Model Canvas can be found in the underlying literature (Osterwalder and Pigneur 2010).

4.3.2.1 Results

Value Proposition
The value proposition defines why a customer chooses one product over another. The value proposition may be linked to specific customer segments.

Becoming and remaining a product leader is certainly difficult. Without any doubt, Apple stands out as a brand; especially with the first versions of the iPhones it was clear that it worked perfectly as a status symbol for a wide range of customer segments. Therefore, a strong brand (see Chap. 3 for a detailed discussion of brands as a significant part of the business model) along with being a leader in design, technology, and usability must be in focus of the business model.

The brand "Apple" is especially associated with design, according to which every part is well thought of. Even if the functionality does not differ from any other devices, Apple's version looks "better" or is "nicer" to touch. It is important to note that the design does not stop with the look; all parts are considered important for the overall impression of the product and are part of the design process. To support its product leadership, Apple focuses on an integrated software/hardware product that delivers optimized usability and performance. This is enhanced by an ecosystem that makes sure that network effects are generated by a high number of users, on the one hand, and app developers and content publishers, on the other hand. In this way, the ecosystem itself becomes an element of the product and has to be managed in order to be best-in-class.

It may be an interesting point for discussion whether novelty should be considered a part of Apple's value proposition. Of course, iPod, iTunes, and iPhone/iPad have been disrupting offers in the market. Nevertheless, considering the size of Apple and the revenue it earns with established products today, you may conclude that Apple's success is not really dependent on inventing something new every year. Therefore, it seems more important to be the best rather than to be the first. Altogether, it can be concluded that the value proposition is linked very well to the value discipline of being a product leader.

Cost Structure
Cost structure defines the priorities of operating a business regarding costs.

Analyzing Apple's cost structure is not that easy. On the one hand, there is the value proposition of delivering best-in-class products; on the other hand, there is the need to minimize costs. Therefore, it is hard to decide whether Apple is cost-driven or value-driven.

For sure, as has been pointed out earlier, Apple favors a value-driven approach for design and development. This fits very well to the approach of being a product leader. Nevertheless, there is the necessity to look at costs. According to the value disciplines, this is a prerequisite demanded by the competition. Apple complies with this by exploiting the possibilities of economies of scale in a cost-driven approach for production and distribution.

Revenue Streams
Revenue streams define how revenues are (to be) generated from the customer segments.

Apple generates the major part of its overall turnover by selling hardware. Nevertheless, there is a substantial part generated through media sales (iTunes, AppStore) and subscription fees (iCloud). Across all product groups, Apple follows a high-price strategy. Being successful as a product leader with a strong ecosystem, Apple can ask for higher prices than the competition [as mentioned earlier, Apple's CEO Tim Cook puts this in focus of Apple's strategy (Grobart 2013)].

4.3.2.2 Demand

Customer Segments
Customer Segments identify the target groups of the business.

In terms of hardware products, Apple addresses the mass market by fulfilling the need for easy-to-use devices with a good brand name. With respect to media content such as songs from iTunes or apps in the AppStore, it looks a little different. Basically, you have two groups of customers for that platform. On the one hand, there is the consumer; on the other hand, there are app developers, record companies, etc. Both customer groups affect each other: no content would mean no consumers and vice versa. Implementing such a multi-sided platform is a challenge, but obviously Apple succeeded and cares for both groups within its business model. One aspect of this is observable at Apple developer conferences. Quite often, independent developers are addressed directly in keynotes to make clear that they are part of the "Apple world" and their apps are part of Apple's success. By doing this, Apple addresses them emotionally and makes them know that they are an important part of the ecosystem. Of course, it is also a fact that it is interesting to develop for iOS from a commercial point of view, as it is still the platform with the most revenue for developers and content publishers (Cole 2013).

Concentrating on the mass market and multi-sided platforms, Apple supports the value proposition of delivering a good ecosystem to the customer. In this way, it is guaranteed that all relevant apps are available for iOS and there are enough users to enable network effects. Nevertheless, it is obvious that this situation is at risk. With the increasing number of users of Android devices, you may wonder if Apple can continue to succeed in this area.

Interestingly, Apple has chosen to more or less ignore the enterprise market ("business-to-business" [B2B]). As Apple can be confident that its products are known well, the products may have success in the enterprise market anyway. A stronger focus on the B2B market may lead to interdependencies that may affect innovation and design. As one can imagine, business customers have an interest in longer product lifecycles and version support. Therefore, it is a consequent decision for a product leader not to care for all possible customer segments.

Customer Relationship

The customer relationship identifies the type of relationship that is intended for a customer segment.

As explained in Sect. 4.2.2, Apple does not focus on customer intimacy but on product leadership as its primary value strategy. Therefore, it is a reasonable choice to enable customer-self-services to address the mass market.

Moreover, Apple chose strategically to stay in direct contact with the customer and, therefore, to foster personal assistance. This is not directly connected to a value discipline but represents an additional choice. Interestingly, Apple does not use market studies for evaluation of its products but relies on feedback collected within the own organization; Apple flagship stores play an important role in this respect.

It is important to note that adding personal assistance to the Canvas does not mean that Apple is driven by customer intimacy. A typical example for a customer intimacy strategy would be a more dedicated personal assistance, as you may find in the private banking sector. In such a business model, you may have a dedicated customer representative for each client.

Channels

Channels define how the business addresses its customer segments to deliver the value proposition.

To deliver the value proposition of a strong brand, it is a consequent decision to promote the products through fully controlled channels, such as the Apple website, iTunes/AppStore, and Apple flagship stores.

Again, you find an element which is not inferred directly by the orientation towards a certain value discipline. In Apple's business motivation you probably find additional information that led to the decision to address the mass market. As a consequence, Apple has to achieve an adequate market appearance. For this purpose, the Apple-owned channels are complemented by cooperations with other enterprises (including telecommunications providers).

4.3.2.3 Supply

Key Partnerships

Key partnerships identify partners and suppliers needed for the business model.

Apple needs manufacturers to build its products (for iPhones this is mainly the Taiwan-based company Foxconn). You may view this as a strategic alliance, as the manufacturers are no competitors for Apple but they enable Apple to deliver products according to its high standards. For some parts (e.g., displays for smartphones, microprocessors), Apple is dependent on competitors such as Samsung. In this case, however, you may not consider it a strategic alliance, since Apple and Samsung are in a direct competition at the market.

As mentioned earlier, app developers play a crucial role and are thus important to consider. It helps to look at them not only as customers for a multi-sided-platform but also as partners who enrich the iPhone/iPad products. The same is true for publishers and record companies. They are customers that Apple has to attract to make sure they use its platform. At the same time, they are partners as they deliver the content Apple cannot provide on its own.

There is one special type of partnership for the iPhone market, in which Apple collaborates with telephone providers. For the first iPhones this was necessary to enable some special functionality that was enabled by these providers (e.g., voicemail). Up to now, these partnerships have developed to become an important distribution channel to address the mass market (see previous section).

Partnerships can be classified by their key advantage. Manufacturing partnerships help to benefit from economies of scale, for example. This is not directly linked to any decision with respect to the value disciplines. Nevertheless, as already pointed out, being operationally competitive is always necessary. Partnerships with app developers and content suppliers expand Apple's capability to deliver a best-in-class product. As such, they can be considered a direct implication of the pursued product leadership (as explained earlier, a strong ecosystem is of relevance for mobile devices). Partnerships with telephone providers expand Apple's distribution capability. As already described, this cannot be linked directly to any value discipline. However, you will probably find a statement in Apple's business motivation that suggests addressing the mass market instead of looking for a niche.

Key Resources
Key resources identify the core assets needed for the business.

It is clear that Apple relies on human and intellectual resources for developing and designing its products. This also includes patents and copyrights. As Apple has just started to build manufacturing facilities in the US over the last 2 years, the Canvas also includes physicals. Strategically, it is not clear to what extent Apple aims to manufacture in Apple-owned factories; however, it seems that it becomes a more important part.

Obviously, you can directly link the need for human and intellectual resources to the business motivation and also other parts of the business model. The development of best-in-class products implies having on board people to do so and the need to protect intellectual property. Again, it is difficult to link the choice for Apple-owned factories to the business motivation as analyzed earlier. One can only assume that Apple decided from a strategic point of view to reduce its dependencies from partners.

Key Activities
Key activities describe the most important activities of the business.

As design is a significant constituent of Apple's value proposition (see above), it is clear that it is also reflected in the key activities. Since Apple aims to deliver integrated hardware/software products, software development is an important part of this.

Of course, another key activity is manufacturing. As mentioned, Apple continues to build products in Apple-owned factories. Nevertheless, the collaboration with hardware suppliers is far more important. For products built by suppliers, quality control is necessary to ensure Apple's standards.

These key activities are directly linked to other parts of the business model (value proposition and cost structure) and, therefore, represent a consequent choice to be made here.

4.4 How to Link Business Motivation to Business Operations?

Thus far, this chapter has looked at the business motivation to identify high-level strategic choices that drive an enterprise. At the business model level, these choices have been detailed in terms of the relevant elements for value creation. One may think that it is now straightforward to design an organization and business processes according to the decisions made. Nevertheless, at least one aspect is missing. For example, if you think of a multi-national enterprise that goes for the operational excellence, it appears reasonable to set up structures that come with a high standardization and centralization, as this may allow a high degree of efficiency. For other value propositions something else may be adequate. Generalizing this thought, it is valuable to analyze in more detail how the business motivation may influence the business execution. This will be based on the operating model concept, which may be considered an additional part of the business model that directly links to the business execution (see Chap. 1).

4.4.1 Domain-Based Analysis of Operating Model

While architecting the domains of an enterprise, it is of good use to know which business processes should be highly integrated and/or highly standardized. Of course, this will determine architectural decisions while building organizations and IT landscapes to a large extent. One major influence on making these decisions may come from the value discipline. If an enterprise follows operational excellence, it may pursue a high level of standardization. In this case, it may exploit economies of scale while building IT systems and implementing processes. In contrast, if an enterprise pursues a customer intimacy strategy, it may rather opt for a low level of standardization. Therefore, it has the flexibility to respond better to the demands of different customers.

One tool to discuss the intended level of *integration* and *standardization* for all relevant business processes is a simple *2 × 2 matrix*. A prerequisite for this is a clear understanding of the business motivation and the other parts of the business model. In particular, there are two top-level drivers affecting the level of integration/standardization (Table 4.2).

Depending on the level of business process integration and standardization, you have four generic options (Ross et al. 2006) for how to build the architecture (Fig. 4.3).

The four variants have different process characteristics, as explained in Table 4.3. Obviously, the choices made with respect to the operating model directly influence the business execution and IT architectures.

Table 4.2 Drivers for business process standardization/integration

Driver for standardization	Cost efficiency: To be cost-efficient, it may be necessary to exploit economies of scale. This may require a higher level of standardization
Driver for integration	Need for data reuse: If different business units address the same customers or if processes are supported by several locations, there is a need for high integration

Fig. 4.3 Business process integration/standardization (cf. Ross et al. 2006)

As an architect, if you apply this way of thinking to your architecture development process, you have to evaluate whether you can position your enterprise as a whole according to these criteria or if it seems a more suitable approach to look at processes of single architectural domains. For example, maybe the architecture domain of financial accounting can be unified in a global enterprise (better reporting, economies of scale through central systems), whereas marketing and/or product development are diversified or coordinated (to improve responsiveness to local trends). You may thus look at the key activities captured in the Business Model Canvas. For each activity, it is useful to analyze the parameters from the value discipline and how this affects integration/standardization. By doing so, you should be able to develop an architecture in which the decisions with respect to the

Table 4.3 Outline of generic operating models

	Process characteristics	Tasks for EA management
Diversification	• All business units are able to design their own processes; there is no shared data throughout the enterprise. • This is most suitable for enterprises with multiple subsidiaries serving different markets with different products.	• Enable economies of scale by facilitating reuse of solutions without limiting local optimizations.
Replication	• Each business unit uses centrally designed processes; nevertheless, the data is not shared between the business units. • This solution is adequate for companies that can replicate their way of working but are not in need of sharing data across different markets (e.g., McDonald's).	• Provide standard solutions for global efficiency.
Unification	• A business process is standardized and used by all relevant business units; all data is shared. • This may be a good approach for enterprises that work highly integrated with complex supply chains (e.g., chemical industry).	• Provide shared applications to reinforce standard processes and global data availability.
Coordination	• All business units have their own business processes; the relevant data is shared between these processes. • This can be of use for enterprises that address the same customers with different products (e.g., insurance companies; processes are designed to fit the needs for automobile or life insurance, core master data about the customer is shared throughout the processes).	• Provide global data access through standard data interfaces, enable local solutions through loosely coupled systems.

operating model are in line with the pursued value discipline and the other parts of the business model.

This way of looking at operating models may also resolve a possible conflict in case the strategy is oriented towards product leadership or customer intimacy, where, however, efficiency should also not be left unconsidered. After having identified key activities that have to be supported by an "expensive" operating model, one may find other domains in which a higher level of standardization is possible. By doing so, one may end up with possibilities to improve efficiency without affecting the value proposition for customers.

Table 4.4 Drivers for responsiveness/integration forces

Drivers for local responsiveness forces	An enterprise may opt for high local responsiveness if there are different local customer needs depending on nationality, culture, etc. Furthermore, it may be necessary to deal with different local legislations or different distribution channels
Drivers for integration forces	High integration may be forced by the need for exploiting economies of scale. Customers drive global integration if there is the need for a globally unified service or if the customers ask for similar products all around the world. If the competition acts globally, this will also reinforce global integration

4.4.2 Enterprise-Based Analysis of Operating Model

The approach outlined in the previous subsection considers business process standardization as one criterion. For top-level stakeholders this may be too operational. Nevertheless, it may still be of good use to analyze effects from the business motivation on the operating model in a more general way. Therefore, this subsection presents an alternative to the previous model [adopted from Prahalad and Doz (1987) and Bartlett and Ghoshal (1991)]. If you look at the dimensions global integration and local responsiveness forces for the whole enterprise, the discussion will have a more strategic focus. The general drivers for these criteria can be found in Table 4.4.

One may wonder what the value of these dimensions is. The good thing is that the value proposition may directly influence them. For example, customer intimacy is probably a driver for high integration (as the reuse of customer data in several processes for different products may improve the customer relationship). So without looking at a more detailed level of the business model, you may be able to infer the "right" level of integration and local responsiveness.

From a retrospective point of view, this may allow for performing a consistency check of your strategy and the operating model. The resulting 2×2 matrix (see Fig. 4.4) again identifies four stereotypes and also indicates a typical structure and strategy in each quadrant. If you think of a company with low *integration* and high *local responsiveness forces* that is managed by a strong head office, you have likely discovered a field for further discussion. The general characteristics of the architecture within this model can be found in Table 4.5.

4.4.3 Example: Apple

As emphasized earlier, Apple's first priority is product leadership. Interestingly, Apple is successful as a global and unified company. In general, the products are the same everywhere, the way of marketing and selling is unified. The following subsections provide some examples of how Apple connected the various elements from business motivation, business model, and operating model (according to this

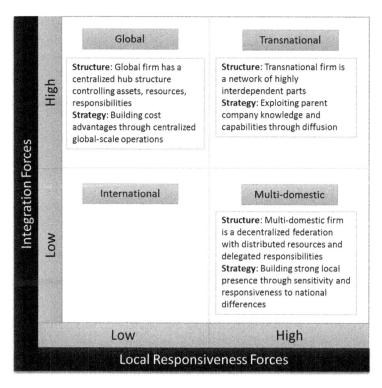

Fig. 4.4 Integration/local responsiveness forces

Table 4.5 Characteristics of operating models with respect to internationalization

Global	Transnational
• Managers with worldwide responsibility	• Try to exploit economies of scale by standardizing processes that are not directly connected to products and services
• Core processes are centralized (marketing, development, etc.)	• Limited number of production facilities
• Small number of product variations	• Reduced number of product variations
• Exploit economies of scale for nearly everything	• Local responsiveness for distribution channels
• Global knowledge sharing	• Processes for marketing and dealing with the competition are coordinated
	• Global knowledge sharing
International	Multi-domestic
• Country/region managers at a lower hierarchy level than managers from headquarter	• Country/region managers, who are more or less independent from headquarter
• Small number of product variations	• High number of product variations
• Localized processes for distribution and marketing	• Localized processes/strategies

framework part of the business model) and implemented these in its business execution architecture.

4.4.3.1 Value Proposition

To implement the value propositions "design" and "usability," Apple has (among others) two main challenges to stay in the product leadership position:

- How can Apple keep building top-quality products?
- How can Apple be flexible and innovative?

Of course, there may be several options for how to successfully build high-quality products; a diversified approach may be as successful as any other. Nonetheless, unification seems to be working for Apple. That means that all products are developed in one design center under central supervision. This is to ensure a common user experience for all Apple devices and coordinated product lifecycles. This can be taken as a good example of how operating model choices are determined or at least affected by the offering part of the business model.

4.4.3.2 Customer Relationship/Channels/Customer Segments

With respect to sales, distribution, and customer communication, you might expect that Apple prefers self-controlled flagship stores to sell and promote its products, since this probably suits best for product leadership. In fact, this may be seen the only way to ensure that the consumer has the best possible experience while purchasing an Apple product. As a matter of fact, these stores do exist, and Apple decided to unify this globally (Apple is placed in the unification quadrant for this capability). At the business execution level, Apple therefore trains sales personnel in addressing customers worldwide in a similar way. Each sales person is supposed to represent the Apple brand through the outfit, the way of talking to customers, and handling problems a customer may have. Apple store personnel thus do not only care about maximizing sales but also about promoting the brand.

Since Apple also addresses the mass market, the operating model also has to facilitate customer self-services. Again, it is a consequent decision to place this capability in the unification quadrant to stay in line with the business motivation. At the business execution level, this is reflected in the provisioning of a worldwide online store (including iTunes and AppStore) and the apple.com website. Through this, the value proposition of a strong brand and outstanding design is supported.

Nevertheless, a consequent implementation of this approach (with Apple products not being available through mass retailers or telecommunications providers) alone would have affected the availability of Apple products in the market. Therefore, Apple expanded the pure unification approach (for marketing and sales) to use market opportunities as they appear. In one market, that may result in cooperations with retailers, in others there may be an alliance with one or several telecommunications providers. It does not necessarily question the unification approach; it just shows that unification does not stand for inflexibility.

This example demonstrates that creating an operating model is influenced by the overall strategic direction and determined to a considerable extent by the customer area of the business model. Additionally, it has to be decided at the business execution level how these elements should be implemented with respect to integration and standardization. Once this is in place, there is a solid ground for the further design of the architecture.

4.4.3.3 Key Activities

Design and Development
It has already been analyzed that Apple generally chose to operate in unification mode and that design and development are key activities. To understand how these choices influence the business execution, one may look at the development and marketing processes. Interestingly, Apple found a very unique way here (Lashinsky 2012). The key aspects are:

- *Start with design*: Apple's designers have the right and responsibility to build a product according to their vision (including hard- and software). The finance or manufacturing departments are not involved in this process.
- *Work as startup*: Once the team for a product has started to work, it does only report to the Monday-meeting-executive-team (ET). The ET consists of members from the top management; it is the final decision committee for all design projects. Every week the ET reviews the progress of Apple's development activities; this is possible due to the fact that Apple only has a limited number of products in the market. Decisions in a development project are made relatively fast without the complex reporting structures of a huge company.
- *Build and test*: Each product is built several times, tested, and then rebuilt with improvements. This process is a very expensive way of development, but it guarantees that every aspect can be considered and maybe replaced if some alternatives are available. Implementing such a process of proactive collection for criticism and product improvement is a well-proven way of fostering innovation and creativity (Burkus 2013). The design process even includes the packaging of a product. The package of a new product is considered as important as any other part of the device.
- *Central marketing*: All marketing activities are coordinated centrally to support the global brand and are already planned within the product development stage. As the brand is one of the value propositions, marketing is not just considered as cost but as something that brings value to the company. Of course, this has to be reflected in the product itself.

Additionally, this way of managing projects is one option to overcome linkage issues within the different management levels of a company. As addressed in the IT engagement model (Fonstad and Robertson 2006), there are three challenges of linkage for IT-related projects:

- *Business Linkage*: With the ET (Monday-meeting-executive-team), it is ensured that development projects are directly linked to top-level objectives.
- *Architecture Linkage*: Through the phases of development it is ensured that each and every part of the new device is developed according to the architectural requirements. If necessary, a new architecture may be developed to offer an integrated solution (consider the introduction of iPod and iTunes that together formed an integrated solution).
- *Alignment Linkage*: This denotes the challenge of how to align projects with the rest of the business. Typically you may have the challenge of how to align development projects with marketing campaigns of different teams. Apple addresses this challenge by organizing marketing centrally and aligning it directly with the CEO and the ET.

These details of the product development process are implemented business architecture and work as an example to show how the decisions about linking business motivation (product leadership) and operating model (unification) determine the parameters for designing the processes at the business execution level. As described, this also helps to overcome some typical alignment issues you may find in other enterprises.

Manufacturing and Quality Control

The choice of working as a global enterprise (according to the enterprise-based analysis of the operating model, see Sect. 4.4.2) directly affects the key activity "manufacturing." This is recognizable in Apple's manufacturing capabilities over the last decades. In the 1990s, Apple had various production plants that built Apple products only. This affected flexibility and exploitation of economies of scale. A typical move for an enterprise with a global operating model would be to reduce the number of products (remember: back then Apple still produced printers and other devices) and minimize the number of production facilities to achieve high production numbers.

To maximize this effect, Apple chose to ally with external manufacturing partners. These partnerships let Apple keep control over the manufacturing process and the tooling of the factories. It provides Apple with huge production capacities without raising the capital costs on its balance sheet. Additionally, Apple controls the whole supply chain. This is necessary to have global product rollouts (the iPhone 5 started in 31 countries simultaneously with 5 million sales in 3 days). The optimization of manufacturing for such global events reflects the global character of the operating model. In any other mode, manufacturing would have to support differentiating activities at a lower scale but perhaps with more variations.

One key aspect here is quality control. Of course, it would be a disaster for Apple if the value propositions of brand/status and design would be compromised by low product quality delivered by manufacturing partners. The necessary processes for this are in place. Due to its bargaining power, Apple obviously managed to have the right contracts in place to put quality issues back to the manufacturing partner. In

2013, Apple sent more than five million iPhones back to Foxconn (the major partner for hardware products) due to quality issues. The cost of around $1.5 billion hit Foxconn but not Apple.

This shows that quality control is a necessary key activity for realizing value propositions such as brand/status and design. Especially for an enterprise in a global operating mode it is of high relevance, as quality issues may affect the brand worldwide.

4.5   Conclusion

This chapter has shown that while working with the three business architecture levels—from business motivation to business model and business execution—it is necessary not to lose sight of the big picture. Each level on its own has its value and is worthwhile to be analyzed as such. Nevertheless, you will need insights from other levels to develop the architecture consistently.

The introduced tools may offer support for this purpose (see Fig. 4.5). However, as the example of Apple shows, this is only a start. It may be "easy" to decide on a global operating model; developing the architecture has its challenges on lower levels though. When detailed processes are to be designed, one may still face the difficult situation of how to find appropriate solutions to comply with the top-level targets (e.g., the Apple design process in its existing form). It heavily depends on the right people and capabilities. Of course, the success of an enterprise is not only determined by strategy or the business model but, at last, by the success of bringing together people, processes, information, and the use of technology.

Can EA development also work bottom-up? One may think that Apple could have also started with its more or less unique design process and built the enterprise around it. Even then, however, Apple would in fact have decided on a strategy in which design—as one of Apple's key capabilities—determines all other elements of the architecture, which brings us back to a top-down development of the enterprise architecture and the cornerstones that are necessary to ensure an integrated architecture.

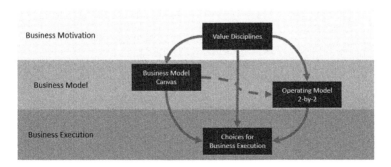

Fig. 4.5 Demonstrated tools in the business architecture framework and linkages

References

Bartlett CE, Ghoshall S (1991) Managing across borders: the transnational solution. Harvard Business School Press, Boston, MA

Burkus D (2013) The myths of creativity. Wiley, Hoboken, NJ

Chen BX (2014) Email from Steve Jobs hints at how Apple ticks. In: The New York Times—Bits. http://bits.blogs.nytimes.com/2014/04/07/email-from-steve-jobs-hints-at-how-apple-ticks/?_php=true&_type=blogs&_r=0. Accessed 16 Apr 2014

Cole S (2013) Apple's iOS brings developers 5x more revenue per download than Android. http://appleinsider.com/articles/13/11/27/apples-ios-brings-developers-5x-more-revenue-per-download-than-android. Accessed 21 Feb 2014

Fonstad NO, Robertson DC (2006) Transforming a company, project by project: the IT engagement model. MIS Q Exec 5(1):1–14

Grobart S (2013) Apple chiefs discuss strategy, market share—and the new iPhones. http://www.businessweek.com/articles/2013-09-19/cook-ive-and-federighi-on-the-new-iphone-and-apples-once-and-future-strategy. Accessed 21 Feb 2014

King R (2012) Business model fishbone for Apple's classic iPod. http://de.slideshare.net/RodKing/business-model-fishbone-for-apples-classic-ipod. Accessed 21 Feb 2014

Lashinsky A (2012) Inside Apple: how America's most admired—and secretive—company really works. John Murray, London

Osterwalder A, Pigneur Y (2010) Business model generation—a handbook for visionaries, game changers, and challengers. Wiley, Hoboken, NJ

Prahalad CK, Doz YL (1987) The multi-national mission: balancing local demands and global vision. The Free Press, New York, NY

Ross JW, Weill P, Robertson D (2006) Enterprise architecture as strategy: creating a foundation for business execution. Harvard Business School Press, Boston, MA

Simon D, Fischbach K, Schoder D (2014) Enterprise architecture management and its role in corporate strategic management. Inform Syst E Bus Manag 14(2):5–42

Treacy M, Wiersema F (1993) Customer intimacy and other value disciplines. Harv Bus Rev 71(1):84–93

Part II

Architecting the Business Capabilities

Matthias Wißotzki

Abstract

Enterprises reach their goals by implementing strategies. Successful strategy
implementation is affected by challenges that an enterprise has to face and
overcome. Enterprises require specific capabilities in order to be able to implement strategies in an effective way and achieve desired results. Thus, the
demand for a systematic capability management approach is growing. This
chapter, therefore, introduces a general process for identifying, improving, and
maintaining capabilities in an enterprise. This is based on an integrated capability approach that results from a number of investigations performed over the
past years. Comprised of four building blocks, the capability management
process represents a flexible "engineering" approach for capability catalog
developers and designers.

5.1 Introduction

Enterprises are complex, highly integrated systems comprised of processes, organizational units, information, and supporting technologies, with multifaceted
interdependencies between each of these (Razavi et al. 2011). Therefore,
organizations have to be more sensitive towards the implementation of business
strategies and their consequences on, e.g., processes, customers, and/or application
systems. In fact, while enterprise structures are becoming increasingly complex,
changes inside such structures have frequently confronted enterprises with
challenges over the last few years (Wißotzki et al. 2013; Wißotzki and Christiner
2012). This issue is emphasized by the fact that "business-critical" projects fail in
two out of three enterprises. A lot of decision makers experience failure in their

M. Wißotzki (✉)
University of Rostock, Rostock, Germany
e-mail: matthias.wissotzki@uni-rostock.de

© Springer International Publishing Switzerland 2015   77
D. Simon, C. Schmidt (eds.), *Business Architecture Management*, Management for
Professionals, DOI 10.1007/978-3-319-14571-6_5

"business-critical" projects because of conflicting interests, insufficient information quality, or decisions being taken elsewhere (Radar 2012). Above all, there are several factors that may influence enterprises in terms of modifications:

- *Mergers & acquisitions* require consolidation and elimination of redundancies to form a "new" architecture that supports the whole business at a high-quality level at lowest possible costs (Alm and Wißotzki 2013; Sonnenberger and Wißotzki 2013).
- *Sourcing strategies* like outsourcing, insourcing, offshoring, or cloud computing create a distributed landscape with completely new requirements for the governance processes (Wißotzki et al. 2014).
- *Internalization & globalization* require a rapid replication of existing best-practice blueprints of how to execute certain parts of the business in a new organizational unit (Alm and Wißotzki 2013).
- *Regulations and fast changing or new business models* might require more agile business operations and IT to provide completely new capabilities (e.g., car manufacturers that become mobility providers or telecommunication infrastructure enterprises that become full service providers) (Sandkuhl et al. 2012).
- *Budget restrictions* especially in the small-to-medium enterprise (SME) context limit the resources that can be used (Wißotzki and Sonnenberger 2012; Sonnenberger and Wißotzki 2013).
- *External regulations* like Dodd-Frank or Sarbanes-Oxley Act (SOX) limit the flexibility while increasing the workload (Wißotzki et al. 2014; Berneaud et al. 2012).
- *High complexity in enterprise architectures* might restrict even highly skilled and competent professionals and also increase costs (Berneaud et al. 2012; Ahlemann et al. 2012).
- *Information quality*: "Information is outdated: 14 months old & 55 % accurate" (Nucleus Research). "Information is weak: On average 20 % of applications are redundant" (Capgemini 2011).

Economic success is dependent on sound strategies that support the realization of defined goals. Therefore, it is not only important to be aware of the existing challenges and problems but also to continuously gather and assess information about organizational knowledge, responsibilities, available resources, and processes required for strategy implementation.

Enterprises are equipped with various capabilities that are specific to their situation and setting, but many are not fully aware of these capabilities. For this purpose, an integrated approach is needed that supports the identification and description of capabilities required for an effective operationalization of enterprise strategies. These capabilities should then be derived systematically through a structured process, gathered and managed in an enterprise-specific repository that we call "capability catalog."

This chapter thus provides a description of a generic capability management process, including a preparation phase, a capability identification and refinement phase to define and manage them in a capability catalog, and an evaluation and maintenance phase for update purposes.

5.1.1   Starting from Strategy

In general, strategies could be understood as impulses for actions to be taken to reach a certain goal (see Chap. 1). The term "strategy" originally comes from the military field and represents an adjustable construct used to convert an actual state into a target state (Hinterhuber 2011). There are many similarities to the idea of a "strategy" within the economical context, as enterprises modify their original plans over time as well. Moreover, the own market positioning in comparison to that of competitors needs to be identified and either maintained or improved in consideration of market conditions, stakeholders, and available/required resources (Hinterhuber 2011). Enterprises are able to achieve defined goals with the aid of long-term planned behavioral patterns.

There are different approaches regarding the specific content of a corporate strategy (i.e., there is no universal consent in the literature). However, modern approaches of strategy formation usually concentrate on the market positioning of products and services and enabling operationalization thereof inside a business model. From an architectural point of view, this is supported by developing representations of enterprises in abstract models.

In line with the description provided in Chap. 1, a strategy serves as a mediator between goals and their realization in terms of, e.g., action catalog packages, considering other motivational elements such as directives, values, constraints, and drivers. Goals of an enterprise and strategies used to achieve these goals may thus lead to the adjustment of, e.g., the business model, which characterizes (among others) the overall value chain, involved stakeholders, core assets, or the operating model. In a next step, the organizational structure, roles, processes, and also the IT landscape (application and technology architecture) is designed (Simon et al. 2014).

However, there are two fundamental challenges when it comes to the realization of strategies to achieve defined goals:

1. According to Wöhe (1990), strategy formulation involves the creation of an action catalog for strategy realization. In order to be effective, such an action catalog requires an enterprise to have a structured view of its capabilities though.
2. Even though a strategy is designed for long-term efforts, there is the need to remain responsive to any changes in the business environment. This flexibility is essential in order to react to new drivers and constraints such as changed customer needs, new technologies, or statutory regulations (Sect. 5.1). This requires the ability to immediately evaluate changes and their implications; again, this can be supported by an overall capability model.

5.1.2 Analysis of Capability Approaches

There are several capability approaches in the literature that cover different disciplines of entrepreneurial experience. According to Bakhtiyari and Adel (2012) and Ulrich and Rosen (2011), capabilities belong to the elements that are strategically relevant for an enterprise, even though there are only a few studies about features and criteria for demarcation of the capability idea.

Based on a literature review of several conference proceedings and journals released after 2002, we thus identified and analyzed similarities of definitions, elements, methods, and theoretical principles.[1] From 189 papers found in our literature search, we classified as 23 papers as relevant.[2]

First, we identified different concepts of capabilities prevalent in the literature. We found "dynamic capabilities" to be the most frequently applied concept. However, universal "business capabilities" and capabilities restricted to information technology ("IT capabilities") are subjects in a considerable amount of papers as well. In addition, few publications addressed so-called "core capabilities" (either advanced or basic) of an enterprise. Other concepts represent very specific objects of research (as they appear in only one paper). Among these concepts are those focusing on the lifecycle of capabilities (1), capabilities in the context of business process management (BPM), innovation (1) and knowledge integration (1) capabilities, as well as strategic capabilities. A definition of the different capability types will be given in the next section.

In addition to these capability concepts, we examined the works in terms of their support for the process of developing and evaluating capabilities. We therefore distinguished methods of development and assessment. Tools that are applied to map defined capabilities onto an interval or ordinal scale fall within the scope of assessment. In contrast, methods of development support the identification and further development of existing capabilities. We identified nine approaches that addressed the process of developing or evaluating capabilities; seven publications focused on the development of capabilities, whereas the other two dealt with methods of assessment.

Teoh et al. (2008), for example, adopt a phase-based model ("capability development process model") to determine important resources and (dynamic) capabilities for system upgrading in SMEs. A more generic approach is pursued by the framework of Helflat and Peteraf (2003). It introduces a general way or, say, pattern for developing (different forms of) capabilities; it thus provides a rough outline instead of a detailed development process. The two stages of the framework are (Helflat and Peteraf 2003, pp. 5–7):

---

[1] Sources included the European Conference on Information Systems (ECIS), the Enterprise Computing Conference (EDOC), the Journal of Management, and the Strategic Management Journal, for example.

[2] It should be noted that both the selection of relevant sources and the method of analysis [in this instance a literature review (Kitchenham and Charters 2007)] have an influence on the results.

- Development stage: This stage begins after a team is organized and assigned to a capability to be developed.
- Maturity stage: The maintenance of a certain capability is performed within this stage, involving measures such as revising a capability in order to keep it in the organizational "memory" of an enterprise. Repeating these measures helps embed a capability within internal structures.

In contrast, the "CPX Capability Framework" introduced by Duhan et al. (2005) provides more details. This framework pursues a new and innovative approach applied to combine the domains of "Dynamics," "Systems," "Cognition," and "Holism," with a focus on knowledge-based SMEs. "Dynamics" relate to both the market an enterprise appears in and the capacities required to be responsive to changes in the market. "Systems" depict relationships between resources and stakeholders of a company. "Cognition" is the responsibility of managers to effectively organize corporate processes. "Holism" represents the gained knowledge about those stakeholders that contribute resources to valued-adding processes (Duhan et al. 2005, p. 4).

In general, the identified approaches for capability development come with comprehensive models. With regard to capability evaluation, this is similar. As the two identified papers dealing with assessment cannot be considered representative, there remains a need for further research.

5.1.3 Capability Definition

Following the presented literature review, this section develops a definition of the term "capability" that will be used as a basis for the integrated capability approach. First, we thus detail the different types of capabilities introduced in the previous subsection. Above all, four types of capabilities are prevalent in the literature, some of which can be divided into certain subtypes. Figure 5.1 presents our classification of the different types.[3]

As can be derived from commonalities in the literature, the individual capability types come with the following characteristics:

- *Dynamic capabilities*: How does an enterprise achieve and sustain competitive advantages in rapidly changing markets and strong competition in consideration of technological innovations? In case an enterprise applies the dynamic capability concept, it should acquire the ability to respond to changes in the enterprise environment by creating, extending, recombining, or protecting assets like resources, processes, or competences. The identification of existing opportunities and potentials belongs to this type of capability as well. The innovative capability subtype refers to the development and supply of both

---

[3] The number in brackets denotes the number of papers the concept appears in.

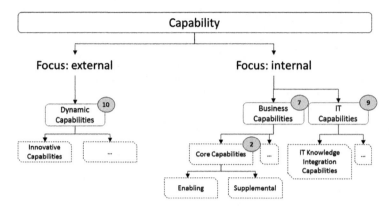

Fig. 5.1 Capability classification

new products and services (Vitari 2009; Barreto 2010; Teoh and Shun 2009) (see Chap. 6 for further details on dynamic capabilities in business architecture management).

- *IT capabilities*: This is where the focus is on technical aspects. IT capabilities enable an enterprise to provide IT services both internally and externally. The "IT knowledge integration capability" represents a subtype that concatenates knowledge management and IT resources (Hecht et al. 2011; Tarafdar and Gordon 2005; Basaglia et al. 2009).
- *Business capabilities*: These capabilities allow an enterprise to combine resources, competences, information, processes, and their environments to deliver consistent value to its shareholders and customers. They describe what the business does and what it will need to do differently to achieve business goals (Helflat and Peteraf 2003; Iacob et al. 2014).
- *Core capabilities*: Core capabilities should be categorized as a subset of business capabilities. They represent the execution of core competencies for the purpose of providing either products or services. In addition, core capabilities are supported by both enabling (capabilities that are necessary but not sufficient) and supplemental (replaceable even though creating an added value) capabilities (Butler and Murphy 2003; Duhan et al. 2005).

The different types of capabilities are combinable. In the case of dynamic and IT capabilities, for example, the focus is on the IT-supported adjustment to environmental changes. To create an overview of similarities and differences between the different capability concepts, we analyzed the identified papers with regard to "descriptive elements" (see Fig. 5.2).[4] In this context, we examined whether such elements are an actual part of the definition (if provided) or simply get a mention in the context of "capabilities."

---

[4] Again, the numbers in brackets indicate the frequency of the elements in the analyzed literature.

Fig. 5.2 Descriptive elements of analyzed capability types

The following characterization of the descriptive elements is predominantly based on the author's view, since most papers do not provide an exact definition. Nevertheless, this overview shall facilitate the understanding of the integrated capability approach introduced later:

- *Resource*: This element aggregates all material and immaterial goods of an enterprise (e.g., financial, physical, human, technological, organizational resources), and thus also includes the people concept of this book's business architecture framework (see Chap. 1).
- *Business Goal*: As an enterprise represents a goal-oriented system, every capability should be assigned to a certain business goal from a logical perspective. It was thus examined whether a reference was made to the goal concept (e.g., competitive advantages, satisfying customer wishes, provide services).
- *Enterprise Context*: The enterprise context is an issue in the context of dynamic capabilities, as their focus is on dynamic enterprise environments. Specifically, the enterprise context relates to the actual field of application.
- *Process*: A process represents a sequence of activities in order to achieve a certain outcome.
- *Knowledge*: Even though knowledge might be classified as an immaterial resource, we consider it as a distinct concept here due to its multiple references.
- *Actor/Role*: Capabilities are assigned to a certain actor. An actor may represent a single person or an organizational unit that is defined by its roles and corresponding responsibilities, decision authorities, and financial capital.

On that basis, we then reviewed specific perspectives or, say, attitudes of the authors with regard to the capability concept. The following paragraph presents capability characteristics as present in specific literature sources that we re-evaluate here:

- *Core Capabilities lead to competitive advantages* (Butler and Murphy 2003, p. 4): Capabilities do not per se lead to competitive advantages but only if capabilities are successfully implemented within the organization in order to provide an increase in value.
- *Capabilities have to be difficult to imitate* (Butler and Murphy 2005, p. 2): Enterprises might have both general and special capabilities, from which only the latter should be hard to imitate.

- *A capability represents a process that uses resources* (Vitari 2009, p. 3): A capability is not a process, as the latter represents a sequence of activities. A process implies an emphasis on how work is done within an enterprise. A capability, instead, specifies a more general concept, focusing on what an organization can or should do.
- *The result a capability yields is sufficient* (Helflat and Winter 2011, p. 9): A capability does not consider input or output items. Accordingly, these are not comparable with each other and thus usable for evaluating whether expectations have been met. In order to evaluate the quality of a capability, e.g., capability maturity models can be applied.
- *Capabilities are adjusted to user needs* (Butler and Murphy 2005, p. 3): Satisfying a user's needs corresponds to the goal orientation of an enterprise. As capabilities are goal-oriented, this statement is supported.
- *Capabilities are used for coordination of activities and utilization of resources* (Hecht et al. 2011, p. 3): Resources have an important function in the context of capabilities. Therefore, both the utilization of resources and corresponding activities represent an essential feature of capabilities.
- *A capability is the ability of a structural unit to use a resource in order to achieve a certain goal* (Azevedo et al. 2013, p. 2): Acquiring an ability has priority in this context, as it indicates that a capability has to be initiated by a human instead of being proceeded automatically.

Eventually, from our analysis (and the concepts identified therein), and closely in line with the definition given in Chap. 1, the following definition of the term "capability" derives:

> **Capability:** Represents the ability of an enterprise to join resources and information in order to support a strategic goal. This combination is applied in consideration of the specific context and executed in a defined and repeatable activity/process for which certain roles/actors take responsibility in order to produce a desired outcome.

The aim is to provide a general definition that copes with the requirements of both the projects and the capability management process introduced in the next section. The definition refers to the six descriptive capability elements introduced above. The concept of "knowledge" has been integrated into the generally accepted concept of "information." Furthermore, the "business goal" has been rephrased to "strategic goal." The concept of "enterprise context," or just "context," characterizes the environment or, say, application area of a capability. The element "actor" has been incorporated into the definition as an operating unit that has the responsibility to "join resources" or "execute processes."

Derived from the introduced analyses, it appears to be common that the terms "capability," "business function," and "business process" are often applied

Table 5.1 Attempt of term classification: capability, function, and process

	Capability	Function	Process
Focus	Strategically, existing and future behavior	Tactically, existing distinct behavior	Operatively
Solidity	Enduring and stable	Not as stable as a capability	Flexible, start/end
Scope	Entire enterprise	Business unit-specific	Task-specific
Origin	Strategy/strategic goals	Capability	Function/services
Purpose	What	What	How
Lowest decomposition level	Capability	Service	Activity
Modeling approaches	E.g., cluster maps, strategy maps, text/templates, archimate	E.g., 4EM, archimate	E.g., BPMN, EPC, etc.

synonymously. Consequently, we identified several criteria that help to clarify the differences between the terms (Table 5.1).

5.2 The Integrated Capability Approach

In line with Santana Tapia (2009), the research approach followed in this chapter consists of two main stages. The first stage is the problem investigation rooted in empirical and conceptual research, e.g., conducting systematic literature analysis, surveys, and expert interviews (Pöppelbuß et al. 2011; Wißotzki et al. 2013). The second stage addresses a project-driven method of resolution that is based on our experiences in three different research projects: EACN Project,[5] CaaS Project,[6] The Open Group Capability Improvement Project.[7]

This chapter presents preliminary project findings combined with the results of first action research cycles; hence, the proposed method is a part of a larger body of a work in progress. The purpose is to develop an appropriate management process for the preparation, identification, organization, evaluation, and maintenance of capabilities in enterprise environments. It should provide clear guidance and accommodate established state of the art and best practices to overcome challenges described in the introduction section of this chapter. As part of this, we propose an integrated capability approach that supports the identification of the capabilities required for an effective operationalization of a strategy. Using this approach, capabilities should then be derived systematically through a structured process and gathered in an enterprise-specific catalog.

---

[5] See http://www.wirtschaftsinformatik-rostock.de

[6] See http://caas-project.eu

[7] See http://www.opengroup.org

In line with this book's architecture framework (see Sect. 5.1.1), both capabilities and the elements capabilities consist of or, say, are realized by can be assigned to the business execution level. We distinguish between three capability types:

1. Business Capabilities (business context)
2. EAM Capabilities (architectural context)
3. IT Capabilities (IT context)

Basically, these types have different kinds of context, which in turn depend on the area of application. For instance, the context of business capabilities represents a combination of objects of the business architecture (e.g., product, market, or customer) and management activities, whereas the EAM capabilities context is defined as a combination of architectural objects (e.g., application, information flow, or component) and management functions (Wißotzki et al. 2013).

However, referring back to the previous subsection, a thorough definition of a capability requires an additional set of elements to be considered: the required information, roles/actors with competences to help create a specific outcome, the relevant activities or process, and appropriate resources (Fig. 5.3).

We now return to the following question:

What kinds of capabilities are required for an enterprise within a certain area of application in order to achieve defined goals?

We deal with this question using the concept of a capability catalog that describes a collection of capabilities necessary to support the implementation of an organization's strategy. The subsequent process is applied to support the identification and creation of a capability catalog.

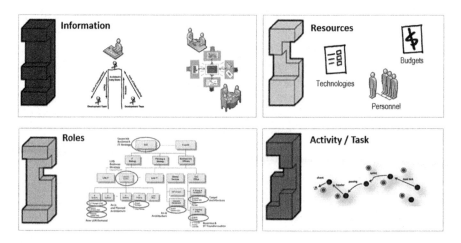

Fig. 5.3 Descriptive elements of a capability

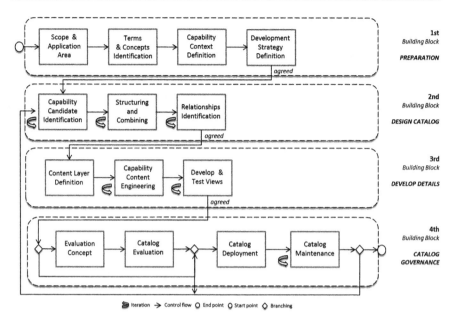

Fig. 5.4 The capability management process

5.3   The Capability Management Process

This section offers a description of our capability management process (CMP). The CMP consists of four building blocks (BBs), each focusing on distinct contents and having distinct outputs. In short, the first building block sets preparation conditions like problem, scope, and stakeholder definition. The second building block designs the capability catalog structure, whereas the third block develops the detailed capability content. The governance building block covers catalog evaluation and maintenance issues (Fig. 5.4).

All in all, the process building blocks thus need to cope with the following requirements:

- Identification of involved parties and definition of terms and preconditions
- Identification of capability types and corresponding capabilities for operationalization of strategic objectives
- Systematic derivation of capabilities, gathered and maintained in a repository called capability catalog

The following subsections provide detailed explanations of each phase and the steps involved in these phases.

5.3.1 Preparation

The first building block defines conditions for the capability catalog to be created and should help meet the following requirements:

- Problem definition & clear scoping of the application area
- Define developer and user groups of the capability catalog
- Negotiate terms & perspectives
- Define capability type & context objects
- Agree on a common development procedure
- Form the outer frame of the catalog

Therefore, the first building block will be divided into the four steps:

1. *Scope & Application Area*
2. *Terms & Concepts Identification*
3. *Capability Context Definition*
4. *Development Strategy Definition*

In the first step, called "*scope & application area*," stakeholders and the focus of the required capability model are clarified. The involved parties have to agree on the application area and the goals of the capability catalog that is to be created. Accordingly, several questions are relevant here, e.g.: what kind of support do stakeholders expect from a capability catalog? Does the catalog cover domain- or context-specific questions or is it used for more general purposes? Who is involved in the development of the catalog (e.g., managers, domain experts, etc.)? So, all in all, the following questions have to be answered in this stage:

- For which purpose are capabilities defined?
- Which strategies need to be supported?
- Which area of application requires a capability catalog?
- Are there any industry-specific capabilities that need to be considered?
- Who is involved and provides input?

As indicated, different stakeholders need to be involved in the preparation of a capability catalog, including the upper management. According to human nature, there is a warily behavior towards change as long as it is not assessable. Consequently, a base of confidence needs to be established by providing information about the starting situation and interests and thus creating so-called "pick-up points" for involved parties. These pick-up points might strongly differ from each other, depending on the position and associated concerns of the participant. A stakeholder analysis supports the identification of parties that are or at least should be involved, their interests, and their corresponding pick-up points. Therefore, the following questions need to be answered:

- Who will have which benefits?
- Who has an influence on the capability catalog development project?
- Who should be involved?
- What are the expectations of involved persons/groups/stakeholders?
- What is the general attitude towards the project (positive, negative, or neutral)?
- How great is the influence of specific persons/groups (small, medium, high, or crucial)?
- Who initiated the project for what reasons?
- Who already is or needs to be informed about project goals/addressed problems?
- Who is essential to initiate the project and who will be affected by project outcomes?
- Will answers to these questions be documented in form of a project description and also approved in some sort of project contract?

Table 5.2 illustrates an exemplary analysis of a capability catalog's application area with respect to a potential goal to improve the business-IT-alignment:

This first step defines just the outer frame of the catalog but does not yet determine the concept of capability in depth, its level of detail, the specific context, as well as the strategy and design of the catalog. The understanding of the capability concept may vary among the relevant stakeholders. Therefore, the step *"terms & concepts identification"* will identify terms and common perspectives to define a consistent capability concept. Starting with a general example of the capability approach may create a common understanding of the perspective at hand. Nevertheless, obtaining an overview of already existing definitions and concepts in the area of capabilities during preliminary stages is advisable in order to either use or extend present standards. The following questions might be helpful:

- Are there existing capability approaches, projects, catalogs, or maps in the enterprise?
- How is the concept of capabilities applied?
- What level of detail do these capability approaches have?

Table 5.2 Example for application area analysis

Goal	Improve our business-IT-alignment	Challenge: "IT is not able to deliver to the business strategy say 75 % of CFOs" (Gartner 2011)
Strategy	Development and maintenance of an architecture inventory	Benefits: Reliable architecture information, standardized communication, cross-company comparability of applications, reduced efforts for current landscape analysis and ad-hoc reporting, ability to identify redundancies and change impacts
Application area	Enterprise architecture management	Actions: E.g., situation analysis, elaborate options, develop target state, roadmapping and migration planning, project portfolio planning, etc.

- In which application areas have these approaches been applied?
- How satisfied are stakeholders with preliminary results?

Results of this particular stage have to be documented and made available for the involved stakeholders. At this point, the global requirements of the capability catalog development are defined and the existing concepts are compared and enhanced by missing components.

In the next step, the *"capability context definition"* is worked out. According to Abowd et al. (1999), a context describes any information that can be used to characterize the situation of an entity. As already depicted, the integrated capability approach is premised not on an entity but on object-based concepts of the enterprise architecture, i.e., descriptive elements such as roles, information, or resources (see Sect. 5.2). Therefore, the context of capabilities is broken down into architectural levels as well. Referring to Buckl et al. (2010), capabilities have either a direct or indirect relationship to (other) architectural objects. The introduced descriptive elements are assigned to a capability within this step in order to determine the actual type (Figs. 5.5 and 5.6).

Attention should be paid to the fact that the context objects for business capabilities could depend on industry-specific aspects, given that business capabilities are meant to sustain and enhance competitive advantages due to their uniqueness, inimitability, and contribution to the generation of higher customer value (Bakhtiyari and Adel 2012). In this context, certain objects or functions such as business objects or management functions are defined as context objects, since their interaction creates customer value. Time horizon (e.g., current, future), activity-based or management aspects (e.g., planning, implementation, audit, maintenance), impacts (e.g., core, support) might be other candidates for context objects as well.

Table 5.3 illustrates a couple of examples of typical industry-related business capabilities that provide guidance for the identification process.

Now, that content-related elements of required capabilities have been explained, the question of how the catalog is constructed and appropriate capabilities are found

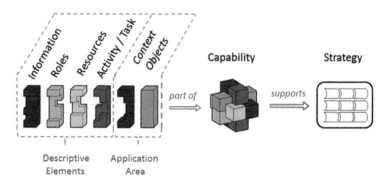

Fig. 5.5 Genes of capabilities

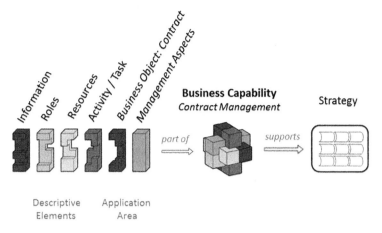

Descriptive   Application
Elements   Area

Fig. 5.6 Example for a business capability definition

Table 5.3 Typical industry-related business capabilities industry

Industry	Examples
Utility	E.g., contract management, policy management, claims management, customer management, network capacity management
Automotive	E.g., production facilities planning, production equipment manufacturing, customer management, supply chain management, incoming goods processing factory
Banking	E.g., safety management, credit management, compliance management, trade management, risk management, order management, real estate management
Software	E.g., product life-cycle management, pre- and after sales, test & validation management, license management
Mining	E.g., production planning, ore extraction, waste management, logistics management, plant management, smelting, materials management

needs to be answered. Hence, this leads us to the "*development strategy definition*" step. Here, two different approaches can be distinguished:

- A new catalog is developed.
- An already existing catalog is extended.

During the development of strategies, it is necessary to obtain management approval and support. In addition, all relevant organizational units and employees have to get access to required information and documents. In fact, informing relevant stakeholders about, e.g., the upcoming activities and the corresponding timeframe is essential in order to obtain the required support.

The relevance of the overall project to the enterprise, the purpose of the capability catalog, a time schedule, planned activities, the involved parties, a common understanding of how capabilities will be applied—all of these aspects need to be clear and/or available right at the beginning. The main objective here is to create openness among the involved parties or, say, stakeholders to upcoming analyses in order to have a positive influence on both quality and correctness of the identified capabilities.

The need for personnel and monetary resources required in the context of a capability development project may have to be justified during the first building block as well. The following aspects may generally support the value justification:

- Added value of the capability catalog in accordance with the overall performance of an enterprise, e.g., cost savings or quality enhancements
- Development of competitive advantages with the aid of capability-based planning and investment
- Improvement of the documentation and auditability of organizational requirements used to achieve goals

The following aspects summarize the most important points of the preparation phase:

1. Define and agree on goals and the application area
2. Ensure to have consent and support of the upper management
   - Involve all relevant organizational units
   - Arrange an adequate period of time and sufficient resources
   - Admit access to already existing documents
3. Consider affected individuals at an early stage
   - Inform about the purpose of the capability catalog that is to be created
   - Make the schedule and planned activities available
   - Communicate who currently is or will be involved for what specific purpose

The quality of a developed capability catalog depends on precise scoping and whether compliance with guidelines for quality management is achieved. These guidelines represent another important component of this phase, as they contribute to quality improvement of the development process and allow an evaluation of the achievement of objectives.

5.3.2 Design Catalog

Subsequent to the determination of content within the preparation stage, the design of the capability catalog is initiated. Hence, capability candidates are identified, collected, structured, and their dependencies are defined:

1. *Capability Candidate Identification*
2. *Structuring and Combining*
3. *Relationships Identification*

Table 5.4 Overview of methods of analysis for capability identification according to Sandkuhl et al. (2013)

Analysis method	Field of application within capability identification
CapStorming	The utilization of creativity techniques such as brainstorming in the course of the initialization process of a capability catalog is helpful for quickly seizing ideas and combining these with existing concepts. The goal is to gather several ideas in a minimum of time with the aid of problem-oriented associations and combinations. As the point of origin there might be, e.g., goals, packages of measures, processes, or a context matrix
Survey	Represents the main technique for gathering information in the context of descriptive capability elements. In particular, these elements are used to either describe the context or improve the comprehensibility of a subject by creating a uniform language
Document analysis	Is used for either preparation purposes or as an initial step within the identification process (e.g., existing strategy maps, process models, domain architectures)
Written cases	Are used in addition to surveys to identify the time and material input necessary to carry out a certain task
Moderated/participative/design thinking workshop	Characterizes identification activities and/or solution development steps that are applied in order to achieve consent among the involved parties. A joint analysis of current as well as prospective capabilities has an influence on quality, feasibility, and acceptance

The phase starts off with the "*capability candidate identification.*" The focus of this activity is the definition of the first capabilities. Prior to any analyses, it is important to accurately define the area of application and coordinate the required work (see BB1). The area of application determines the content and concepts that are significant for the identification process.

Therefore, the output of BB1 provides the basis for the planning of required identification activities, involved experts, and the effort estimation. For the actual identification process, there are several possibilities that have been successfully used in other fields such as enterprise modeling. Table 5.4 summarizes different methods of analysis with respect to their field of application within the capability candidate identification stage.

The initial activities for identifying capabilities should be kept as short as possible. In general, these initial activities result in a roughly structured collection of individual capabilities or at least capability ideas.

The origin of the identification process is a so-called "*capability solution matrix.*" At the X-axis and Y-axis of the matrix, you find the context objects. For a business capability "market analysis," for example, the X-axis contains a context object called "market" (business object). At the Y-axis, there are simplified management processes like "planning," "execution," and "controlling." Consequently, the matrix cell at the intersection of the "market" object and an analysis step of the

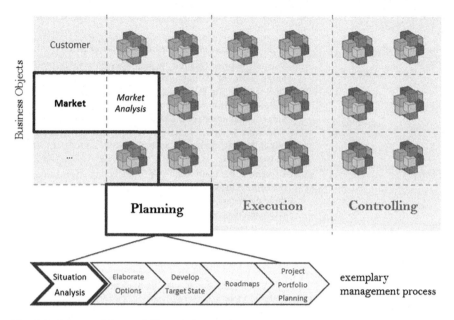

Fig. 5.7 Concept of the capability solution matrix

"planning" phase would then represent the "market analysis" capability. Figure 5.7 illustrates this example.

After collecting initial capability suggestions, the results need to be analyzed (with regard to their context), discussed, and, if necessary, restructured. Within the step "*structuring and combining*," redundant elements are removed and capabilities that have a strong coherence as to content are aggregated or further specified. Within this stage, content-related aspects are combined to create a catalog that is both easy and clear to understand. A capability catalog does not serve its purpose if users are not able to gain a certain understanding of the catalog after an initial training. In case there is a large amount of capabilities, these could be aggregated or categorized. Accordingly, similar capabilities are either pooled or integrated using appropriate decomposition levels. It is of course necessary to have this agreed by the involved stakeholders and to document questions and critical comments that may occur. Subsequent to first refinements of the capability catalog, participants work on additional iterations with the aid of the collected questions and critical comments in order to suggest further changes and enhancements.

In the course of several iterations, it is necessary to create a suitable document or description of the capability catalog in order to achieve a better understanding and to support involved stakeholders. The documentation should be digitized during initial activities, using, for example, a document such as the one depicted in Fig. 5.8. The capability solution matrix could provide a structuring concept for this stage. Still, any other type of structuring is possible (note that this mainly depends on the area of application as well as the applied context [see BB1]).

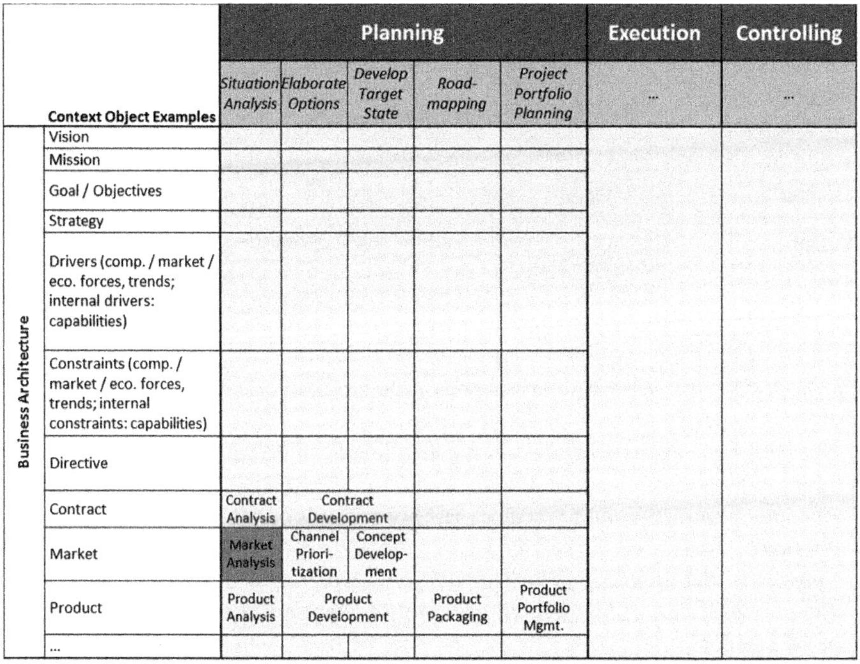

		Planning					Execution	Controlling
Context Object Examples		*Situation Analysis*	*Elaborate Options*	*Develop Target State*	*Road-mapping*	*Project Portfolio Planning*	...	...
Business Architecture	Vision							
	Mission							
	Goal / Objectives							
	Strategy							
	Drivers (comp. / market / eco. forces, trends; internal drivers: capabilities)							
	Constraints (comp. / market / eco. forces, trends; internal constraints: capabilities)							
	Directive							
	Contract	Contract Analysis	Contract Development					
	Market	Market Analysis	Channel Priori-tization	Concept Develop-ment				
	Product	Product Analysis	Product Development		Product Packaging	Product Portfolio Mgmt.		
	...							

Fig. 5.8 Structural concept of a capability solution matrix

Additional criteria that might be subjects of further refinements (e.g., the level of content and detail) are explained in BB3.

The objective of this step is to classify identified capabilities, create a consistent structure, and fix capability names and prepare stable descriptions. The capability catalog can be characterized as follows at the state of this building block:

- Represents the first substantial results of the brainstorming activities
- Redundant elements that state similar points are pooled
- The catalog is may still be incomplete
- Relationships between capabilities are either fragmentary or missing

Since the collected improvement suggestions usually may not guarantee a sufficient, complete, or consistent capability catalog, it is necessary to conduct further analyses and reorganizations. In addition to an improved level of detail that is achieved in BB3, dependencies among capabilities need to be identified and documented. During the step *"relationships identification,"* different relationships are documented and analyzed. As a result of identifying missing relationships, removing inconsistencies, and discovering gaps, there is an enhancement of both the knowledge represented by the catalog and the understanding of capabilities being available within an enterprise. Implicit, undesired, or overlapping relationships between capabilities have to be detected and adjusted (Fig. 5.9).

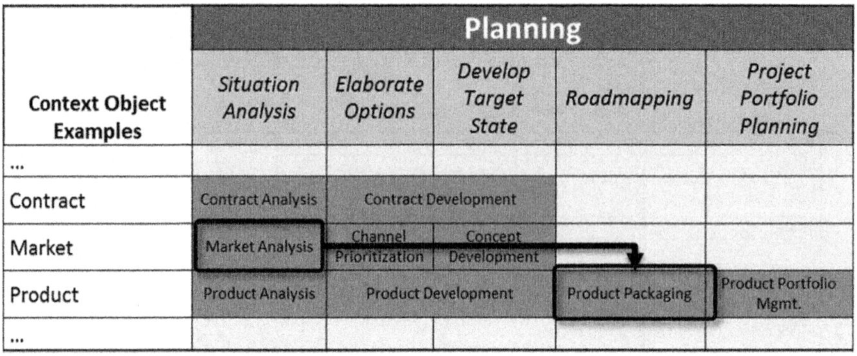

Context Object Examples	Planning				
	Situation Analysis	Elaborate Options	Develop Target State	Roadmapping	Project Portfolio Planning
...					
Contract	Contract Analysis	Contract Development			
Market	Market Analysis	Channel Prioritization	Concept Development		
Product	Product Analysis	Product Development		Product Packaging	Product Portfolio Mgmt.
...					

Fig. 5.9 Visualization example for relationships in the capability solution matrix

The different relationships between capabilities can be classified as follows:

- *Informative Relationship*: Which capability depends on information provided by another?
- *Supportive Relationship*: Which capability is a prerequisite for another?
- *Functional Relationship*: Which capabilities represent different aspects in the same category?

5.3.3   Develop Details

Creating a capability catalog is typically an iterative process that is completed once every capability is described in a sufficient level of detail for supporting the strategy implementation of an enterprise. Thus, the third building block is responsible for the refinement of already achieved results by applying the following steps:

1. *Catalog Content Layer Definition*
2. *Capability Content Engineering*
3. *Develop & Test Views*

The initial step of the third building block, "*catalog content layer definition*," addresses the definition of the content and associated depth in order to provide both a final structure and order of the capability catalog. This step is important in case the catalog needs to achieve a high level of detail in terms of content (e.g., by specifying descriptive elements and defining evaluation criteria). Figure 5.10 illustrates a three-level approach for the content layer definition. The capability solution matrix represents the first level and is used to identify contextual capabilities. At the second level—the capability content—descriptive elements are specified. Last but not least, different kinds of evaluation criteria are developed at the third level.

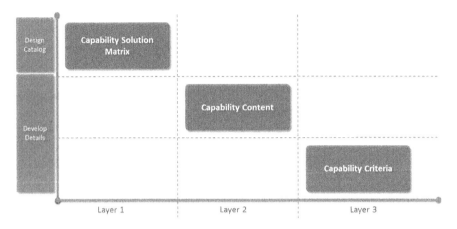

Fig. 5.10 Exemplary catalog content layers

After specifying the number of content layers covered by the catalog, a systematic analysis of the identified capabilities as part of the "*capability content engineering*" step is advisable. Here, the capabilities are actually described in further detail.

According to Ulrich and Rosen (2011), the following list presents a number of basic principles for the capability content engineering process:

- Capabilities define what is done, not how to do something.
- Capabilities are nouns.
- Capabilities are defined in terms of their application area (i.e., there should be no technical terms for describing business capabilities).
- A capability should be enduring and stable, not volatile.
- Capabilities are not redundant.
- There is one capability map for an application area.
- Capabilities can have relationships to other capability types.

During the engineering process, the entire capability catalog appearance may still be subject to substantial changes. The catalog's structures are depicted with the help of models that support a clear and consistent conception of the catalog.

Prior to any adjustment, a review of previous work is required. Afterwards, an elaboration or refinement of the descriptive elements can be carried out. An elaboration of the "market analysis" capability, for example, would be performed with respect to the following questions:

- What information is required in order to conduct a market situation analysis?
- Which roles are able to provide information and make decisions with respect to this object?
- What resources are required to perform a market situation analysis?

- How is a market situation analysis performed and what kind of output is produced?
- Are there already predefined activities or a standard process for market analysis?
- Are there any references of already defined capabilities to logical objects of the enterprise?

The third building block is completed by the "*develop & test views*" step. When describing capabilities in detail, it is necessary to ensure that every capability is formulated in a general manner, i.e., there should not be any connections to objects such as particular applications or markets. However, capabilities may well be linked to logical elements. For instance, the connection between goal, strategy, and corresponding capabilities for realization could be captured in a view. Figure 5.11 illustrates this example.

In general, views might be applied to present specific sets of capabilities to different kinds of stakeholder groups. In particular, one of the following sample views might be created: required maturity level vs. current maturity level of a capability used for strategy implementation, costs of creating a capability, dependencies between capabilities, financial aspects (revenue, profit), or just a business capability overview (see Fig. 5.12 for an example).

For presentation purposes, different tools and technical measures (multiple video projectors or monitor screens, special software tools) may be used. This is to name just a few examples: data and tree maps, radar charts, parallel coordinates, cone trees, or layer charts (Lengler and Eppler 2007).

5.3.4 Catalog Governance

The last building block describes an important, remaining stage in the context of creating and introducing a capability catalog. In fact, the governance process addresses the quality management of a created capability catalog. It thus includes activities referring to the evaluation, deployment, and maintenance of a catalog. The paragraphs below describe these activities in detail:

1. *Evaluation Concept*
2. *Catalog Evaluation*
3. *Catalog Deployment*
4. *Catalog Maintenance*

Even though there are a lot of approaches dealing with quality criteria and valuation methods in the context of, for example, business processes (Sandkuhl et al. 2013), there is still little progress in the application area of evaluating capabilities, in which approaches most often build on ordinary methods for quality control or are impractical for the designated purpose (Sect. 5.1.2). This might have originated from an omitted preparation phase, which is normally used to describe the quality criteria a catalog has to satisfy.

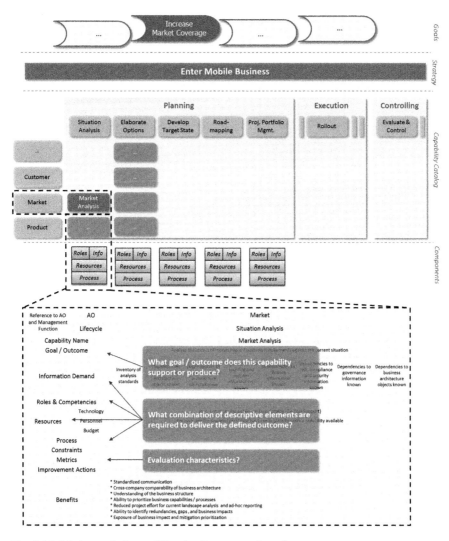

Fig. 5.11 Market analysis capability details—content layer 3

In order to both counteract deficient quality and promote the functionality of a catalog, the optional steps "*evaluation concept*" and "*catalog evaluation*" can be used.

The subject of the "*evaluation concept*" step can be the development process (the way the catalog is constructed), the designed result (the catalog itself), or both, i.e., a differentiation between "model verification" and "model validation" is necessary (de Bruin et al. 2005). In line with Duhan et al. (2005), the catalog verification determines if the artifact represents the developer's concept accurately and it tests the model against a set of theoretic evaluation methods. The catalog

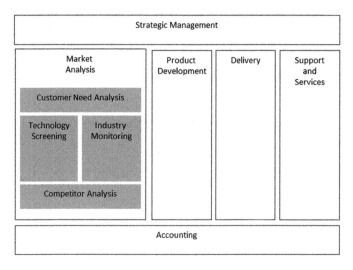

Fig. 5.12 Exemplary fragment of a business capability catalog visualized in a cluster map

validation examines from the perspective of the intended catalog usage if the artifact corresponds to the real world. This can be achieved by applying case studies, assessments, and expert interviews. An example of a verification method is described by Wißotzki and Koç (2014). Due to practice-oriented reasons, this section exclusively covers the validation of capability catalogs. Accordingly, the quality level and quality criteria have to be elaborated during this stage (unless it has been done BB 1) to make a measurement possible. Appropriate criteria can normally be derived from the goals predefined in the scoping of the capability catalog (Sect. 5.3.1). In addition to conducting an overall review of general quality standards such as completeness, accuracy, flexibility, linkage, simplicity, intelligibility, and usability, it is recommended to apply comprehensive evaluation tools, e.g., capability maturity models, in case of large capability catalogs.

Maturity models are specific management instruments that define various degrees of maturities in order to evaluate to what extent a particular competency fulfills the qualitative requirements for a set of competency objects (Wendler 2009) and/or development processes in an organization (Back 2010). Having their origins in the software industry, maturity models are designed to measure the current state—the achieved level of competence—by means of assessment methods (Meyer et al. 2011; de Bruin et al. 2005). Maturity models may be applied in the "*catalog evaluation*" step. After such an evaluation, the second building block can be revisited and the feedback can be used as an input for further iterations of catalog development.

The way of integrating a catalog into an enterprise has a vital influence on the success of this catalog. To this end, the "*catalog deployment*" step addresses the implementation/roll-out of a catalog in the organization. As specified earlier, creating a capability catalog is only reasonable in case the management approves and supports the process. Accordingly, both upper and middle management need to be convinced. That being said, the success of integrating a capability catalog depends on two major elements:

1. The capability catalog has a high-quality level
2. Stakeholders (e.g., board level, business developers, line managers) are satisfied with both the approaches and achieved results.

The completed capability catalog thus needs to be formally presented to the steering committee and contracting authority, respectively. This should be delivered either in the form of an intermediate presentation or as part of the project completion. It thus needs to be ensured that the needs of the stakeholders are satisfied. To achieve this, accurate planning and preparation is required. The project team needs to be able to enhance the results of the capability catalog creation process, i.e., converting the final catalog version, descriptions, and illustrations into an appropriate form of presentation. Relevant stakeholders might, for example, obtain a copy of the document in order to prepare themselves for approval. The subsequent aspects need to be considered in the context of catalog deployment:

- Obtain feedback from users and the steering committee
- Obtain decisions about the maintenance of the catalog and the allocation of resources
- Integrate the catalog into existing processes

All in all, the catalog deployment needs to pursue the goal of achieving an acceptance of the results and creating an activity plan in terms of additional elaborations or unresolved issues. Even though an initial evaluation of the achieved state should have been conducted in the preceding building blocks, it is unlikely that a single iteration is sufficient. The second goal is to receive user feedback provided by individuals or working groups in order to improve the catalog utilization. In this regard, it is recommended to perform internal surveys or workshops after a certain period of time. Such feedback can result in a change in the structure and/or in the function of the capability catalog. Besides, changes in the domain knowledge and management approaches can create the need for improvements in the catalog (Lahrmann and Marx 2010). For these reasons, and given that an enterprise may have to meet new challenges over time and capabilities need to be modified accordingly, there is an ongoing "*catalog maintenance*" process in addition to the aforementioned evaluation methods applied to create a high-quality capability catalog. This step comes with the following advantages:

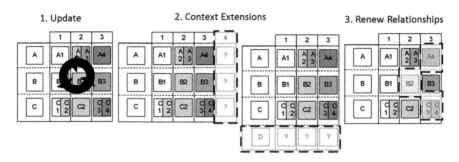

Fig. 5.13 The catalog extension patterns according to Lahrmann and Marx (2010)

- Structure and comprehensibility
- Precise descriptions
- Simplified modifications and reorganizations of the created catalog
- Contributes to the organizational learning and securing of organizational knowledge

Consequently, an improvement of both quality and usage period of the catalog is addressed within the last step of this building block. Modifications in the catalog structure as well as slight changes may occur in this step. From Lahrmann and Marx (2010), we adopted three of four extension patterns for the purpose of catalog maintenance, illustrated in Fig. 5.13.

A general update of capability catalog elements by adding new descriptive elements or updating the evaluation mechanism (e.g., maturity assessment procedure) may be examples of the first pattern. It is also possible to add new context objects or reorder their configurations, e.g., by changing attributes that might influence the identification process (Sect. 5.3.2) or at least reconfigure the relationships between different capabilities. Although these extension patterns challenge the metastructure of the capability catalog to some extent, they would not require passing the first building block and beginning the development process again by redefining the scope, as this would go beyond the scope of maintenance.

5.4   Conclusion

Enterprises reach their goals by implementing strategies. Successful strategy implementation is affected by challenges that an enterprise has to overcome. Enterprises require specific capabilities in order to be able to implement strategies efficiently and achieve a specific outcome. A demand for a systematic management approach to identify capabilities is growing.

We presented a generic approach that can be used to derive capabilities through a structured process and gather them in an enterprise-specific catalog for an effective operationalization of enterprise strategies. A capability here describes a certain combination of information, roles, activities/procedures, and resources to support issues like strategy implementation, planning purposes, or transformation processes.

Following a four-building-block approach, we described a straightforward and flexible process for capability catalog developers and designers, which allows the integration of descriptive elements for different capability types. The capability management process is based on the approach of Wißotzki and Koç (2013) and it forms a tool that facilitates the development of scientifically well-founded capability catalogs aligned with the design science research guidelines (Hevner et al. 2004). In particular, our approach provides a building block covering the continuous evaluation and maintenance in order to maintain capability and catalog quality.

Additional detailed content of the building blocks and corresponding steps are still in development and have only been mentioned to some extent in this chapter. Our future research will elaborate on this topic and demonstrate more practical use cases of capability catalog development projects. In fact, our aim is to focus more on use cases and/or possible applications in order to indicate the tradeoffs of our approach and to evaluate and potentially extend the process.

References

Abowd GD, Dey AK, Brown PJ, Davies N, Smith M, Steggles P (1999) Towards a better understanding of context and context-awareness. In: Proceedings of the 1st international symposium on handheld and ubiquitous computing, Karlsruhe, Germany, 27–29 Sept 1999

Ahlemann F, Stettiner E, Messerschmidt M, Legner C (eds) (2012) Strategic enterprise architecture management: challenges, best practices, and future developments. Springer, Berlin

Alm R, Wißotzki M (2013) TOGAF adaption for small and medium enterprises. In: Adbramowicz W (ed) Business information systems workshops, lecture notes in business information processing, vol 160. Springer, Berlin, pp 112–123

Azevedo CL, Iacob ME, Almeida JPA, van Sinderen M, Ferreira Pires L, Guizzardi G (2013) An ontology-based well-founded proposal for modeling resources and capabilities in ArchiMate. In: Proceedings of the 17th IEEE international enterprise distributed object computing conference (EDOC), Vancouver, Canada, pp 39–48

Back A (2010) Reifegradmodelle im management von enterprise 2.0. In: Proceedings of KnowTech 2010, Bad Homburg, Germany, 15 Sept 2010, pp 105–112

Bakhtiyari R, Adel M (2012) Business capability and its strategic impacts. In: Proceedings of Australasian conference on information systems (ACIS) 2012, Geelong, Australia, 3–5 December 2012

Barreto I (2010) Dynamic capabilities: a review of past research and an agenda for the future. J Manag 36(1):256–280

Basaglia S, Caporarello L, Magni M (2009) The mediating role of IT knowledge integration capability in the relationship between team performance and team climate. In: Proceedings of the 17th European conference on information systems, Verona, Italy

Berneaud M, Buckl S, Diaz-Fuentes A, Matthes F, Monahov I, Nowobilska A, Roth S, Schweda CM, Weber U, Zeiner M (2012) Trends for enterprise architecture management and tools. Technical Report, TU Munich, Munich, Germany

Buckl S, Dierl T, Matthes F, Schweda CM (2010) Building blocks for enterprise architecture management solutions. In: Harmsen F, Proper E, Schalkwijk F, Barjis J, Overbeek S (eds)

Practice-driven research on enterprise transformation, lecture notes in business information processing, vol 69. Springer, Berlin, pp 17–46

Butler T, Murphy C (2003) Unpacking dynamic capabilities in the small-to-medium software enterprise: process, assets, and history. In: Proceedings of the 11th European conference on information systems

Butler T, Murphy C (2005) Integrating dynamic capability and commitment theory for research on IT capabilities and resources. In: Proceedings of the 13th European conference on information systems

Capgemini (2011) Application landscape report 2011 edition. http://www.capgemini.com/resource-file-access/resource/pdf/Application_Landscape_Report_2011_Edition.pdf. Accessed 08 Oct 2014

de Bruin T, Rosemann M, Freeze R, Kulkarni U (2005) Understanding the main phases of developing a maturity assessment model. In: Proceedings of the 2005 Australasian conference on information systems (ACIS), Sydney, Australia, 30 Nov–2 Dec 2005

Duhan S, Levy M, Powell P (2005) IS strategy in SMEs using organizational capabilities: the CPX framework. In: Proceedings of the 13th European conference on information systems

Gartner (2011) Technology issues for financial executives: 2011 annual report. Gartner and Financial Executives International (FEI), Morristown, NJ

Hecht S, Wittges H, Krcmar H (2011) IT capabilities in ERP maintenance—a review of the ERP post-implementation literature. In: Proceedings of the 19th European conference on information systems

Helflat CE, Peteraf MA (2003) The dynamic resource-based view: capability lifecycles. Strateg Manag J 24(10):997–1010

Helflat CE, Winter SG (2011) Untangling dynamic and operational capabilities strategy for the (n) ever-changing world. Strateg Manag J 32(11):1243–1250

Hevner AR, March ST, Park J, Ram S (2004) Design science in information systems research. MIS Q 28(1):75–106

Hinterhuber HH (2011) Strategische Unternehmensführung, 8th edn. Erich Schmidt, Berlin

Iacob ME, Meertens LO, Jonkers H, Quartel DAC, Nieuwenhuis LJM, van Sinderen MJ (2014) From enterprise architecture to business models and back. Softw Syst Model 13(3):1059–1083

Kitchenham BA, Charters S (2007) Guidelines for performing systematic literature reviews in software engineering. Technical report EBSE-2007-01. School of Computer Science and Mathematics, Keele University, Keele, UK

Lahrmann G, Marx F (2010) Systematization of maturity model extensions. In: Winter R, Zhao JL, Aier S (eds) Global perspectives on design science research, lecture notes in computer science, vol 6105. Springer, Berlin, pp 522–525

Lengler R, Eppler M (2007) Towards a periodic table of visualization methods for management. In: IASTED Proceedings of the conference on graphics and visualization in engineering (GVE 2007), Clearwater, FL

Meyer M, Helfert M, O'Brien C (2011) An analysis of enterprise architecture maturity frameworks. In: Grabis J, Kirikova M (eds) Perspectives in business informatics research, lecture notes in business information processing, vol 90. Springer, Berlin, pp 167–177

Pöppelbuß J, Niehaves B, Simons A, Becker J (2011) Maturity models in information systems research: literature search and analysis. Commun Assoc Inf Syst 29(1):505–532

Radar (2012) The impact of data silos on IT planning. Whitepaper Radar Group, Winchester, MA

Razavi M, Shams Aliee F, Badie K (2011) An AHP-based approach toward enterprise architecture analysis based on enterprise architecture quality attributes. Knowl Inf Syst 28(2):449–472

Sandkuhl K, Borchardt U, Lantow B, Stamer D, Wißotzki M (2012) Towards adaptive business models for intelligent information logistics in transportation. In: Proceedings of the 11th international conference on perspectives in business informatics research, Russia, 24–26 Sept 2012, pp 43–59

Sandkuhl K, Wißotzki M, Stirna J (2013) Unternehmensmodellierung: Grundlagen, Methode und Praktiken. Springer Vieweg, Berlin

Santana Tapia R (2009) Assessing business-IT alignment in networked organizations. Ph.D. thesis, University of Twente, Drienerlolaan, The Netherlands

Simon D, Fischbach K, Schoder D (2014) Enterprise architecture management and its role in corporate strategic management. Inf Syst E-Bus Manage 12(1):5–42

Sonnenberger A, Wißotzki M (2013) Adoption of enterprise architecture management in small and medium enterprises. Whitepaper, University of Rostock, Rostock, Germany

Tarafdar M, Gordon SR (2005) How information technology capabilities influence organizational innovation: exploratory findings from two case studies. In: Proceedings of the 13th European conference on information systems

Teoh SY, Shun C (2009) Innovative capability development process: a Singapore IT healtcare case study. In: Proceedings of the 17th European conference on information systems, Verona, Italy

Teoh SY, Tng QH, Pan S-L (2008) The emergence of dynamic capabilities from a SME-enterprise system upgrade. In: Proceedings of the 16th European conference on information systems

Ulrich W, Rosen M (2011) The capability map: the rosetta stone of business/IT alignment. In: The enterprise architecture advisory service executive report 14(2), Cutter Consortium, Arlington, TX

Vitari C (2009) Sources of IT dynamic capability in the context of data genesis capability. In: Proceedings of the 17th European conference on information systems, Verona, Italy

Wendler R (2009) Reifegradmodelle für das IT-Projektmanagement. Technical University Dresden, Germany

Wißotzki M, Christiner F (2012) Enterprise architecture visualization: techniques for complexity reduction. AV Akademikerverlag, Saarbrücken

Wißotzki M, Koç H, Weichert T, Sandkuhl K (2013) Development of an enterprise architecture management capability catalog. In: Kobyliński A, Sobczak A (eds) Perspectives in business informatics research (Lecture notes in business information processing), vol 158. Springer, Berlin, pp 112–126

Wißotzki M, Koç H (2013) A project driven approach for enhanced maturity model development for EAM capability evaluation. In: Proceedings of the 17th IEEE international enterprise distributed object computing conference workshops (EDOCW), Vancouver, Canada, pp 296–305

Wißotzki M, Koç H (2014) Evaluation concept of the enterprise architecture management capability navigator. In: Proceedings of ICEIS 2014, Lisbon, Portugal

Wißotzki M, Sonnenberger A (2012) Enterprise architecture management—state of research analysis & a comparison of selected approaches. In: Short paper proceedings of the 5th IFIP WG 8.1 working conference on the practice of enterprise modeling, Rostock, Germany, 7–8 Nov 2012

Wißotzki M, Timm F, Wiebrig J (2014) Investigation of IT sourcing, relationship management and contractual governance approaches: state of the art literature review. In: Proceedings of ICEIS 2014, Lisbon, Portugal

Wöhe G (1990) Einführung in die allgemeine Betriebswirtschaftslehre, 17th edn. Vahlen Verlag, Munich

Using Capability Models for Strategic Alignment

6

Wolfgang Keller

Abstract

In many enterprises there is a gap between strategies and their implementation by business processes and information systems supporting those processes. Capabilities can bridge this gap by offering a common language (for business and IT) and a means to systematically map strategy (expressed in business models) to capabilities, which are then implemented using, e.g., people, business processes, and also information systems. Therefore, capabilities form a central element in business architecture management, easing the execution of a business strategy as expressed, e.g., in various forms of business model canvases. This chapter explains the general concept of capabilities. These can be divided into so-called operational capabilities, which are the ones to implement and execute a strategy, and dynamic capabilities, which are needed to formulate business models, to develop strategies, and to configure the right set of operational capabilities. The main part of the chapter deals with methods that help manage a portfolio of operational capabilities, such as so-called heat mapping, or the use of capability footprints, and provides hints on how to obtain a capability map for an enterprise in some given industry.

6.1 The Role of Capabilities in Business Architecture Management

The term "capabilities" is being used quite a lot in discussions on business architecture and IT investment planning (see, e.g., Bredemeyer et al. 2006; Cameron and Kalex 2009; Homan 2008; Ritzenhöfer 2008). It is somehow strange that, on the one hand, people are using the term in an inflationary fashion, while, on the other

W. Keller (✉)
objectarchitects, Lochham, Germany
e-mail: wk@objectarchitects.de

© Springer International Publishing Switzerland 2015
D. Simon, C. Schmidt (eds.), *Business Architecture Management*, Management for Professionals, DOI 10.1007/978-3-319-14571-6_6

hand, the body of literature on capability-based investment planning in business architecture is comparably small. Maybe this is because a lot of the players, who actively apply capability-based planning, still consider it some form of competitive advantage.

This chapter will first give a short clarification of relevant terms such as capability and capability model in as much depth as needed in practice. If you ask three people about capabilities in business architecture or even business capability management, you might get five answers. It may thus be a good idea to start by looking up the basic terms in a dictionary. Merriam Webster's Dictionary (Merriam-Webster 2014) defines *capability* as follows:

1. the quality or state of being capable; also: ability
2. a feature or faculty capable of development: potentiality
3. the facility or potential for an indicated use or deployment

Taking this further to the notion of business capabilities, Cameron and Kalex (2009) provide the following definition:

A *business capability* defines the organization's capacity to successfully perform a unique business activity. Capabilities:

- are the building blocks of the business,
- represent stable business functions,
- are unique and independent from each other,
- are abstracted from the organizational model,
- capture the business interests.

One might say that this is not really revolutionary new. Some people might argue that they do not see a real difference to functional decomposition here. Comparing capabilities, components, and, e.g., functional decomposition is indeed a rewarding exercise for ongoing academic research (see Chap. 5). However, it is not a necessity to go through such an exercise in order to get practical benefits from using capabilities in business architecture management.

Some might argue that the term capability is not sufficiently well defined here. From a rather academic point of view this is more than valid; from a practical standpoint, however, the above level of precision proved to be sufficient, facilitating communication between business and information technology (IT) people.

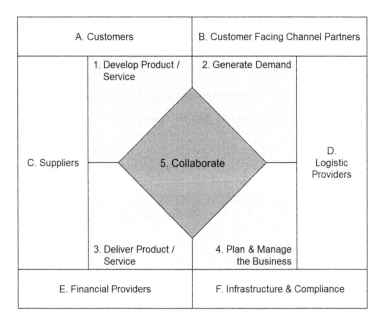

Fig. 6.1 Exemplary top-level capability model [adopted from Merrifield and Tobey (2006)]

6.1.1   Capabilities and Domains

Some professionals opine that top-level capabilities are nothing else than the top-level domains of the business architecture of a company. This comes close to the truth. Figure 6.1 offers an example for illustration.

As an architect, if you compare the rather generic model illustrated in Fig. 6.1 (which is applicable to all industries) to your own company's domain model, you will typically be able to properly map these two models onto one another. Deviations may come at a more detailed level. Let us assume that risk management is a top-level capability of insurance. Then underwriting (the acceptance of risk) can be seen as a subcapability of risk management. However, looking at the enterprise more from a supply chain perspective, one would rather say that underwriting belongs to the processing capability. You could now spend a lot of time discussing whether to put underwriting in the processing corner or the "manage the business" area of the model. Experience says that this is not really worth the effort. At some level in the hierarchy of capabilities, the views will merge again. No matter what the path from the root of a capability tree to an underwriting capability looks like, you will find an Underwriting Capability in an insurance capability model. So, in different capability models for the same industry there are very similar capabilities at very different places in the capability tree. However, capabilities remain a useful planning instrument as long as a given enterprise agrees on a single tree of capabilities for its business architecture management (BAM). This does not have to be a "universally true" capability tree for an industry. Most practitioners will not invest too much effort in finding a universal capability tree. Instead, they will use the models they have at hand and then mix these models (see Sect. 6.3.3) to be able to have something applicable in a relatively short time.

6.1.2 Capabilities in Business Model Canvases

Business model canvases provide classification schemes for the necessary ingredients of a business model. In general, these come in different variants (e.g., King 2012; Osterwalder and Pigneur 2010); however, what they have in common is that they usually comprise both "key resources" and "key activities." Such key activities, in turn, directly relate to capabilities needed to implement the business model, as described using a business model canvas.

As explained in Chap. 1, business models and capabilities are closely related to each other. An enterprise implements at least one business model. It can also implement more than one business model if it has, e.g., more than one division where each division might have its "own" business model. Implementing one or more business models requires a set of appropriate "operational capabilities"—a term that is not meant to say that those capabilities may not have any strategic importance, but to point out their relevance for running the business and allow a proper demarcation to so-called dynamic capabilities, as introduced in the following section.

In most enterprises there is already a set of capabilities implemented that is more or less aligned with the actual set of capabilities needed to implement all business models. This might not have happened as a conscious or planned activity; however, with the concept of capabilities in mind, it will be possible to identify and describe a set of capabilities currently implemented. In order to help establish a managed process for dealing with actual and planned sets of capabilities, Sect. 6.3 will introduce a few methods that may support business architects in properly planning and implementing the set of operational capabilities that is needed to implement all relevant business models of an enterprise.

From time to time—say, in periods of up to 3 years—some of the following might happen:

• The enterprise wants to adopt new business models or change existing ones.
• Existing business models are optimized.
• Changes of the environment may lead to new ways of how to best source or implement capabilities.

In each case, changes of the optimum set of operational capabilities may be required. For example, capabilities may become obsolete and should then be removed from an enterprise's capability portfolio. It may also turn out that a capability could better be outsourced or that the implementation of certain capabilities needs improvement.

6.1.3 Capabilities as a Common Language in the Enterprise

As has been outlined in this book's introductory chapter, capabilities represent significant portions of what the business is able to do and encompass various aspects, e.g., people, processes, and, potentially, the information technology used to support the activities needed to offer a capability.

In many businesses you will find a large percentage of capabilities that might not be automated by IT at all. In such cases, there may just be a support by common office solutions such as email, word processing, and spreadsheets, but not by specialized business applications. Examples are the "capability to imagine new products" or the "capability to report regulatory compliance."

It is quite common for capability names to start with a verb. For example, you may have a capability "manage life insurance contracts." Again, in case of a small-scale or a start-up operations, this capability might not be supported by any IT system at all.

Relevant aspects that can be integrated into the concept of a capability are [e.g., according to Kumar (2006)]:

- performance metrics and cost information for a capability,
- service level agreements for a capability,
- compliance criteria,

and any other attributes that may be helpful for managing a set of capabilities. As an enterprise IT architect, if you have practiced application portfolio management, this will sound familiar, except that the subject of interest is a business capability instead of an IT application.

Referring back to the previous subsection, it is also clear why having capabilities as the subject of discussion should be favored over mere discussing at the level of business processes. This is because in the latter case you may omit important strategic aspects and consider only those aspects that are already implemented.

Activities that will contribute to future business success might not yet be implemented. In other words, as some enterprise architect may claim, business processes represent the past. To express future needs, additional concepts are required. This is where capabilities offer assistance, as they serve the purpose of reasoning about future sources of success much better than other concepts do.

6.2 Dynamic Capabilities

Up to this point, this chapter's discussion of capabilities has revolved around the context of how to implement a business model or strategy. There is one further notion of capabilities that is related closer to an earlier step in strategic management or, say, the creation of a sustainable competitive advantage, that is, strategy formation. With reference to the business model canvases discussed above, one could also say that strategic management is, amongst other topics, about how to identify and define the business models needed to make a venture successful. So-called dynamic capabilities are those capabilities needed to identify and implement a proper set of business models and operational capabilities to create sustainable competitive advantage and evade a "zero profit condition" (Teece 2009, p. 85 ff.) of strategic management.

Dynamic capabilities are defined as "*the firm's ability to integrate, build and reconfigure internal and external competences to address rapidly changing environments*" (Teece et al. 1997). This may also be restated as the firm's ability to integrate, build, and reconfigure internal and external operational capabilities. Hence, dynamic capabilities can be seen as meta-capabilities.

According to the dynamic capability concept as described by Teece (2009) (see also Fig. 6.2), an enterprise

- must be able to *sense* new opportunities for products or services (which has a lot to do with technology management and management of innovation)
- must be able to *seize* them (which has a lot to do with business model design);
- and, finally, must be able to *manage threats* on the way to exploit the opportunities. (which also comprises disciplines such as solid governance or, e.g., knowledge management).

Hence, dynamic capabilities have a far wider scope than just designing business models. They also deal with systematic ways how to come across new business models and how to defend them against competitors or any other threats. Managing operational capabilities is a part of implementing business models, while defining and successfully maintaining a business model is one outcome of the application of dynamic capabilities.

6.3 Managing a Set of Operational Capabilities

Based on the previous sections, we can conclude that a proper management of one's set of operational capabilities can be considered as a use of dynamic capabilities or as a dynamic capability itself; in particular, one may thus perceive BAM as a dynamic capability. The remainder of this chapter focuses on some patterns according to which enterprises manage their portfolios of operational capabilities.

In a typical large scale enterprise there might be some 200–300 operational capabilities that are the subject of planning exercises at a senior management level. They might be decomposed into a few thousand fine-grained operational capabilities, which will be dealt with by lower levels of management to implement those capabilities that have been identified as important by the senior management. Depending on the hierarchy levels used for capability decomposition, one may end up with catalogs (or call them trees) of up to 2.000 and more capabilities, grouped hierarchically from the top-level domains down to maybe level 5–7. Senior management will deal mostly with levels 1–3, while the lower levels are typically used to design implementations of the capabilities at levels 2–3 (as level 1 just represents

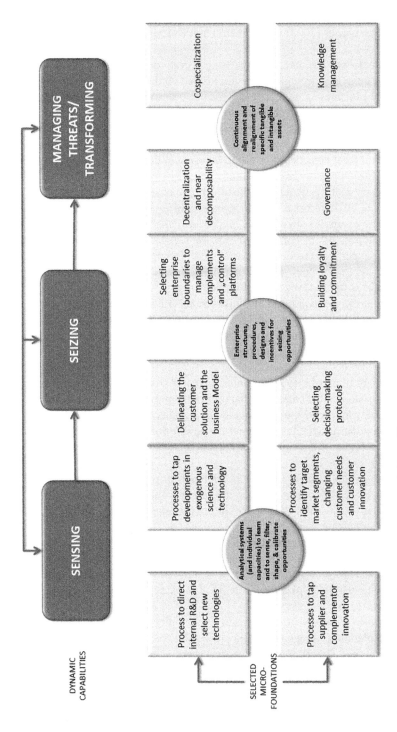

Fig. 6.2 Dynamic capabilities according to Teece (2009, p. 49)

the domains). More specifically, typical use cases of such capability models according to Ritzenhöfer (2008) and Cameron and Kalex (2009) are:

- *Investment decisions*: One can assess existing operational capabilities in terms of whether they have any strategic importance based on the support of the business strategy and/or business model. One can then also scrutinize the capabilities' IT support and compare this to their strategic importance. This may lead to the identification of mismatches: strategic capabilities with insufficient IT support and less important capabilities with best-in-class IT support. This should then be addressed or at least considered in future investment decisions.
- *Business-IT-alignment*: An assessment of a capability portfolio can also be used to conduct a gap analysis with respect to the implemented business processes and IT support in an enterprise. On that basis, different deficiencies may be identified. For example, strategically important capabilities might lack high-quality IT support or, in contrast, unimportant capabilities are implemented using far too expensive business processes and IT support.
- *Outsourcing decisions*: Non-strategic capabilities with high operating costs are prime candidates for any wave of outsourcing.
- *Demand and portfolio management*: This is more or less a variant of the above. Mapping change demands onto capabilities, it may be straightforward to find out whether those demands contain more or less unimportant features or whether they help improve strategically important capabilities.

A main strength of capability management is that it creates a common language for various professions in an enterprise that allows them to discuss common issues, e.g., where to best invest financial resources in an enterprise. Against this background, the following subsections will present a description of three procedures that illustrate the handiness of the capabilities approach:

- *Heat Mapping*: This is a very universal approach to produce colorful material that helps prepare decisions, e.g., for the use in capability-based investment allocation. Heat maps show "*hot spots*" in the operational capability landscape and help communicate them.
- *Footprinting*: This is a variant of heat mapping that can be used for solution planning and comparison across, e.g., several subsidiaries. IT applications, for example, have a footprint that can be expressed in terms of capabilities. Making such footprints visible helps to compare solutions and make their scope easily discussable.
- *Mix the Models*: It shows how to obtain a capability model, as the basis for analysis and planning using capabilities (such as in the previous procedures). In most cases, it will not be possible to download a "ready-to-use" capability model, but it will have to be developed for the specific purposes at hand. A typical approach is to mix the models.

In a logical order of sequence, we would have to look into the development of a capability model first ("mix the models"). However, as this has already been addressed in detail in Chap. 5, we deal with the application of a capability model first (i.e., heat mapping and footprinting), before returning to the development part and giving some further advice on how to get started with a capability-based approach.

6.3.1 Heat Mapping: Using Capabilities to Direct Investments

Imagine you want to know the spots where your house could require some investments in additional insulation. You could have a so-called thermal infrared building survey carried out. Now consider the (re-)allocation of investments in business activities (or, in a second step, in their IT support), which may be triggered by some changes in the business model. It thus needs to be reviewed where it might be worth putting money. For this purpose, one needs some sort of a bird's eye view, which also allows for communicating facts to the upper management in a visual, easy-to-understand style. So the question here is: *What is the equivalent to an infrared building survey in business architecture management or enterprise investment planning?*

When trying to answer this question, one has to deal with a set of conflicting forces:

- *Managers want one slide, while architects may want the details*: For management meetings like investment committees, it is essential to have relevant facts on a single or at least only few slides. On the other hand, architects want accurate facts, and they want decisions to be based on these facts. They want things to be true or right. Operationally minded people would typically say that PowerPoint slides used at the management level are inaccurate, while managers would say that too much detail would blur their vision and hence hamper their ability to decide.
- *Sometimes also managers want a drill down*: The fact that managers want a one-slide overview does not mean that they would not like to have more details at hand if required. Hence, whatever planning method should allow drill-downs like thermography allows zooming.
- *Time consumption versus accuracy*: The "higher the resolution" of the images that also allow zooming in, the more expensive the technology to make the pictures. This holds for thermography, photography, and this also holds for the use of capability-based heat maps in investment planning. One can apply any level of functional decomposition in order to increase accuracy. The drawback are rising costs.

A straightforward approach is to produce a so-called heat map of the capability landscape. Figure 6.3 depicts a sample heat map at a domain level. Such a map could also be refined to lower-level capabilities. Red color coding could, e.g., stand for high maintenance costs combined with low customer satisfaction for the implementation and support of a capability. The basis for producing such heat maps thus

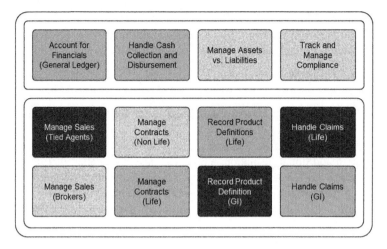

Fig. 6.3 Sample heat map

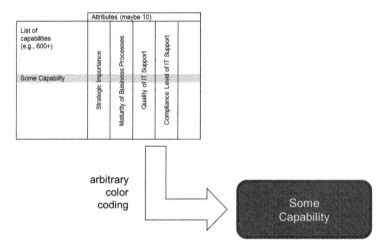

Fig. 6.4 From evaluated capabilities to a heat map

is a list of capabilities together with a set of attributes used to go through the current situation of the enterprise in a bunch of expert sessions (Fig. 6.4). Therein, experts can tell you, e.g., how important they rate a capability for the enterprise's success.

Business managers could judge whether the capability has any strategic importance. Users can evaluate the quality of, e.g., business processes for a given capability. Enterprise IT architects can contribute insights into how many applications are used to implement the capability, thus indicating the degree of redundancy.

Once such an information base has been set up, it can be used to generate far more than one heat map. If you define that

$$color\ on\ map\ =\ some\ function\ (\{attributes\ of\ capability\}),$$

then it will be possible to generate an arbitrary set of heat maps, depicting different aspects, depending on the attributes some stakeholders are interested in (Fig. 6.4).

6.3.1.1 Variants

As indicated, heat mapping allows a high variability in itself. You can basically define arbitrary sets of attributes that you want to have included in the evaluation as well as an arbitrary evaluation function that assigns colors or other map attributes to the graphical representation of the capability on a heat map.

One option is to use border color to indicate the result of a second evaluation function (Microsoft Services 2006). Certain tool sets also make the size of boxes variable to indicate, e.g., application costs (cf. Cameron and Kalex 2009). There are hardly any limits to one's fantasy.

6.3.1.2 Consequences

Capability heat mapping implies the following:

- *Both managers and operational people can be satisfied*, if enough efforts are invested in evaluating capability catalogs down to the level that is wanted or needed for a decision.
- With a proper tool set, *one can drill down to an arbitrary level*, as deep as a given set of capabilities is modeled.
- The method is *as time consuming or accurate as one wants it to be.* You can thus start at a high level of capabilities and model or evaluate deeper in areas, in which there seem to be "hot spots."

6.3.1.3 Known Uses

The business engineering method set called "Motion" (Homan 2008; Microsoft Services 2006) makes extensive use of configurable heat maps. In fact, heat mapping is supported by various tool sets, as has been demonstrated by Cameron and Kalex (2009). The "Business Domain Based Capability Roadmap" (Buckl et al. 2009a) is a specialization of heat mapping, used by companies such as Nokia and Siemens. Prominent consultancies also promote the use of heat maps and capability-based planning (see example maps in Ritzenhöfer 2008).

6.3.2 Footprinting: Using Capabilities for Solutions Planning

Consider the execution of a globalization strategy for a large scale financial service company, in which you have to synchronize operations in regions such as Northern America, LATAM (Latin America), EMEA, (Europe Middle East Africa), and APAC (Asia Pacific). You are tasked with a comparison of the different solutions (incl., e.g., processes, roles) in the subsidiaries in the various regions. Those subsidiaries have completely different histories. Hence, they may have different solutions, which may implement different capabilities. Here, the question is: *How do you get a sufficiently accurate overview of numerous solutions that implement a few hundred fine-grained capabilities each?*

Again, if you aim to answer this question, you have to deal with a set of conflicting forces:

- *Ease of use versus sufficient accuracy*: A method that allows quick comparisons should also allow enough accuracy to not end up with wrong decisions because important facts were not taken into consideration. Ideally, one should be able to drill down to the lower level of detail if required.
- *Speed versus accuracy*: Managers are impatient, while operational people often want details and sufficient time to prepare optimum decisions. A method that allows comparing process ecosystems should be able to support both, that is, fast screenings, on the one hand, and also longer, but more accurate examinations, on the other hand. At best, the quick check should allow to be taken to a more detailed level later.

An often employed method is to compare the solution footprints. To this end, a common catalog of capabilities should be used to identify the capabilities that are implemented by each solution and then map, e.g., the processes and applications in focus onto the capability catalog. Color coding finally allows an indication of those capabilities that are implemented by a solution (and those which are not). The resulting maps are called "footprints" (Fig. 6.5).

6.3.2.1 Variants
Instead of simply using a boolean value for "X implements capability Y," it may also be reasonable to use a scale with respect to the degree of quality to which X implements Y.

6.3.2.2 Consequences
System footprinting based on capabilities comes with the following characteristics:

- *Ease of use*: Once a common capability model is available, using it for footprinting is really straightforward. If a heat mapping tool is in place, it can also be used for footprinting.
- *Fast and accurate enough*: Footprinting can be used down to any level of a given capability tree. If initially a coarse footprint has been used to exclude a few of the candidate solutions first, it is also possible to refine the evaluation at a later stage and then put more efforts in the evaluation only for favored solutions.

6.3.2.3 Related Procedures
Footprinting can be seen as a special form of heat mapping, using one property or relationship ("is implemented by process or application X") and hence a trivial coloring function. By mapping a given set of processes and IT applications onto a capability catalog you end up with their footprints, which can be easily visualized using a "degenerate" heat map.

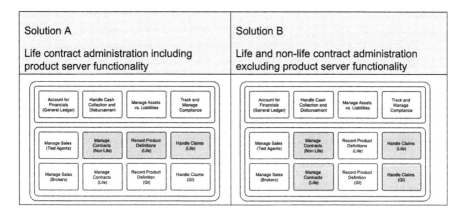

Fig. 6.5 Comparison of two system footprints

In order to be effective with footprinting, a high-quality capability model of the relevant area of interest is required. This can be mixed from various sources (see next subsection). Footprinting can also be combined with kiviat diagrams (Buckl et al. 2009b).

6.3.3   Mix the Models: Obtain an Own Capability Map

Consider an upcoming capability-based planning activity for which a catalog of business capabilities is required and for which you thus need to come up with, say, around 200–400 capabilities. In addition, the capability model should be structured into different levels. The issue here is: *How can you obtain a "good enough" capability model for your future planning efforts?*

When trying to obtain a capability list, you typically have to deal with the following set of conflicting forces:

- *Speed versus quality*: Typically time is a scarce resource when a new strategy is about to be defined. Developing a catalog of maybe 300 capabilities, as (initially) needed for a typical international enterprise, and discussing this with all relevant stakeholders may take far more than a year. Typically, these are time spans that the upper management does not accept. On the other hand, by an initial brainstorming in a small group under high time pressure, it might be possible to produce a result much faster. However, the quality level may suffer; the catalog might be incomplete, redundant, might not capture the strategically important capabilities, and so on.
- *Patience versus accuracy*: In a management workshop there will not be sufficient time to discuss 2.000 single capabilities. Perhaps it might be possible to discuss 50–70 important top-level capabilities and their respective state and importance to the enterprise.

- *Full custom versus reference model*: To obtain a capability model for a given enterprise, one can try to "invent" the whole catalog, which means that capabilities are derived from some theoretical or other models by applying whatever business engineering techniques. This will typically take lots of time and the results might initially not have the quality of best-in-class models. On the positive side, such models have the potential to be relatively well tailored to the specific enterprise. Alternatively, one could also consider the purchase of an industry-specific capability model from external sources, with which it might be possible to save a lot of time. The downside of this is that it may result in a list of capabilities for the average of the industry, that is, non-standard capabilities that are important for the specific enterprise might be missing.
- *Clean design versus pragmatism*: The literature offers various business engineering methods that would allow the development of a functional domain model, capability model, and also service model more or less from scratch by gathering in front of a whiteboard and applying design principles (Engels et al. 2008). On the other hand, it is also possible to obtain models from various sources and design one's own model on that basis by discussing at a domain expert level. Those experts will also have design principles in their mind when synthesizing their enterprise-specific model; however, they will not start with a blank sheet of paper or a blank whiteboard. In contrast to a method specialist who is good at design procedures, they will also know the industry they operate in.
- *"Good enough and fast" versus "perfect and slow"*: One could spend years developing the "perfect" capability catalog for a given enterprise. For the upper management, however, it will not seem worthwhile to produce a 100 % solution but to achieve timely results. Apart from that, the "perfect" catalog would be outdated soon because business changes faster than engineers can apply real methodical engineering. The usual 80 % of the maximum possible results by employing maybe 10–20 % percent of the effort for a 95 % perfect solution should do the job. This is well known as applying the Pareto principle.

Therefore, as a best practice, people mix their capability models from various sources. Typically, you would start by identifying the top-level domains. This level can be developed using the following sources:

- *Folklore from the own company:* Often companies do have maps of a certain structure from previous planning efforts.
- *Industry maps:* For many industries there are industry reference models maintained by groups who foster knowledge exchange and promote best practices in the respective industry. eTOM (TM Forum 2014) is a typical example of such models for the telecommunications industry. Reference material for the insurance business, on the other hand, may be provided by a given country's association of insurers.
- *Standard software solution maps:* Often there is also standard software available for a specific industry. These often come with a "solution map" or something similar for the relevant industry, which also comprises typical industry domains. As such, they may represent a very good source here.

- *Maps provided by specialized consultants:* Consultancies typically organize themselves according to industry sectors, e.g., banking, telecommunications, chemicals, or manufacturing. Typically, they also possess capability lists from previous engagements that can help kick-start the setup of a capability model.
- *Generic maps:* On a high level, to start with, one can use models like Porter's value chain (Porter 1985), or a top-level domain map as already mentioned earlier.

Once a high-level domain map has been set up, you would continue in an iterative way to break down the capabilities to a level 2 or 3, for example. Typically, the internal sources start to dry up here and it will be required to mix stuff from industry maps [such as eTOM (TM Forum 2014)] and experts with generic capability models.

6.3.3.1 Variants
There are too many variants to be counted. Any combination of sources for a capability model could be seen as a variant, depending on what sources are accessible in a given industry.

6.3.3.2 Consequences
If one obtains a capability model as a synthesis of various sources, this has the following typical consequences:

- *Speedy and good enough:* Typically a time box will be set for the development of a capability model. If quick results are required, one can rely on a bigger proportion of external material, often resulting in higher costs. However, if the aim is to save money and there is no serious time pressure, the primary use of internal experts may be favored.
- *Sufficient individuality:* Models provided by industry experts are good enough in many cases. If additional capabilities are needed that are not covered by such models, they can often be found in generic capability models or also in those for similar industries. Particular strategically important capabilities might be known oneself (if they are considered important in a given enterprise). Therefore, a mixed capability model will be "individual enough" in most cases.

6.3.3.3 Known Uses
There is one international telecommunications provider based in Germany who has a mixed capability model based on sources such as its own group domain model, eTOM, and also capabilities lists from a large software vendor. Another large telecommunications company operating in Germany also makes extensive use of eTOM and complements this with own considerations. There are more than a handful of German insurance companies who have developed their domain architectures based on VAA, an initiative of the German Association of insurers GDV.

6.4   Summary

In this chapter, we could demonstrate that operational capabilities are needed to implement business models. So-called dynamic capabilities are a meta-concept which can be used to sense, seize and defend opportunities to generate sustainable competitive advantage. Business model generation is one discipline in applying dynamic capabilities. Operational capabilities are needed to bring business models to life. Operational capabilities can be managed using methods of portfolio management in order to align them with an enterprise's strategy. This also comprises questions of sourcing and performance management for operational capabilities.

References

Bredemeyer D, Krishnan R, Lafrenz A, Malan R (2006) Enterprise architecture as business capabilities architecture. http://bredemeyer.com/pdf_files/Presentations/EnterpriseArchitectureAsCapabilitiesArcE.pdf. Accessed 12 Nov 2009

Buckl S, Ernst A, Kopper H, Marliani R, Matthes F, Petschownik P, Schweda CM (2009a) EA management patterns for consolidations after mergers. In: Proceedings of the 2009 workshop on patterns in enterprise architecture management, Kaiserslautern, Germany

Buckl S., Ernst A, Lankes J, Matthes F (2009b) Enterprise architecture management pattern catalog. http://eampc-wiki.systemcartography.info/wikis/eam-pattern-catalog/v-83. Accessed 12 Sept 2014

Cameron B, Kalex U (2009) Webinar (web seminar) on business capability management. Forrester Research & alfabet AG, June 2009. http://www.alfabet.de/news/veranstaltungen/webinar_driving_productive_it_investment. Accessed 13 Nov 2009

Engels G, Hess A, Humm B, Juwig O, Lohmann M, Richter J-P, Voß M, Willkomm J (2008) Quasar enterprise. dpunkt Verlag, Heidelberg

TM Forum (2014) eTOM Business process framework. http://www.tmforum.org/Overview/13763/home.html. Accessed 06 Sept 2014

Homan L (2008) Enterprise architecture: connecting business and IT. Presentation at GI-Jahrestagung 2008, Munich, 9 Sept 2008

King R (2012) Business model fishbone. http://de.slideshare.net/RodKing/business-model-fishbone-for-apples-classic-ipod. Accessed 12 Sept 2014

Kumar D (2006) Motion—a framework for SOA adoption in the enterprise. Presentation at Microsoft TechEd conference 2006, Pasadena

Merriam-Webster (2014) Capability. http://www.merriam-webster.com/dictionary/capability. Accessed 26 Sept 2014

Merrifield R, Tobey J (2006) Motion lite: a rapid application of the business architecture techniques used by Microsoft Motion. http://msdn2.microsoft.com/en-us/library/bb736727.aspx. Accessed 12 Sept 2014

Microsoft Services (2006) Microsoft Motion heat mapping tool. blogs.microsoft.co.il/files/folders/2034/download.aspx. Accessed 26 Sept 2014

Osterwalder A, Pigneur Y (2010) Business model generation—a handbook for visionaries, game changers, and challengers. Wiley, Hoboken, NJ

Porter ME (1985) Competitive advantage: creating and sustaining superior performance. The Free Press, New York

Ritzenhöfer G (2008) SOA-basierte IT-Strategien für Banken. Presentation at GI-Jahrestagung 2008, Munich, 9 Sept 2008

Teece DJ (2009) Dynamic capabilities & strategic management—organizing for innovation and growth. Oxford University Press, New York

Teece DJ, Pisano G, Shuen A (1997) Dynamic capabilities and strategic management. Strateg Manag J 18(7):509–533

Part III

Architecting Business Capability Realization

Can Culture Be Designed?

7

David W. Gray

Abstract

Culture is widely recognized as one of the prime foundations of a successful business, yet it is still poorly understood, especially as an element of business architecture management. This chapter explores the following questions:

1. What is culture and why is it important?
2. Is there such a thing as an inherently "good" or "bad" culture?
3. What is the role of culture in change?
4. Can culture be designed?
5. If these things are possible, how might they be achieved?

This chapter also introduces a diagnostic tool, the "Culture Map"—designed to help groups of all sizes improve their understanding of their culture, diagnose issues and work toward resolutions, along with some instructions for its use.

7.1 Introduction: What Is Culture and Why Is It Important?

No company escapes the need for change. Numerous studies have found that more than 50 % of change initiatives fail to meet their objectives. Resistance to change is cited as the number one reason for these failures. And what most leaders call "resistance to change" is actually culture (Schein 1992).

If you want to understand the dynamics of change, you have to understand the dynamics of culture. They are an essential part of the business architecture, yet they are not so easy to understand. In fact, culture does a really good job of hiding in

D.W. Gray (✉)
Webster Groves, MO, USA
e-mail: dave.gray@gmail.com

© Springer International Publishing Switzerland 2015
D. Simon, C. Schmidt (eds.), *Business Architecture Management*, Management for Professionals, DOI 10.1007/978-3-319-14571-6_7

plain sight. For example, if people know what needs to happen, yet they fail to do it, that is a culture problem.

Culture is collective behavior. It is the habits that we form as a group. That is all it is. And it is emergent; a living, dynamic thing. In any company you do things. As you find ways to do things that are consistent and repeatable, habitual behaviors and routines form. This is inevitable. It is part of a natural process that enables an organization to scale, so it can become more efficient.

Any behavior that is rewarded consistently over time will become a habit, and will become embedded in the collective habits we call culture. Some of these habits are good for the organization as a whole, but some might also be harmful. In any group, people attempt to influence each other's behavior in a variety of ways. For example, if political or backstabbing behavior is rewarded, say by promotions or pay increases, then you will see that behavior continue and, if it is rewarded persistently over time, it will become a part of "how we do things around here."

Rewards might be formal or informal. Formal rewards include things like pay increases, promotions, bonuses, and formal recognition such as awards or a corner office with a nice view. Informal rewards can be such things as being appreciated by peers, a sense of accomplishment, or feeling like you "fit in" as a respected member of a group.

Over time, "the way we do things around here" comes to be seen as the only valid way to do things. There is a right way to see the world, to think about things, a right way to manage tradeoffs, to solve problems, to make decisions and judgments, as well as acceptable ways to rationalize, justify, and explain them. Because culture is also a group dynamic, it has a shared history and a group identity. It has rules and norms about who is included, who is excluded, who has status and power, what can be discussed and what is undiscussable. The longer an organization has existed, the more deeply embedded its culture will become. And the longer an individual has lived and worked in a given culture, the more invisible the culture will become over time. It is the deeply rooted habits as well as the relative invisibility of culture that gives it its power. New people who are just joining such a culture may feel disoriented at first. Understanding the formal rules as written in policy manuals and handbooks is only part of the story. They must "learn the ropes" so they can navigate the social system and find their place in it.

Typically, the people who have the most power in a culture also have the most to lose if that culture changes. So the culture itself has a tremendous power to resist change. In fact, every significant change in the routine habits and behaviors of an organization will involve cultural resistance and cultural change. To fight change, organizations employ a variety of conscious and unconscious defenses, known as "organizational defensive routines" (Argyris 1990).

7.2   Is There Such a Thing as an Inherently "Good" or "Bad" Culture?

Culture evolves through the interplay of dynamic forces inside and outside the organization. On the one hand, any group needs to organize and work together as a group (internal integration). On the other hand, it needs to adapt to market forces and other outside influences (external adaptation) (Schein 1992), as has been explained earlier in this book (Chap. 1).

A successful culture is one that has achieved a good fit between the two. That is, the way it is integrated internally is a good fit for the external environment. Most companies that have achieved sustainable success in their markets have such a fit. As long as those market conditions remain relatively constant, a strong culture can be a significant asset. However, if the market environment shifts, the same strong culture that was once an asset can quickly become a liability.

Consider Nokia, which was, as recently as 2008, the largest player in the mobile phone market, with 40 % market share (Malykhina 2008). Nokia was celebrated for its organizational values and culture, and rightly so. Over its more than 100-year history, Nokia had achieved excellence as an innovative, entrepreneurial manufacturing company, evolving from a rubber and paper manufacturer to electronics, cables and telegraph equipment, and emerging in the 1960s and 1970s as a mobile phone manufacturer.

However, as the company entered the twenty-first century, the role of the mobile phone in society was shifting. Phones were no longer simply communication devices. Increasingly, the phone was becoming a computing device. And while the earlier "dumb phones" were differentiated based on things that were based on manufacturing excellence, like industrial design, reliability, and performance, the newer "smart phones" were differentiated by the operating system and applications. In other words, when all you could do with a phone was talk and text, customers cared more about things like color, size, and reliability. But when new devices like the iPhone emerged, and customers found they could access whole new functions and capabilities, they cared less about what a phone looked like and more about what they could do with it.

Nokia's culture was successful in a world centered on manufacturing, where new models required heavy R&D investment and high risk. But the company floundered when faced with technology giants like Apple, who could mobilize an entire ecosystem of developers who created new applications at a pace Nokia could not hope to match.

Nokia's culture hadn't changed. But the culture that had once made Nokia great would prove a liability as Nokia adopted a strategy that was driven mostly by software, making hardware more of a commodity. A corporate culture that was once celebrated became "a culture of complacency" (O'Brien 2010).

Was Nokia's culture inherently good? Yes and no. The culture was so strong that culture change would have been a major undertaking. Resistance would have been high. And in fact, Nokia did go through a series of cultural change exercises to become "more like an internet company" (Willigan 2009). But that bridge, it seems, Nokia was not able to cross.

The more successful a company has been in the past, the more difficult it will be to change, because in a strong culture people tend to persist in believing that the habits and routines that made them successful in the past will continue to work. They will also tend to employ organizational defensive routines, denying the validity of reports and observations which are inconsistent with deeply-held beliefs about their group and its identity. However, an organizational culture can only be great if it is not only internally integrated, but also a good fit with its external environment.

7.3   What Is the Role of Culture in Change?

When the market shifts, companies must adapt. With respect to culture there are two options: You can change the culture to fit the new business strategy, or you can change the business strategy to leverage a strong culture that already exists.

Consider Samsung, another mobile phone manufacturer that took a radically different approach to the changing market landscape. Samsung focused on making devices that could run every operating system that was available. Although they could not build devices to run proprietary operating systems like Apple's iOS or Nokia's Symbian, they made sure that Samsung phones could run any operating system that was available to them, like Windows and Android. They made phones with small screens and big screens. They also sold components to other smart phone makers, including Apple.

In short, they recognized that the mobile-device market would be driven by software, and they did everything possible to ensure that no matter what the software was, it would be able to run on a Samsung phone. Recognizing that smartphones will in turn become commoditized, the company is also spending $20 billion to develop its capabilities in medical devices, solar panels, LED lighting, batteries for electric cars, and biotech.

Nokia was acquired by Microsoft in 2013, and Samsung now sells more mobile phones than any company in the world, including Apple. A company with a strong culture, like Nokia, might have been more successful with option two (see above)—a Samsung-like strategy. However, when strategic options are limited, sometimes the only option left is culture change.

Consider IBM in 1993. A once-proud company, with a very strong and storied culture, was on the brink of bankruptcy. As a last resort, the board of directors hired a customer—Lou Gerstner, formerly CEO of American Express—to take over the failing company.

IBM's values, "Excellence in all we do," "Superior customer service," and "Respect for the individual" had become ossified over time. What had once been living, dynamic values had, over time, deteriorated into platitudes, habits and routines. The company's culture was internally integrated, but after holding a virtual monopoly on mainframe computers for many years, it had lost touch with the market.

In Gerstner's words, "'Excellence' became an obsession with perfection... 'customer service' became largely administrative... like a marriage that had lost its passion... 'respect for the individual' came to mean an IBMer can pretty much do whatever they want, with little or no accountability."

What had once been a customer-oriented culture had become stultified and bureaucratic. As Gerstner points out, "This codification, this rigor mortis that sets in around values and behaviors, is a problem unique to—and often devastating for—successful enterprises. I suspect that many successful companies that have fallen on hard times in the past—including IBM, Sears, General Motors, Kodak, Xerox, and many others—saw perhaps quite clearly the changes in their environment. They were probably able to conceptualize and articulate the need for change and perhaps even develop strategies for it. What I think hurt the most was their inability to change highly structured, sophisticated cultures that had been born in a different world" (Gerstner 2003).

Gerstner did everything he could to get IBM re-focused on customers and the market. One of his first moves was to send senior executives out to meet directly with customers and give him a one-page report on their issues and concerns. He also changed IBM incentives and reward systems to align with the new strategy. In other words, he not only talked about culture and values, he changed the structure and focus of the company so that the behaviors he wanted to see were reinforced and rewarded. In spite of massive organizational resistance, including senior managers actively fighting his agenda, he eventually succeeded in turning IBM around.

Gerstner recognized that his turnaround of IBM was successful largely because he put culture front and center. "Culture isn't one aspect of the game," he wrote. "It is the game." Culture change at this scale is exceedingly difficult. In fact, Gerstner only decided to address IBM's culture as a last resort:

Frankly, if I could have chosen not to tackle the IBM culture head-on, I probably wouldn't have... changing the attitude and behavior of hundreds of thousands of people is very, very hard to accomplish. Business schools don't teach you how to do it. You can't lead the revolution from the splendid isolation of corporate headquarters. You can't simply give a couple of speeches or write a new credo for the company and declare that the new culture has taken hold. You can't mandate it, can't engineer it. What you can do is create the conditions for transformation. You can provide incentives. You can define the marketplace realities and goals. But then you have to trust. In fact, in the end, management doesn't change culture. Management invites the workforce itself to change the culture. Perhaps the toughest nut of all to crack was getting IBM employees to accept that invitation (Gerstner 2003).

7.4 Can Culture Be Designed?

Gerstner understood that culture is not something that can be changed by mandate. To initiate culture change, leaders must create the conditions that will allow it to emerge, and then invite the workforce to change.

The conditions that give rise to culture are typically not consciously designed. Rather, they emerge over time as a natural by-product of business operations, processes, habits and routines. However, the relentless advance of technology has accelerated the pace at which businesses must adapt to changing markets and circumstances. Traditional sources of competitive advantage and barriers to entry erode faster today and are no longer sustainable over the long term. Thus, learning, adaptiveness, creativity, and design have now become key sources of sustainable competitive advantage.

This has led to the emergence of design tools for developing business models and strategies, a new suite of business mapping frameworks that, in line with architectural thinking, create structured spaces within which strategists can visualize complex and dynamic relationships, identify gaps, and explore possibilities. Two examples are the "Service Blueprint," to design services (Shostack 1984), and the "Business Model Canvas," a tool to explore and develop innovative business models (Osterwalder and Pigneur 2010).

The Service Blueprint creates a space that organizes service interactions along a timeline, distinguishing between a front stage (where customer interactions take place) and a back stage (internal operations), divided by a line of visibility (the degree and depth which customers can observe backstage operations) (see Fig. 7.1).

As outlined in further detail in other chapters of this book, the Business Model Canvas contains nine building blocks in a structured spatial relationship that codifies the relationship between nine key elements of any business model (see Fig. 7.2). It thus represents a tool to capture main (though not all) aspects of the business model as presented in Chap. 1.

A good design tool should have the following characteristics[1]:

1. It solves a clear and relevant business problem.
2. It is based on sound research and theory.
3. Its categories are mutually exclusive and collectively exhaustive.
4. It uses plain language and concepts that are easy to understand.
5. It is content-agnostic and solution-agnostic.
6. It is simple and practical enough to be used in real-life work situations.

All of the preceding characteristics were carefully considered in the development of the tool presented in the next section.

---

[1] These characteristics were identified in a personal interview of Alexander Osterwalder—as the creator of the Business Model Canvas—by this chapter's author in 2014.

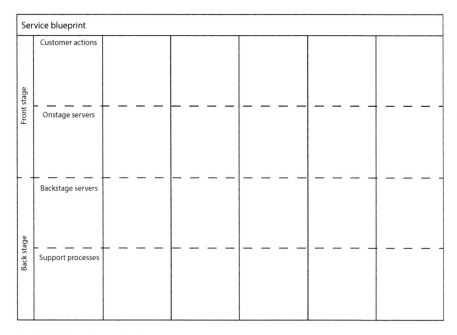

Fig. 7.1 Example service blueprint

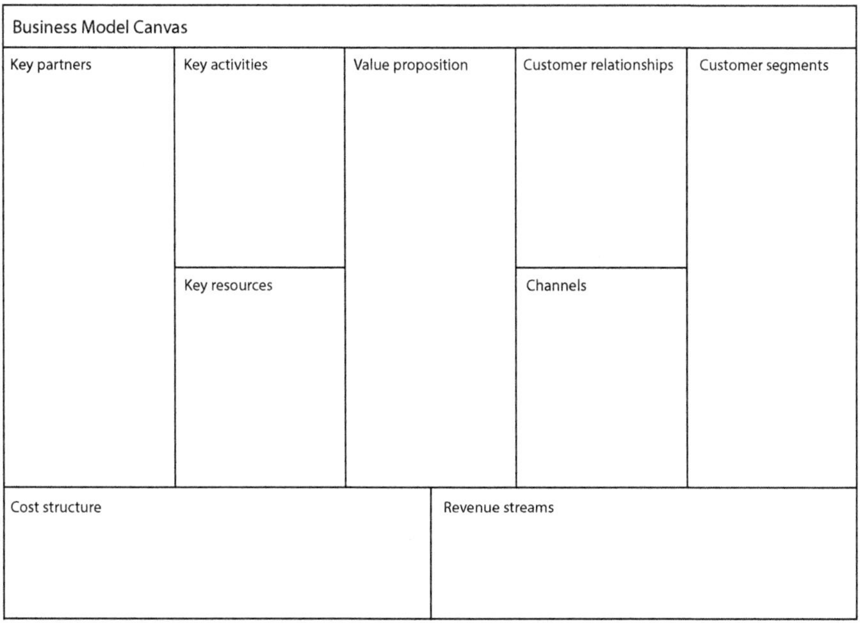

Fig. 7.2 Business model canvas template

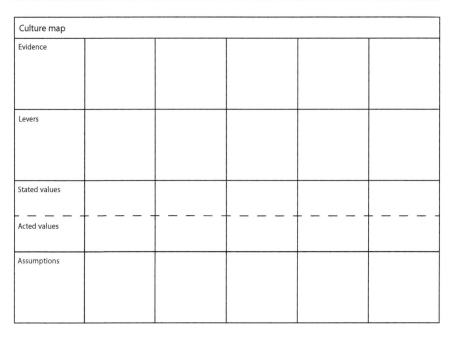

Fig. 7.3 Culture map template

7.4.1 The Culture Map and the Principles of Its Design

The *"Culture Map"* is a business design tool for exploring and understanding the culture of an organization, industry or profession. It is a structured, spatial framework that codifies the important components of an organizational culture (see Fig. 7.3).[2]

The Culture Map is based primarily on the research and theories of Edgar Schein (MIT Sloan School of Management) and Chris Argyris (Harvard Business School), specifically, Schein's model of organizational culture (Schein 1984), and Argyris's theories of action (Argyris 1976).

Schein's model of organizational development divides culture into three cognitive levels, often visualized as an iceberg (see Fig. 7.4), because two of the levels are not directly observable. At the first level are those things that are directly observable, such as facilities, furnishings, dress code, observable interactions, the way that meetings are structured, visible rewards and recognition, language, the stories people tell, and so on. Schein calls this level *"artifacts."* At the second level are the group's *shared values*, which constitute the core identity of the group. Values are preferences for one way of acting over another, for example, valuing

---

[2] The map was designed with the assistance of Alex Osterwalder and conforms to his criteria for a good business tool. In addition to Alex Osterwalder, significant contributions were made by Larry Irons, Chris Finlay, Marcia Conner, and Alan Smith.

Fig. 7.4 Schein's iceberg

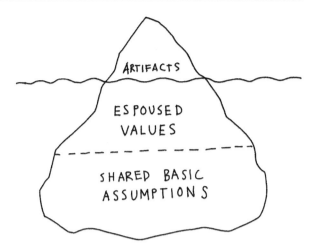

teamwork over outstanding individual contributions, or vice versa. At the third, deepest level are the group's *tacit assumptions*, which are not easily recognized and do not come up in daily conversation or interactions because they are often not consciously realized. These are the elements, like "unspoken rules" which are taboo, undiscussable, and otherwise not easily accessed.

Schein's model of organizational development forms the core structure of the Culture Map. The top row of the Culture Map, labeled *"Evidence,"* corresponds with Schein's top level. The second level of the Culture Map, *"Levers,"* is the addition of the author. The reason for this is that making strategic changes to an organization's culture will require changes to rewards, incentives, organization structure, and so on (i.e., other elements of business execution as outlined in Chap. 1). Thus, the "Levers" row is the space for considering organizational design decisions that are necessary in order to create what Gerstner calls "the conditions for the transformation." The third and fourth levels of the Culture Map, *"Values"* and *"Assumptions,"* conform to the second and third levels of Schein's iceberg.

Argyris's theories of action postulates that people have mental models about the way the world works, which they use to decide how to act in various situations. He calls these theories of action. In his research, he discovered that when people were asked to describe their theory of action, it often did not correspond with their observable actions. He suggested that people have two theories of action: one that they will describe to themselves and others, and a second, often unconscious theory which can be inferred by their actions. He called these the espoused theory and the theory-in-use. The espoused theory is the explanation that someone will offer when asked how they will act in a given situation. The theory-in-use is how that person actually acts when that situation arises.

The difference between an espoused theory and a theory-in-use is the difference between what people say and what they do, which is easily observable in any office environment. In fact, as Argyris points out, most people can detect the gaps between the two theories in other people, even though they can rarely do so for themselves.

In the interest of politeness, or getting along, however, most people refrain from pointing out these gaps.

Because people generally avoid conflict, and prefer not to do things that embarrass or threaten others, these gaps tend to fall in the "undiscussable" category. If the boss says she has an open door policy, but every time someone complains they are shut down or ignored, people will quickly learn to stop complaining.

So over time, people will learn to avoid such pitfalls, in fact, they will quietly collude with each other, while at the same time they will refrain from discussing them openly. Organizational culture is often rife with such inconsistencies, which is one reason culture has to be "learned" by new employees. When confronted by information which seems incongruous or inconsistent with their theories, individuals and groups within a culture will engage in defensive reasoning, such as blaming others, questioning the reliability of sources, and so on.

In his book "The Future of Management" Gary Hamel reports a conversation he had with senior executives in a big American auto manufacturer. He asked them why, after 20 years of benchmarking studies, the company had been unable to catch up to Toyota's productivity. The answer is a perfect example of the kind of defensive reasoning that "protects" an organization from learning the truth:

> Twenty years ago we started sending our young people to Japan to study Toyota. They'd come back and tell us how good Toyota was and we simply didn't believe them. We figured they'd dropped a zero somewhere—no one could produce cars with so few defects per vehicle, or with so few labor hours. It was 5 years before we acknowledged that Toyota really was beating us in a bunch of critical areas. Over the next 5 years, we told ourselves that Toyota's advantages were all cultural. It was all about wa and nemawashi—the uniquely Japanese spirit of cooperation and consultation that Toyota had cultivated with its employees. We were sure that American workers would never put up with these paternalistic practices. Then, of course, Toyota started building plants in the United States, and they got the same results here they got in Japan—so our cultural excuse went out the window. For the next 5 years, we focused on Toyota's manufacturing processes. We studied their use of factory automation, their supplier relationships, just-in-time systems, everything. But despite all our benchmarking, we could never seem to get the same results in our own factories. It's only in the last 5 years that we've finally admitted to ourselves that Toyota's success is based on a wholly different set of principles—about the capabilities of its employees and the responsibilities of its leaders (Hamel 2007).

To account for possible inconsistencies between theories of action and observable action, the third level of the Culture Map has been divided by a dashed line to distinguish between espoused theories (called "*Stated values*" on the map) and theories-in-use (called "*Acted values*" on the map). Acted values are those that may not be explicitly stated but can be inferred from evidence.

The language of the Culture Map has been carefully chosen. It is designed to be clear, simple and easily understandable and has been tested in a variety of business environments.

7.4.2 Using the Culture Map

The Culture Map is designed to help business people explore, discuss, and interact with the cultural dimensions of their workplace. It can be used by an individual, a team, a larger group like a department or a division, or by the company as a whole, to capture the cultural aspects of their overall business architecture.

Culture is complex and dynamic, and there are many cultures that exist, simultaneously and overlapping, in any organization. For example, people in a profession or an industry, such as accounting, affiliate with the culture of their profession as well as that of their company. People in a region will affiliate with regional cultural preferences as well as those of their company. Therefore, before using the Culture Map, it is important to discuss which culture you want to examine. For example, do you want to examine the culture of your department or the company as a whole?

It is important to create a space for discussion such that people feel safe discussing things that are usually undiscussable. For this reason, it is best if culture mapping can take place in a calm, refreshing, neutral environment, outside the normal office realm, in a casual, informal environment, with as few of the usual cultural trappings as possible. It is especially important to include new people, and to make sure they feel as safe as possible. People who have not yet "learned the ropes" can often see incongruities that have become invisible or undiscussable to others.

People should be asked to take on the role of "culture detective" and told that we are here to examine and look critically at our culture. They might need help to understand why this is important, by pointing out, for example, that "we are merging two groups and want to ensure we get the best of both" or "our market has changed and we want to deepen our understanding of our culture's strengths and weaknesses."

It can be helpful to start with Argyris and Schön's "Two-Column Exercise" to demonstrate the difference between espoused theories and theories-in-use (Argyris and Schön 1996).

1. Have participants divide a page into two columns, a left-hand column and a right-hand column.
2. Ask them to think of an important, emotionally difficult, conversation they had at work.
3. In the left-hand column, have them write down the conversation as they remember it, like a script in a play.
4. In the right-hand column, have them write down what they were thinking and feeling but did not express at the time.
5. Have people compare the two columns and consider what was taboo or undiscussable and why.
6. Ask people to share their insights.

If people are not willing to discuss their emotional conversations and their insights, you have not yet created a space that is safe enough for culture mapping.

Once this exercise has been successfully completed, the Culture Map can then be used to see and explore the relationships between

1. The things you do and see every day (Evidence),
2. The systems, rules and structures, both formal and informal, that reward the behavior (Levers),
3. The underlying values, both stated and acted (which are often quite different) that are expressed in the systems, rules and structures (Values), and
4. The tacit or unconscious assumptions and beliefs (often based on experience) that the values are based on (Assumptions).

A culture mapping exercise is partly like an archeological excavation, and partly like therapy. You want people to look for clues, and, by comparing across categories, to try to make linkages and connections, as well as identify gaps and incongruities. At the same time, because you are looking at people, behavior, motivations and often conflict, the process can be deeply emotional, sometimes gut-wrenching, and even cathartic.

It is recommended to use an outside facilitator who is not overly familiar with your culture. The facilitator should be told that the role is to act as a lead culture detective, to look for clues, make connections, and ask what might seem like difficult questions. The role of the facilitator is to dismantle your group's organizational defenses, to untangle the defensive logic. To get to the root of the following:

1. What do we do? (Evidence)
2. What do we reward and punish (Levers)
3. What do we say we value, and how is it different than what we truly value? (Values)
4. What do we believe? (Assumptions)

When in doubt, keep asking why. "Nothing is more powerful than the dumb question." (Schein 1992).

There are numerous ways to approach the Culture Map, but after the "Two-Column Exercise" it often makes sense to put the group's stated values up for examination. Most companies have some kind of official statement of values (see Chap. 1), which can often be found on the company web page. If not, people should be able to come up with a list.

You can tell people that these are the group's stated, or espoused theories, and that we are here today to discover and discuss our theories-in-use—the theories that actually drive the dynamics of the workplace, which may often be unstated, taboo or undiscussable. The group's stated values can be put on sticky notes and positioned in the row titled "Stated Values."

Next, the group should be asked to brainstorm evidence that either confirms or contradicts those values. For example, if a group values "openness" but has very high cubicle walls and offices with closed doors, that would be evidence that is in contradiction to the values.

Once the "Evidence" row is filled in, you can have people think about the levers—rewards, incentives and punishments—that have a direct causal link with the behaviors. How exactly does the group benefit from high walls and closed doors? On examination, you might find a number of levers. People do not do things unless they are rewarded over time. So, one should look for those rewards. They may be formal, like pay, bonuses and awards, or they might be informal, like being appreciated. But they will be there.

Next, you could move to the "Acted Values" column. It is not unusual to find that the acted values are in direct opposition to the stated values. The author's experience includes companies who said they valued simplicity, only to find that, judging by their actions, they clearly valued complexity. It also includes companies who said they valued entrepreneurship and risk-taking, while their actions demonstrated a clear value for bureaucratic, risk-averse structures.

The lowest level of the map, "Assumptions," is perhaps the most difficult for the culture detective. It requires deep reflection and thoughtful consideration of the tacit assumptions that underlie the group's values. Any group will have shared assumptions about the external world and the marketplace. In a cult, for example, the outside world is assumed to be antagonistic, to be feared and shunned. Some companies see customers as targets, to be captured, stolen from competitors and owned, while others see them as peers or collaborators.

The important thing to remember about the "Assumptions" level is that assumptions are beliefs about the way the world works. People will have a tendency not to realize they are assumptions, because, within the context of a culture, they often seem obvious and axiomatic.

For example, a company that is highly competitive and avoids partnerships may believe that the world is fundamentally competitive and cooperation is for fools. Such beliefs are usually based on experience. However, external environments often change faster than organizations can keep up, and, for example, if a market has become fundamentally more complex and interdependent, cooperation may be the only way to survive. By questioning fundamental assumptions, you can open the door to new ways of thinking about the market.

One way to think about assumptions is to ask people to design an experiment that could test whether those assumptions are correct—an experiment they could conduct themselves. In the example above, and experiment might begin by asking, "How would we act if our market was fundamentally cooperative instead of competitive?" If you can describe those actions, then you can act as if they were true, in a small, low-risk way (even if you do not believe it), and observe the kinds of results you get.

There are many ways to use the Culture Map. The approach described above is an exploratory approach, a kind of diagnostic, designed to help a group examine and reflect on their culture, as part of their current architecture. From a target architecture perspective, you can also use the Culture Map as a design tool, to imagine a desired culture and create the systems and structures most likely to support it. You can use it to think about the design of your physical work environment. You can use it when launching a new venture that will require radically

Culture map for Nokia

Evidence How do we behave? What is observable? · how we work together · the language we use · How we collaborate, compete, create, and control?	We innovate but don't launch much	We decide by consensus	Everyone has a voice	We move slowly	CEO & workers eat in same cafeteria
Levers What are the "rules of the game" (formal and informal) that drive our behavior? · Who controls what · How we make decisions · How we allocate resources · What we reward · The spaces we work in	Need layers of approvals to launch / Many brakes, few accelerators	We must agree to proceed / Anyone can block something / If we don't agree we can't move forward	Many can say no, few can say yes / Many opportunities to block	Hundreds of SVPs and VPs / Strong unit fiefdoms / We avoid competition between units / Many opportunities to block	Decisions are political / We need each other to get what we want
Values What do we say that we stand for? What do we care about? · Stated, public values (What we say we value) · Unstated or undisclosed values (Values we demonstrate by our actions)	Passion for innovation // We fear and avoid risk	Collaboration // Standing out is discouraged / Consensus lets us avoid responsibility	We value diversity // Our leaders are almost all Finns / Everyone is welcome to act Finnish	Fast, flexible decision making / Flat, networked organization // We should be able to block threats / We compete for resources	Respect the individual / We value people // Don't step on anyone's toes / You might need them someday
Assumptions What do we believe about the world, and how it works? What is the reasoning behind the values?	Experiments are costly / Most innovations fail / No action is better than wrong action	It's safer to be part of the herd / Standing out can get you punished	The Finnish way is the best way	We dominate the market / The biggest competitors are internal	We have plenty of time / Nokia IS the world

Fig. 7.5 Nokia culture map

different values than the parent company. You can use it when you have a strong, successful culture, in order to better understand the dynamic elements that make it great.

Because culture mapping is a strategic and sensitive exercise, it is not possible to share real-life examples at this time. However, for the purposes of study and conversation, below is a sample Culture Map, populated based on the Nokia case study described earlier (see Fig. 7.5). Note that there are many gaps and incongruities. For example, there is a clear gap between the stated value "passion for innovation" and the acted value "we fear and avoid risk."

7.5   Conclusion

Meaningful conversations about culture are difficult to have. Most such discussions are superficial, "rah-rah" affairs. Most enterprises are not safe places in general, and to create a space that is safe enough for deep reflection and emotional conversations is challenging. But an organization's culture is its center of gravity, its most powerful latent force, and where most of the potential can be found for organizational success.

Organizations are like people. They have experiences, and based on those experiences they form theories about the world and how they should act. And, if successful, those theories become deeply embedded habits and behaviors. When the world changes, sometime something that used to be a good habit becomes a bad habit. But habits, good or bad, are difficult to change.

A company trying to change its culture is like a 1,000 people trying to quit smoking at once. It is exceedingly difficult. But it can be done. This has been demonstrated by Lou Gerstner and others. But as Gerstner said so well, "You can't mandate it, can't engineer it. What you can do is create the conditions for the transformation."

Culture is not necessarily something that you need to worry about. It is not something that necessarily needs to change. But you should be aware of it. You should understand it and you should be intentional about it, just as with other elements of the overall architecture.

In most companies the current condition is a mass of organizational rules, rituals, systems, and structures that have accumulated over a long period of time. But the conditions that lead to a successful culture are not arbitrary. The conditions for cultural transformation are not arbitrary.

If you want to understand a culture you can map it. If you want to design the conditions that will lead to successful behavior, or successful change, you can do it. Those conditions must be designed.

References

Argyris C (1976) Theories of action that inhibit actual learning. Am Psychol 31(9):638–654

Argyris C (1990) Overcoming organizational defenses: facilitating organizational learning. Prentice Hall, Upper Saddle River, NJ

Argyris C, Schön D (1996) Organisational learning II, theory, method and practice. Addison-Wesley, Reading, MA

Gerstner L (2003) Who says elephants can't dance? Leading a great enterprise through dramatic change. HarperBusiness, New York, NY

Hamel G (2007) The future of management. Harvard Business School Press, Boston, MA

Malykhina E (2008) Nokia grabs 40 % of mobile phone market. In: Information Week, 24 Jan 2008. http://www.informationweek.com/nokia-grabs-40--of-mobile-phone-market/d/d-id/1063712?. Accessed 17 Oct 2014

O'Brien KJ (2010) Nokia's new chief faces culture of complacency. In: The New York Times, 26 Sept 2010. http://www.nytimes.com/2010/09/27/technology/27nokia.html?pagewanted=all. Accessed 17 Oct 2014

Osterwalder A, Pigneur Y (2010) Business model generation—a handbook for visionaries, game changers, and challengers. Wiley, Hoboken, NJ

Schein E (1984) Coming to a new awareness of organizational culture. Sloan Manag Rev 25 (2):3–16

Schein E (1992) Organizational culture and leadership: a dynamic view. Jossey-Bass, San Francisco, CA

Shostack GL (1984) Designing services that deliver. Harv Bus Rev 62(1):133–139

Willigan G (2009) Nokia: values that make a company global. In: Society for human resource management. https://www.shrm.org/Education/hreducation/Documents/Nokia_Values_Case_with%20teaching%20notes.pdf. Accessed 17 Oct 2014

From Value Chain to Value Network: Reinventing the Enterprise in the Light of Technology Forces

8

Tarmo Ploom

Abstract

Cloud, mobile, social, and analytics technologies are changing the environment in which today's industries operate. It takes only few employees to start a globally scalable business. It may be that such startups are currently still in their infant phase. But what will happen if these new enterprises achieve massive cost reduction and flexibility advantages over the coming years due to new technology application? It is clear that current enterprises have to adapt to the revolution initialized by the new technologies. How can existing enterprises respond to the new entrants who use the latest technology to their advantage? Should they just copy technology? Or should they take a knowledge-based approach and ask the question "what special know-how do they have that new entrants do not have?" What would be the "new" competitive advantage of today's enterprises? To answer these questions, this chapter analyzes four general business architecture views (value chain, process view, information view, and structural view) of an example financial service company. In particular, it discusses the impact of technology-driven changes on these four views. Based on this analysis, it proposes a scenario that could help financial service companies to respond to technology-driven changes. This scenario is based on process management techniques and the application of domain-specific industry standards. The combination of process management with elements of information architecture can act as a catalyst in transforming value chain oriented enterprises over to value network-oriented enterprises, which focus on orchestration of value creation activities in the value network. Rather than fighting new entrants in their strength areas (technology), existing enterprises can use their business process know-how for reconfiguring their business to adapt to changed external circumstances.

T. Ploom (✉)
Credit Suisse, Zurich, Switzerland
e-mail: tarmo.ploom@credit-suisse.com

© Springer International Publishing Switzerland 2015   141
D. Simon, C. Schmidt (eds.), *Business Architecture Management*, Management for
Professionals, DOI 10.1007/978-3-319-14571-6_8

8.1   Introduction

Fifteen years ago, enterprises faced changes caused by a new technology—the World Wide Web. Enterprises worked out their e-commerce strategies, implemented them and started using the World Wide Web for their benefits and growth. Now, 15 years later, companies face not only one new technology, but a combination of cloud, mobile, social, and analytics technologies. Today's impact of the combination of new technologies is significantly stronger than the impact of one single technology 15 years ago. Back in these days, enterprises found a way to respond to technological challenges accrued from the World Wide Web. But how can today's enterprises respond to changes caused by a combination of four game-changing technologies instead of just one?

Against this background, this chapter:

- takes a closer look at environmental changes of today's enterprises,
- analyzes the current state in an example industry—the financial industry,
- describes the high-level business architecture of an example financial company—Credit Suisse,
- analyzes how the value chain could change due to a perfect technology-driven storm caused by cloud, mobile, social, and analytics technologies,
- analyzes how the overall business architecture may change as a result of value chain changes,
- describes how enterprises could adapt to the changed value chain, and
- discusses how a transformation towards the new value chain could be carried out.

8.2   Environmental Analysis

This section starts off with a description of the context in which today's enterprises operate. First, social, technical, economic, and political forces surrounding existing enterprises are analyzed. Second, to become more specific, an example industry—the financial industry—is analyzed to illustrate how an industry can be impacted by "*the technology-driven storm.*"

The following analysis focuses more on consumer-based businesses (for example, retail or private banking) and less on non-consumer-based businesses (for example, re-insurance or investment banking). However, it should be noted that results of the following analysis are partially applicable also to non-consumer-based industries.

8.2.1   Social, Technical, Economic, and Political Changes

The main social challenges companies face today result from technology-based social networks. In the past, enterprises could take central control of their branding, marketing, and communication initiatives. Today, information in social networks is no longer controlled centrally but it is distributed across the graph of network participants. By linking together different social networks, information can be spread across the world at an unprecedented speed. In addition, the communication sender no longer has to have a multi-million dollar budget for global communication; it is enough to have Internet-connected devices and an understanding of how social marketing works. For today's enterprises this means the following:

1. Enterprises are no longer in full control of their communication. In the past, enterprises could control centrally which target group receives which message. However, today's social networks give their members the means to communicate as effectively as enterprises with globally distributed target groups. Enterprises have lost their ability to control which information about themselves is distributed in social networks.
2. New entrants can use social networks for viral marketing (social marketing which crosses different social subgroups) and build their customer base in days from zero to millions of users. If the communicated message resonates with members of the social network and is subsequently transmitted from one social group to another, then brands can be built in days instead of decades.
3. Fortunately, social networks are not simply a threat. Existing enterprises can use social networks for sentiment analysis and adjust their products and services accordingly.

Cloud-based service offerings are having a dramatic impact—increasing the speed at which companies can scale, and significantly lowering the capital expenditure to enter the market. Today it is possible to build up a multimillion users company with only a small budget. This has never been possible before. Fifteen years ago, when the World Wide Web technology started to be adopted, building up a multimillion users company needed financing in the order of millions of dollars. Today's cloud technology combined with social network-based marketing has made setting up a new business more straightforward than ever before. And it is not only about the cost of setting up a new business but also about scaling the business. Cloud technology allows fast and cheap scaling-up for capital-constrained startups.

Two economic forces shaping today's world are globalization and the emergence of free information facilitated by the Internet. The labor market has become substantially global (due to outsourcing options). Enterprises can profit from global labor arbitrage. Value creation activities that cannot be automated with algorithms can be assigned to cheap labor force all around the world. Another side effect of the Internet has been the emergence of free information. Business-relevant information (market researches, customer contacts, prices, addresses, service ratings, product comparisons, CAD blueprints, geographical information systems, financial information, etc.) is freely available on the Internet. The combined effect of globalization and the emergence of free information is that entry barriers for new businesses become even lower than before.

A political force could be the wish to control the Internet. In the past, the main target of political control were natural resources like oil or gas. Currently, the intention of control in the world has extended from real assets to the virtual assets— i.e., to the Internet. Highly scalable technologies for analyzing information in the Internet have been created for control purposes. But these technologies (big data analytics and machine learning) can be applied not only for surveillance but also for customer analytics. For enterprises it represents an opportunity; they can learn to know their customers better than the customers themselves.

8.2.2 Impact of Technology-Driven Changes on the Financial Industry

To become more specific as to how changes in the environment impact existing enterprises, this section continues by analyzing an example industry, i.e., the financial industry, with the main focus on retail and private banking. Porter's *"Five Forces Framework"* (Porter 2008) identifies industry profitability or, say, attractiveness as an interplay of the bargaining power of suppliers, the bargaining power of buyers, the threat of new entrants, the threat of substitute products, and that of industry rivalry.

Suppliers of the financial industry are employees and various service providers. As the supply of qualified commoditized labor grows globally, the bargaining power of the labor force should drop. Also, as the number of service providers grows, their bargaining power drops. In combination, these two effects positively influence the profitability of the financial industry.

Particular attention should be given to the bargaining power of buyers. As information becomes free, buyers are better informed than ever before; if they need a bank for transactional retail banking rather than for long-term private banking, it is easy for buyers to find cheaper alternatives. Also lock-in barriers of customers are continuously reduced by regulators, who demand the possibility of an easy transfer of bank accounts from one bank to another.

Concerning substitute products, financial industry products themselves remain what they were; however, there are changes in the delivery channels (for example, mobile channels replace "old" online channels), in content (for example, more specific reports are offered to the customer), or in the speed of execution of payments.

Main forces of change for the financial industry come from new entrants. New technologies have reduced the entry barriers for new entrants massively. To build up a multimillion user business, only a few thousand dollars are needed. It has never ever before been possible to set up companies as "easy" as today. And we see new entrants in nearly every sectors of the financial industry, such as currency exchange, payments, swaps, asset valuation, customer relationship management, or risk calculation services.

What does it mean for the profitability of the financial industry? In the short term, the cheaper supply should have a positive effect and increased customer power a negative effect on profitability. Probably these two effects will cancel each other out in the short term. However, from a mid- or long-term perspective, new entrants, who use cloud technology, mobile technology, and viral social marketing, could lead to an erosion of profitability.

Business opportunities for new entrants are restricted by regulations, in particular by banking license and capital requirements. In fact, it is expensive to get and maintain a banking license. Increased regulation makes the maintenance of a banking license even more expensive and forces many banks to exit the business as they don't have the capability to fulfill various regulations.

What it means for the area of the financial industry that is protected by the need for a banking license is that its profitability grows as there will be fewer players. Another implication is that existing banks will remain account holders of customers, as new entrants are financially not capable to obtain a banking license. However, as new entrants take over financial industry business lines that are not protected by banking licenses, the profitability of the financial industry will erode substantially in the middle and long term.

8.3   Analysis of the Current State of an Example Enterprise

The main threats to the financial industry are new entrants who leverage cloud, mobile, analytics, and social technologies. Before analyzing the impact of this massive attack of new entrants on our example industry—the financial industry— this section describes the current state of an example bank, namely Credit Suisse. Specifically, the next section looks at the following architectural views used by Credit Suisse:

1. Value chain view
2. Domain model (functional view)
3. Business process view
4. Information view

8.3.1   The Porter Value Chain

The *Porter value chain* describes the main activities of value creation inside an enterprise (Porter 1985) (Fig. 8.1) in a linear and rigid way. It starts with inbound logistics and ends with service provisioning to customers. Contact with suppliers takes place in the inbound logistic stage, after that processing takes place inside an enterprise.

The Porter value chain focuses on company-internal processing and not that much on the orchestration of activities between suppliers and the enterprise. As the majority of today's large enterprises are monolithic companies that carry out a substantial part of their value creation activities internally, this kind of value chain is an appropriate framework for their analysis. The question of course is if this

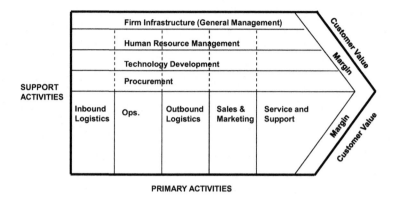

Fig. 8.1 The Porter value chain (Porter 1985)

approach would still be applicable in a hypothetical scenario in which a substantial part of value creation activities is outsourced to external suppliers.

8.3.2 Structural View: Banking Component Model

A banking *component model* describes how the business functionality is aggregated into components, based on the principle of high cohesiveness within components and low coupling between components (Parnas 1972).

An example banking component model—the "Credit Suisse Combined Domain Model"—is presented in Fig. 8.2. This model represents a comprehensive view of diverse banking activities, including retail banking, private banking corporate banking, wealth management for institutional clients, and wealth management for private clients.

Classical blue chip banks today carry out most of their activities themselves. Outsourcing of activities has been a topic in areas like human resources management, information technology (IT) support, or IT application development. However, most of the functionality presented in Fig. 8.2 is carried out bank-internally based on internal IT systems.

The Credit Suisse Combined Domain Model, as illustrated in Fig. 8.2, represents building blocks of general functionality that are independent from financial asset classes (equity, bond, fund, and derivative). As such, it can also be applied by banks specializing in specific financial asset classes.

Today, most of the activities represented in the Credit Suisse Combined Domain Model are carried out internally in the enterprise. Even if (in the future) a substantial part of the value creation activities was outsourced to new suppliers or new entrants, the overall functionality in the model would remain the same. What could change is, of course, the distribution of activities between internal and external suppliers.

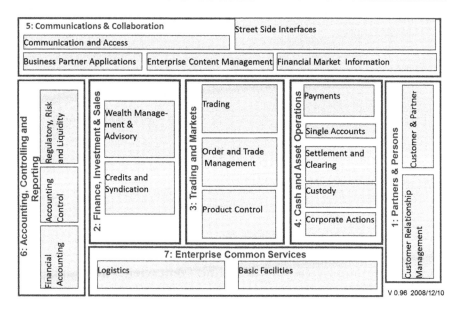

Fig. 8.2 Credit Suisse combined domain model (Murer et al. 2011)

8.3.3   Behavioral View: Banking Business Process Model

The behavioral view explains how activities represented in the structural view act together in the value chain. It represents a dynamic view on enterprise operations contrary to a static view given by domain models.

An overview of an exemplary behavioral view—the Credit Suisse *process repository*—is shown in Fig. 8.3. Business processes at Credit Suisse are classified into five different categories. While business processes at level 0 represent end-to-end enterprise business processes, those at level 4 are operational processes that describe the flow of fine-grained tasks in everyday operations.

Often the behavioral view shows only abstract high-level business processes; in this case, the behavioral view of an enterprise looks quite compact and simple. For example, at Credit Suisse there are 200 business processes at level 0. A business architecture view that focuses only on that level may be overly simplistic though.

The overall size of the behavioral view can be illustrated better not by the numbers of business processes at the highly abstract level 0 but by those at the "tangible" level 4. At Credit Suisse, there are more than 30,000 distinct business processes at level 4. Business processes at that level are thus very fine grained. They represent sequences of activities in the daily operations of the enterprise.

How would such a model be transformed in the future when new entrants start offering specialized services covering core banking activities? Which business processes would then remain in enterprises and which would be procured from low-cost suppliers?

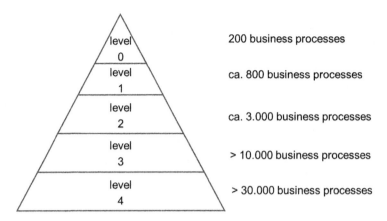

Fig. 8.3 Credit Suisse business process repository

8.3.4 Information View: Orchestrating Components in Business Processes

The information view represents business objects, data types, and attributes that are provided and needed by components of the domain model and are needed in the execution of business processes.

Often the information view is represented in the form of *business object models*. Business objects are relatively stable concepts in the enterprises. Business services, business rules, or business processes change continually; business objects, however, remain relatively stable. As such, business objects form the cornerstone of the business architecture.

However, the weakness of business objects is abstraction. Similar to the behavioral view, in which, e.g., the top level has 200 business processes at Credit Suisse, a focus on only the business objects may create an oversimplified view of the enterprise. To see the real size of the information view two characteristics are needed: the number of *unique attributes* and that of *overall attributes* in the enterprise. For example, for overall banking activities approximately 11,000 unique attributes are needed. Of course, due to redundancy (the same unique attribute is defined multiple times, often with different name or format), there are significantly more attributes used in current banks than just the unique attributes.

Services and domains in today's banks communicate predominantly over in-house-defined data standards. As mentioned, a side effect of such internal definition is redundancy; often for the same business purpose there are many different in-house data standards available that can cause semantic interoperability challenges. Therefore, it is not only the redundancy of information that current enterprises fight with, they also face non-interoperable internal standards that are defined by different departments or organizational units of enterprises.

Of course, enterprises are slowly learning and understanding that information redundancy and semantic interoperability can cause some issues. For example, information redundancy leads to data quality issues which can in turn lead to low-quality reports or forecasts. On the other hand, semantic interoperability issues come with higher integration efforts and reduced agility. These topics have often been ignored in the past.

But what will happen in the future? When banks start integrating web services of external service providers, with each external service provider offering its own proprietary data standards, how can banks then figure out the meaning of information, as it would not only be in-house standards that have to be integrated but also proprietary standards of vendors? And how can enterprises facilitate a seamless flow of information in their business processes?

8.4   Prediction of the Future: A Possible Scenario

As seen in the previous sections, free information and new technologies facilitate the emergence of a large number of new entrants into the financial industry. Never ever has it been easier to set up a new business and scale it up to one with millions of customers.

Thus, the game is changing. Before shedding light on how to play the new game, this section shows what the new game is about. In fact, to point out the effects of the new game on existing enterprises, this section takes a closer look at:

- changes in the value chain of the financial industry,
- changes in the behavioral view of the financial industry, and
- changes in the information view of the financial industry.

8.4.1   The New Game

What is the new game and how to play it? The new game is characterized by the following effects:

1. Emergence of information economy
2. Network effects
3. Free information

The transformation from an agricultural economy to an industrial economy took over 5,000 years. The transformation from the industrial economy to a service economy took over 100 years. The next transformation takes place from the service economy to an information economy. While the core production factor in the old economies was land, machines, or labor, the main production factor in the new economy will be information. Information is the new oil.

Old economies were characterized by production factor distribution based on Gaussian standard deviation. The new economy will be different; distributions of wealth or production factors will be determined by scale-free distribution, resulting in a magnification of network effects. Companies that have the right product at the right point of time and do effective "viral" marketing may grow from dozens of users to millions of users in just a short period of time.

In old economies, production factors had a price. In the new information economy, information itself as the core production factor will become free to some extent. For example, Yahoo and Google offer free financial information to their customers; likewise, a comparison of different financial products or service providers is freely available on the Internet. Information that was expensive years ago has become free. For today's financial industry players this means that entry barriers to the financial industry are disappearing.

8.4.2 How to Play the New Game?

How should companies respond to the "new normal," in an economy that is based on free information and network effects? First, it should be clear that current enterprises cannot stop the transformation of the service economy to the information economy; current enterprises have to adapt and find a way how to do business in the "new normal" and how to use the "new normal" for their own advantage.

Second, as barriers to entry disappear, there will be a plethora of new service providers that offer their services at a fractional cost of current enterprises. As these new entrants leverage new technologies and use free information, they will be able to offer their services at very competitive prices.

Third, new entrants to the financial industry may not have a banking license and may not have the know-how of end-to-end banking business processes. New entrants can acquire know-how about business processes in a specific fine-grained business domain but it will be unlikely for them to understand the complexity of all banking activities.

That is, the financial industry can use the new situation for its own benefit. Existing players in the financial industry can integrate new entrants into their end-to-end business processes and, in this way, reduce their processing costs massively and thus increase their margin.

The key in the new game is the integration of new suppliers and new entrants into the financial industry end-to-end processes and preserving end-to-end processing know-how at the side of the existing players. Customer relationship and knowledge of financial end-to-end processing will be a competitive advantage in the future financial industry.

8.4.3 Changes in the Value Chain

Does the classical value chain approach of Porter still hold in the "new normal"? As more and more activities will be outsourced to new entrants or new suppliers, this is questionable. It becomes even more questionable when taking into consideration that new entrants do not offer their (web) services only to existing enterprises but also to other new entrants. The current monolithic enterprises will thus be replaced by a network consisting of existing enterprises and new suppliers.

As a result, the classical value chain that starts with inbound logistics and ends with customer response transforms itself and becomes more an orchestration of different players with their specific services. Consequently, there will no longer be a linear "internal" value chain but instead a network that connects value creation activities inside and outside of existing enterprises. The role of banks is to preserve their power in such a network, and that is the key to future profitability.

Of course, in the "new normal" existing enterprises may not only consume (web) services from external suppliers, they can also become (web) service providers themselves. For example, there are good chances for financial institutions to provide tax calculations, regulatory reporting, or risk calculations via web services. As all financial enterprises somehow need these services, first movers may obtain a significant market share.

8.4.4   Changes in the Behavioral View

Changes in the value chain will impact the enterprises' behavioral view. As the currently linear and rigid value chains are transformed towards dynamic value networks, the internal processing of existing enterprises should adapt to the changed value network.

In the past, activities in enterprise value chains were predominantly carried out internally. However, new industry entrants can offer the same activities at an unpredictable low price due to leveraging new technologies. It is probable that for cost reduction reasons existing enterprises will partially replace activities that have thus far been provided internally with those externally provided.

Fortunately, new entrants focus on specific activities in the value chain and not on the overall financial *end-to-end processing*, as they miss corresponding knowledge. Only established enterprises have such end-to-end processing knowledge.

This means that parts of lower-level business processes (e.g., level 4 at Credit Suisse, Fig. 8.3) could be carried out by new suppliers, but the overall end-to-end business processes (e.g., levels 0, 1, and 2 at Credit Suisse, Fig. 8.3) will remain under control of the existing players.

In turn, the number of internal business processes will drop; likewise, there will be a greater focus on end-to-end business processes that orchestrate (web) services from external providers. In the "new normal" (web) services relevant for business processes are procured in substantial parts from the outside, not from the inside. The role of existing enterprises becomes the orchestration of these external services rather than that of internal services.

8.4.5   Changes in the Information View

Changes in the value chain will also impact the information view of the enterprises. As a substantial part of internal processing could be replaced by (web) services offered by new entrants, the question arises as to how to integrate all these new service providers? It is probable that information models that today are predominantly internally focused will change to facilitate the integration of new entrants into the new value network in the future.

As there will be a huge number of new web service suppliers for the financial industry, it will be interesting to know which underlying information model may be appropriate for the future.

1. Will new suppliers use their own proprietary data models?
2. Alternatively, will there be consensus in the industry to adopt industry data models?

For suppliers, proprietary data models help to create additional entry barriers to protect their business; in consequence, they may achieve higher margins. It would be a reasonable competitive strategy for new entrants to protect their market share.

However, can this strategy actually be a successful one? As entry barriers for new financial service providers disappear, there will probably be other suppliers who may rather base their services on industry *standard data models*. If existing enterprises aim to reduce costs, then of course they will choose suppliers who do not come with a risk of being locked in; they will choose web service suppliers who offer standard industry data models. Such a development has already started. A number of financial software providers like "Charles River" or "Clear to Pay" have made the support of financial industry standards their strategy.

A strategy that is based on industry standard data models would be beneficial for existing enterprises, as integration costs of new service providers would drop significantly and external service providers would become easily replaceable. If there is only a small set of industry standards data models that have to be considered, integration efforts for current financial enterprises will be reduced. On the other hand, new suppliers that use industry standard data models can increase their market share as their (web) services are easy to integrate.

To sum up, it is highly probable that existing enterprises in the financial industry will face massive transformation from proprietary in-house standards to financial industry standards. Today, the main financial industry standards are:

- ISO 20022 (financial industry message scheme)
- FIX (Financial Information eXchange)
- XBRL (eXtensible Business Reporting Language)
- BIAN (Banking Industry Architecture Network)
- FpML (Financial products Markup Language)
- IFX (Interactive Financial eXchange)
- HR-XML (HR Open Standards)
- RWF (Reuters Wire Format)

These standards alone provide approximately 8,300 unique attributes, which covers approximately 75 % of the needs in the financial industry (11,000 attributes).

Among the benefits of a massive adoption of industry standards by existing enterprises in the financial industry are:

- a simplified integration with new suppliers,
- reduced redundancy in the internal attribute universe, and
- reduced semantic interoperability problems.

Note that the presented information view based on industry standards primarily addresses the integration point of view. Still, an abstract information view, that is, a business object model remains necessary. Fortunately, business objects are stable concepts; business objects and their relations remain relatively stable over time, while other artifacts like business processes or business rules may undergo changes. As such, the business object model of a transformed enterprise is likely to stay relatively similar to the current one.

8.5   Transformed Enterprise in the New Normal

8.5.1   New Value Network

As discussed earlier in this chapter, the classic Porter value chain transforms to a value network (Fig. 8.4) in the financial service industry. The role of existing enterprises in this value network will be:

- to orchestrate suppliers of web services in end-to-end processing,
- to preserve know-how of their end-to-end business processes, and
- to preserve power in value networks by building up capabilities for flexible switching of web service providers.

The value network is not a far from being a reality. The directory service "ProgrammableWeb" has registered more than 10,000 public APIs published over web services today. And not only new entrants register their web services in ProgrammableWeb. Also established players in the financial industry, such as ING (Langlois 2012), have started publishing their own web services to the public. The value network is already in its infancy.

8.5.2   New Structural View

What will be the changes in the structural view of existing enterprises? For example, will there be changes in the Credit Suisse Combined Domain Model introduced earlier?

Fig. 8.4 Value network

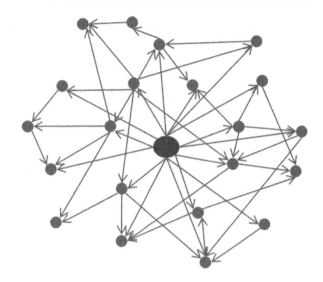

The overall business functions offered by existing enterprises may not change. What changes is that functions will increasingly be *outsourced to external service providers* rather than providing these in-house. This is also prevalent in the domain model of Credit Suisse (Fig. 8.2). Already today there are specialized providers for client trading, custody, payments, settlements, risk calculations, trade finance, tax calculations, etc. That is, most of the functions covered by the Credit Suisse Combined Domain Model can already be procured from external suppliers.

So, while the overall functions provided by today's enterprises will remain unchanged, there may be a frequent change of service providers in the future. After all, the structural view will remain as it is today. For existing enterprises this comes with less in-house infrastructure, less applications, and less operations personnel; however, more people will be required who can handle the new financial value network and manage contracts and service level agreements with web service providers.

8.5.3 New Behavioral View

As mentioned earlier, the behavioral view represented in a business process repository may become flatter and will have less business processes. The main focus of enterprises will be on the *high-level end-to-end business processes* (Fig. 8.3).

To manage the new behavioral view of their operations, enterprises will need the following components in the future:

- a business process execution platform,
- a business process dashboard, and
- a business process repository.

A *business process execution platform* will become a core infrastructure component of future enterprises. Such a platform orchestrates web services provided by the internal and external service providers in the end-to-end processing of business processes. An objective of future enterprises should be to execute all their end-to-end business processes on one central platform to calculate key performance indicators (KPIs) and to be able to switch external service providers and thus preserve control of the end-to-end processing. An example of an end-to-end business process execution platform is described by Ploom et al. (2013).

A *business process dashboard* will present KPIs of all end-to-end business processes, including the option to drill down by specific supplier, web service, business process types, or business process instances to investigate their performance. When companies performed all value creation activities in-house, they were in direct control of their operations. However, in the future, a huge part of operations will be outsourced to a variety of web service providers. To keep sufficient control and to steer external web service providers, strong monitoring of operations is needed. A business process dashboard has to provide a real-time view on the operations of future enterprises.

Finally, a *business process repository* is the place to store the end-to-end business processes. Today, business process repositories are usually only for documentation purposes and often drift away slowly from the actual operational business processes. In the future, there should be a direct link between business processes in the business process execution environment and those in the business process repository, and both should contain the same up-to-date business processes. End-to-end business processes are the new "gold" of future enterprises, it is their DNA that describes how enterprises work and perform.

8.5.4 New Information View

In the past, companies spent significant efforts to define their in-house information standards. Somehow this approach worked despite tremendous side effects in form of redundancy and semantic interoperability problems.

The future financial value network will have a large number of suppliers; the only way these suppliers can interoperate is by collaborating and by using the same set of *information standards*. As outlined earlier, in the financial industry these are standards like ISO 20022, FIX, FpML, RI-XML, XBRL, BIAN, and IFX.

Figure 8.5 illustrates the Credit Suisse Combined Domain Model along with the relevant financial industry information standards. It is apparent that most domains have a corresponding financial industry standard available; only utility functions like archiving or basic facilities are without a supporting financial industry standard.

So, financial industry standards already cover all finance-related domains in the Credit Suisse Combined Domain Model today. There is no need for existing

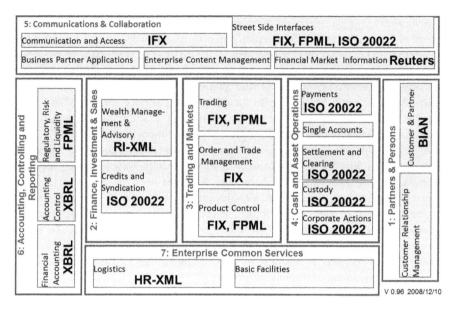

Fig. 8.5 Credit Suisse combined domain model domains with corresponding financial industry standards

enterprises in the financial industry to continue the development of their proprietary in-house standards. Globally agreed standards that facilitate interoperability with new web service providers are available and ready for use.

8.6   Role of Business Architecture Management

From the previous parts of this chapter we can conclude that the perfect technology-driven storm causes a change from a value chain to a value network and, as a result, current enterprises will have to transform significantly:

- Several internal activities will be replaced by external web services.
- Proprietary information standards will be replaced by industry standards.
- Focus of operations become end-to-end business processes, their execution, and their monitoring.

It is massive change—probably the biggest externally driven change current and past enterprises have faced over their history. Existing enterprises have to reinvent themselves. The question is whether such a change is going to happen by chance. In addition, it will be interesting to see whether such a change can be carried out in one large project. Both questions are likely to be answered negatively.

The industry ecosystem will be in change, so it is not fully clear when (and which) internal activities can be replaced by external (web) services. As a result, the transformation from a service economy to an information economy will be very hard to plan, as we do not have an exact picture of the future.

The only viable way for doing so is by making use of the concept of managed evolution (Murer et al. 2011) at the end-to-end business process level. By automating end-to-end business processes using a business process execution platform, by collecting KPIs with respect to their performance, and by improving these business processes, operations can be transformed in a controlled approach from a linear value chain to a collaborative value network.

Such a concept is represented in Fig. 8.6. It is nothing completely new itself. Such an approach has been applied by many companies in the past 15–20 years to improve parts of their business processes. What is new is the focus on the end-to-end business processes and the application of continuous optimization for these end-to-end processes.

To manage end-to-end business processes and to identify best performing interoperable (web) services, *business architecture management* plays a crucial role. Specifically, business architecture management has to

- continually evaluate the mix of in-house and outsourced business activities and find the best mix for each point of time,
- manage a catalog of business services that can be procured externally,
- continually evaluate end-to-end business processes based on KPIs, and
- continually identify necessary changes in end-to-end business processes.

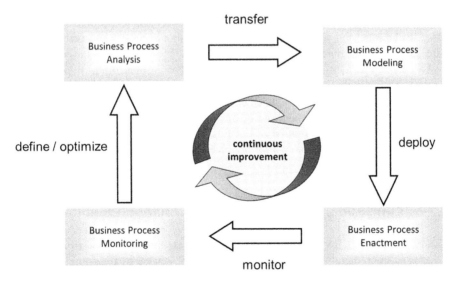

Fig. 8.6 Continuous optimization of enterprise-level business processes

The good news is that the managed evolution (Murer et al. 2011) concept helps carry out the required transformation. However, the bad news is that there are certain preconditions that have to be met:

- A business domain model has to be in place.
- A business activity model has to be in place.
- Business processes have to be known and documented.
- KPIs for business processes have to be defined.
- A business object model has to be in place.
- Information models at the integration level have to be available.
- Finally, all of these models have to be connected with each other.

This means that there is substantial homework before current enterprises can go to the next step, that is, the transformation using a managed evolution (Murer et al. 2011) approach.

It is hard to generalize the current state of business architecture management in today's enterprises. Despite its enormous importance, business architecture management is still a relatively young discipline and its benefits may still not be fully clear to CXOs. Also, the architectural focus in enterprises has thus far mainly been on technology standardization (to reduce the number of technologies in the enterprises) or cost reduction in the form of application rationalization programs (to reduce the number of applications). Widespread business architecture management programs with a focus on the preparation of the enterprise for its hardest transformation are still not very common.

The current state of business architecture management may be understandable though. Without technology and application standardization, current enterprises miss an important stepping stone for the next-level transformation, that is, real business transformation. In other words, before starting business transformation, some technology and application standardization should have taken place to prepare the ground for business transformation.

The role of business architecture management may thus initially also be to support and facilitate technology and application standardization. The transformation from a service economy to an information economy, then, is where business architecture management can show its real value. In fact, business architecture management is the only function in existing enterprises that can guide and plan transformation towards the new information economy.

8.7 Conclusion: "Welcome to the Information Economy"

The transformation from the service economy to an information economy takes place at an unpredictable speed. The "perfect storm" caused by the combination of new technologies (cloud, mobile, social, big-data-based analytics) and changed customer behavior (rise of social information gathering, rather than centrally controlled information push from companies) has changed the world and existing enterprises.

Consequently, the game has changed. The information economy is based on (Lanier 2013):

- free information,
- customer analytics,
- network effects, and
- value networks instead of linear value chains.

Current enterprises can adapt to this new situation, they have the chance to survive this perfect storm of technologies. Business architecture management can help guide enterprises in the transformation from a service economy to an information economy and provide the flexibility for enterprises that they need for the future.

To conclude, it is neither the strongest of the species nor the most intelligent that survives, it is the one that is the most adaptable to change (Darwin 1859).

References

Darwin C (1859) On the origin of species. John Murray, London

Langlois C (2012) ING opens customer data to 'Good Developers' via banking API. http://www.visiblebanking.com/ing-opens-customer-data-good-developers-banking-api. Accessed 22 Sept 2014

Lanier J (2013) Who owns the future. Simon & Schuster, New York, NY

Murer S, Bonati B, Furrer FJ (2011) Managed evolution: a strategy for very large information systems. Springer, Berlin

Parnas DL (1972) On the criteria to be used in decomposing system into modules. Commun ACM 15(12):1053–1058

Ploom T, Glaser A, Scheit S (2013) Platform based approach for automation of workflows in a system of systems. In: Proceedings of the 7th international symposium on the maintenance and evolution of service-oriented and cloud-based systems. Eindhoven, The Netherlands, pp 12–21

Porter ME (1985) Competitive advantage: creating and sustaining superior performance. The Free Press, New York, NY

Porter ME (2008) The five competitive forces that shape strategy. Harv Bus Rev 86(1):78–93

Liberate Your Business Potential via Actionable Patterns

Alexander Samarin

Abstract

Business processes and organizational structures are integral parts of the business architecture. In fact, they are essential when it comes to the configuration of business capabilities. Although the core business processes and structures of each enterprise are unique, they are "constructed" from typical business working practices, e.g., delegation of authority, group approval, four-eye check, etc. When these working practices are implemented in an optimal manner, this leads to less stress, less risk, higher performance, higher security, and higher predictability of results. This chapter presents typical business working practices as formalized and optimized actionable patterns (executable, proven, easy-to-deploy, and reusable working methods).

9.1   Introduction

It has been widely acknowledged that business processes and structures play an important role in the configuration of the capabilities needed to realize a certain business model. Although each enterprise has its specifics in terms of processes and structures, there are some typical practices/approaches that may be used across different enterprises to address certain strategic choices or, in general, business concerns. This chapter therefore presents a selection of patterns (as high-level, general solutions to common "problems") to provide ready-to-use, actionable solutions for the "execution" area of the business architecture that is conceptually defined in Chap. 1 (also see Simon et al. 2014).

A. Samarin (✉)
SAMARIN.BIZ, Arzier, Switzerland
e-mail: alexandre.samarine@gmail.com

© Springer International Publishing Switzerland 2015   161
D. Simon, C. Schmidt (eds.), *Business Architecture Management*, Management for
Professionals, DOI 10.1007/978-3-319-14571-6_9

In general, such actionable patterns provide the following benefits:

- staff members can concentrate on the unique challenges of their business and not waste time re-inventing the wheel;
- armed with actionable patterns, different staff members will employ similar processes and/or activities to implement similar capabilities, thus increasing the level of re-use;
- re-usable patterns facilitate the automation and gradual elimination of routine activities, thus increasing the scope for value-adding contributions;
- disjointed solutions and systems will fuse into a coherent platform for business execution, which will act as a catalyst for business innovation.

The patterns in this chapter are described according to the following schema:

1. the business concern to be addressed by the pattern;
2. the logic of the pattern;
3. the implication(s) of the pattern;
4. example(s) of the pattern.

The use of these patterns is similar to following a recipe. In the first instance, you should follow the recipe. Later, once you have gained some experience, you can adapt it to your "taste" and needs. Based on the schema outlined above, the remainder of this chapter describes the following patterns:

- Anisotropically Decentralized Organization (ADO)
- Customer eXperience As A Process (CXAAP)
- Delegation of Authority Matrix (DAM)
- Maturity Of Process System (MOPS)
- Structuring IT Organization (SITO)

9.2 Pattern: Anisotropically Decentralized Organization (ADO)

9.2.1 Business Concern to Be Addressed by the Pattern

Suppose an organization is growing and decentralizing by creating branch offices (BOs) at various locations to serve more customers (e.g., following a re-design of the business model). The BOs have different capacities, as they have different levels of staffing, different availabilities of skills, and different levels of competencies. At the same time, all BOs have to carry out similar core business processes, so the Central Office (CO) should provide adequate support to the BOs.[1]

---

[1] Alternatively, the other way around, a shared service center is established to support already existing branch offices that were previously fully autonomous.

From an information technology (IT) support perspective, it is practically impossible to automate the activities of such an organization since the work may be dynamically distributed between the CO and BOs; thus, the users cannot provide up-front the full specifications of all variations. The pattern shows how to structure the lower-level business architecture of such a distributed organization (primarily by aligning its overall business processes with the individual capabilities at each business location) to overcome this IT bottleneck.

9.2.2 Logic of the Pattern

This pattern is intended to present formally a business activity as a limited set of combinations of coordinated work between the BOs and the CO.

It is considered that any business activity can be decomposed into four logical steps [similar to the PDCA cycle (Deming 1986)] connected as shown in Fig. 9.1:

1. PLAN: preparation for the work to be done;
2. DO: execution of an indivisible unit of work;
3. VALIDATE: checking the correctness and quality of the work carried out;
4. REFLECT (or "re-factor"): analysis of the work experience and results to see whether it is useful to propose or implement any improvements for future work.

In a decentralized organization, the participants in each step can vary and may comprise branch office ("B") and/or central office ("C") resources. For example, if a particular BO has no experience with the procurement of a particular type of service, then that step should be carried out by the CO. It is assumed that CO resources are capable of carrying out all activities (which includes also any step within any activity).

The possible combinations of participants in a step are:

- C—the step is carried out fully at the CO (i.e., there is no delegation)
- B—the step is carried out fully at a BO (i.e., there is complete delegation)
- BC—the step is carried out at a BO with some post-control by the CO to make sure that it has been done correctly
- CB—the step is carried out at a BO with some pre-advice by the CO to make sure that it will be done correctly
- CBC—the step is carried out at a BO with pre-advice and post-control by the CO

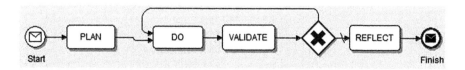

Fig. 9.1 Simple process for any business activity [see OMG (2011) for the BPMN notation]

Only certain of these combinations are actually applicable in each of the four steps:

- PLAN—C, B, BC, CB, CBC (although informal consultations between BOs and the CO resources are always possible, the last three combinations make consultations between the BO and CO explicit and mandatory);
- DO—C, B (the work can be carried out only at a BO or the CO);
- CHECK—C, B, BC (the check can be carried out only after the actual work has been completed; results of the check may be validated by the CO [thus the combination "BC"]);
- REFLECT—C, B, BC (reflection can be carried out only after the actual work has been completed; improvement ideas from a BO may be validated by the CO [thus the combination "BC"]).

These combinations are not independent, and they are combined in a few variants which represent the degrees of decentralization of a particular activity at a particular BO (see Table 9.1).

These variants may also be considered as a BO's "capability maturity level":

- none (level 0)
- technical (level 1)
- managerial (level 2)
- controlled (level 3)
- managed (level 4)
- optimizing (level 5)

Table 9.1 Degrees of decentralization

Level	PLAN	DO	CHECK	REFLECT	Description
0	C	C	C	C	No BO capabilities are available for a particular activity
1	C	B	C	C	The BO has some technical capabilities for a particular activity
2	CBC or BC	B	BC	C	The BO has some management and technical capability but the staff members need some proactive guidance to carry out a particular activity
3	B	B	BC	C	The BO has some management and technical capabilities but the staff members need some reactive guidance to carry out a particular activity
4	B	B	B	BC	The BO has sufficient management and technical capabilities to carry out a particular activity except for reflection
5	B	B	B	B	The BO has sufficient management and technical capabilities to carry out a particular activity without guidance or technical assistance, and it is capable of continual improvement/optimization via reflection

The crux is how to choose the best variant that should be applied for a particular activity in a particular process instance within a particular BO to be carried out by a particular staff member. The choice can be made using some kind of business decision management (BDM) which

- "knows" processes, activities, and local specifics,
- traces the actual skills and performance of staff members, and
- estimates different risk factors (political, financial, etc.) and degrees of compliance.

Such a business decision management should be systematically consulted "between" normal activities, since some characteristics of a particular process (e.g., complexity and urgency) may change over time. To some extent, it is responsible for overall planning, control, and guidance during the course of execution of normal activities, and measurement of outcomes. The business decision management should be carried out by central resources, as it should have access to enterprise-wide knowledge.

The business decision management may work together with the DAM pattern described in Sect. 9.4.

9.2.3 Implications of the Pattern

The capability maturity level of a particular BO to carry out efficiently and effectively a particular activity depends on many objective and subjective factors. Enterprise-wide business processes, their activities, and BO locations (thus local cultures) may be considered relatively static entities.[2] By contrast, there is greater variance with staff members—they can be hired, temporarily contracted, relocated, trained, and guided very quickly. Another variable factor is the provision of adequate supporting tools (HR services, IT environment, logistics, linguistic services, and general services) to staff. Among those, the IT environment should be sufficiently flexible to provide for a BO standard configuration as well as some optional extensions on demand. The latter may improve the maturity level by implementing localized versions of standard processes.

Another factor is the ability to work fully electronically (digitally) within the organization. This implies that staff members are able to exchange in electronic form both information (e.g., data, documents) and actions (e.g., signing an electronic document with an electronic signature).

---

[2] This is not meant to infer that these factors cannot be changed to increase the capability maturity level (see, e.g., Chap. 7 for cultural design).

The following topologies can be considered:

- each BO can exchange data and documents with the CO (star communication);
- the CO and all BOs can exchange data and documents (network communication);
- staff members can carry out some types of work from outside offices having a limited mobile communication;
- staff members can carry out all types of work from outside offices having full mobile communication.

As there are many factors that affect the capabilities of a particular BO, it is important to accept that not all BOs will be able to "jump" immediately to the top capability maturity level—they will advance at their own pace.

9.2.4 Examples of the Pattern

The ADO pattern was inspired by the decentralization of an international financial organization known to the author. Historically this organization was very centralized; to get closer to its customers, the organization has started to transfer staff to field offices.

Another example is the introduction of e-government services at local (communal and regional) levels. As some local administrations are less advanced and less capable than other ones, the central administration must support the former during some transition period.

9.3 Pattern: Customer eXperience As A Process (CXAAP)

9.3.1 Business Concern to Be Addressed by the Pattern

The provision of excellent customer experience is one way for an enterprise to obtain loyal customers who will tell their friends, colleagues, and networks how well the enterprise treats its customers. In fact, it may be a fundamental part of the value proposition to the customer, as captured in the business model (see Chap. 1). To realize this value proposition, other business architecture elements then need to be closely aligned to it. Therefore, it is essential to put oneself into the position of the customer and to consider the business from that point of view.

9.3.2 Logic of the Pattern

The following quotation provides a clue to the logic of this pattern: "The reason customers use our products and services is to get jobs done in their lives" (Campbell 2010). Imagine a hierarchy of nested (in some senses) processes:

Fig. 9.2 Life-span of some business objects

- a person's life as a process (actually a system of processes);
- a person's circumstance as a process (e.g., expecting a baby);
- a person's job as a process (e.g., buying a bigger car);
- customer experience as a process (e.g., a person who is buying a car acts as a customer for a car dealer).

The better the fit of an enterprise's products and services with those processes (e.g., the enterprise reduces the hassle surrounding a particular process for a customer), the more attractive will be the enterprise's products and services for customers.

The purchase of a car from a car dealer is a process comprising pre-selection, testing, and negotiation between two roles (the customer and the car dealer). Actually, each role has its own individual process, and both individual processes are working together as co-processes. If the car dealer's process fits perfectly to the customer's process then the customer may not only buy the car, but may also reuse the services of this garage again (and also recommend it to their friends, colleagues, and networks), as shown in Fig. 9.2.

Obviously, each "customer experience as a process" is unique, but is constructed from some process patterns [with respect to, e.g., appointment making, comparison, decision making (Samarin 2013a), etc.]. The ability to recognize the pattern that is the most appropriate in a particular situation and the knowledge of how to efficiently apply that pattern is crucial for an enterprise to be able to optimize its own processes and to respond to the needs of a particular customer.

A better understanding of the "higher" processes of a particular customer is also very beneficial. It is important to ask the right questions to "milk" the right information from a customer.

For example, a civil architect should not ask a customer (who wants the architect to build his or her house) "How many rooms would you like to have?", but "Will you need to entertain visitors?", "How many children do you have?", or "How long do you intend to stay in this house?". Then the architect can work with the customer to find the best design that meets the customer's stated needs.

9.3.3 Implications of the Pattern

Although the creation of a fascinating customer experience may be considered as an "art," it can be facilitated by the use of process patterns. In addition, the life cycle of certain resources involved in "customer experience as a process," e.g., a customer's file, may be described as processes as well (Samarin 2013b). In fact, all core and supporting processes of an enterprise can be presented as a system of interlinked processes (Samarin 2014). The use of one common concept (namely, processes) along with corresponding techniques to describe the functioning of an enterprise enables better overall monitoring and optimization.

9.3.4 Example of the Pattern

Traditionally, business processes are viewed and measured from the point of view of internal staff members (inside-out view). Considering business processes from the point of a customer (outside-in view) adds additional measures related to the customer experience. An excellent example of what is important to measure in the case of customer experience is provided by Olbrich (2009).

9.4 Pattern: Delegation of Authority Matrix (DAM)

9.4.1 Business Concern to Be Addressed by the Pattern

Consider an operating model (see Chap. 1) that mandates a high degree of centralization. As it is not possible (for practical reasons) for the top management to make all decisions itself, it is necessary to formally specify how the decision-making power is delegated from the top management "downwards" to other roles. Some delegation is defined statically via the organizational structure, whereas some other is defined dynamically depending on the financial impact. For example, a director may approve the purchasing of assets up to a value of US$50,000, while more expensive assets must be approved by a vice president.

9.4.2 Logic of the Pattern

The DAM logic should be expressed in accordance with BDM methods (if existing). All parameters (e.g., the cost of an asset, the type of the asset, priority, etc.) are evaluated in accordance with certain conditions. Each rule comprises one or many conditions, and one decision. A rule in which all conditions are true is itself considered as true.

For example, an approval of procurement may be governed by the authority matrix shown in Table 9.2. The column in Table 9.2 "Action for the role of" actually presents three different variants of a decision process: approval in one step (rows 1 and 4), approval in two steps (rows 2 and 5), and approval in three steps (rows 3 and 6).

Table 9.2 Example of authority matrix

	Conditions		Action for the role of		
	Procurement type	Contract value	Manager	Director	Vice-president
1	Services	<US$10,000	Approve	N/A	N/A
2	Services	≥US$10,000 and <US$50,000	Check	Approve	N/A
3	Services	≥US$50,000	Check	Check	Approve
4	Goods	<US$20,000	Approve	N/A	N/A
5	Goods	≥US$20,000 and <US$80,000	Check	Approve	N/A
6	Goods	≥US$80,000	Check	Check	Approve

9.4.3 Implication of the Pattern

Three business architecture concepts are at the core of this pattern: (1) organizational roles, (2) business process for actions, and (3) business decision for rules. The latter two should be well implemented with adequate tools to allow full control over these artifacts for the business. In addition, cultural aspects (see Chap. 1) should be taken into consideration for a reasonable setup or change of a delegation structure.

9.4.4 Example of the Pattern

As mentioned above, the procurement process is the most prominent example of the DAM pattern. Other examples can be found in the client service area, e.g., with respect to decisions of how to serve particular customers (according to the segment they belong to and its position in the business model).

9.5 Pattern: Maturity of Process System (MOPS)

9.5.1 Business Concern to Be Addressed by the Pattern

Suppose an enterprise wants to reach a particular level of maturity in accordance with the "Capability Maturity Model Integration" (CMMI) (SEI 2009) (e.g., as a response to an insufficient realization/support of the business model) and the functioning of the enterprise is represented as a system of processes. From a process management perspective, the MOPS pattern identifies the operations on business processes that are required to help the enterprise advance to a certain level of maturity (see Table 9.3):

- *Model* refers to the fact that the enterprise makes a representation of the complete (end-to-end) process to support communication about the process.

There is no single standard way to model, but the model must encompass the process.

- *Implement* means that the enterprise creates certain "aids" that are designed to help support the process. Today this often means developing some software that aids in information exchange (it does not have to be software though).
- *Execute* means that the process is performed or enacted in accordance with the agreed model (which acts as a contract or guideline).
- *Control* refers to the fact that there is some means of ensuring that the process follows the designed course. This may be strict control and enforcement, or it may be loose control in the form of guidelines, training, and manual practices.
- *Measure* means that effort is made to determine quantitatively how well the process is working.
- *Optimize* refers to an ongoing activity which builds over time to improve steadily the measures of the process. Improvement is defined according to the goals of the enterprise.

CMMI states that institutionalization is an important concept in process improvement. When mentioned in the generic goal and generic practice descriptions, institutionalization implies that the process is ingrained in the way the work is performed and there is commitment and consistency in the performance of the process. An institutionalized process is more likely to be respected during times of stress.

9.5.2 Logic of the Pattern

The logic is built on a mapping of the introduced process operations onto the CMMI levels.

9.5.2.1 Performed Process (Level 1)
A performed process is a process that accomplishes the work necessary to produce work products.

Interpretation from a process management point of view: Process templates are considered as black boxes (inputs, governance, outputs, resources) with some information about some process-related concepts such as roles and business objects. The relationships between these artifacts are not fully explicit. The outcome of a process instance is unpredictable (because it strongly depends on how people are doing the work together).

9.5.2.2 Managed Process (Level 2)
A managed process is a performed process that

- is planned and executed in accordance with the policy,

- employs skilled people who have adequate resources to produce controlled outputs,
- involves relevant stakeholders,
- is monitored, controlled, and reviewed, and
- is evaluated for adherence to its process description.

A critical distinction between a performed process and a managed process is the extent to which the process is managed. In comparison with a performed process which has no explicit planning, a managed process is planned and the performance of the process instance is managed against the plan. Corrective actions are taken when the actual results and performance deviate significantly from the plan. A managed process achieves the objectives of the plan and is institutionalized for consistent performance.

Interpretation from a process management point of view: Process templates are defined explicitly but not in detail—they comprise the macro-activities. Such a template is based on some locally agreed conventions (as opposed to enterprise-wide conventions). Typically, a template specifies who (roles) is producing what (business objects), how (macro-activities), and when (some coordination). Although this is actually a skeleton of the process, it is sufficient to plan process instances and to have some key performance indicators for managing this instance against the plan.

The enacting of process instances may be performed either manually or with the help of some tools (e.g., project management software). The handling of some artifacts, e.g., project documents, performance data, and resource allocation, may be partially automated. Since each macro-activity involves a significant amount of human interpretation, the outcomes from process instances are not highly repeatable.

9.5.2.3 Defined Process (Level 3)

A defined process is a managed process that

- is tailored from the organization's set of standard processes according to the organization's tailoring guidelines,
- has a maintained process description, and
- contributes work products, measures, and other process improvement information to the organizational process assets.

One critical distinction between a managed process and a defined process is the scope of application of the process descriptions, standards and procedures. For a managed process, the process descriptions, standards, and procedures are local, i.e., they are applicable to a particular project, group, or organizational function, while for a defined process they are enterprise-wide. As a result, the managed processes of two similar projects within the same organization may be very different.

Another critical distinction is that a defined process is described in more detail and is performed more rigorously than a managed process. This distinction means that improvement information is easier to understand, analyze, and use.

Finally, management of a defined process is based on the additional insight provided by an understanding of the interrelationships of the process activities and detailed measures of the process, its work products, and its services.

Interpretation from a process management point of view: Process templates are defined in accordance with enterprise-wide agreed standards. In addition, process templates are defined explicitly at the granularity of well-defined small activities. Typically, a process template specifies who (roles) is producing what (business objects), how (activities), why (rules), and when (exact coordination). This is actually a normal executable process template which mixes human and automated activities. The latter are rather comprehensive and can be common between different business domains.

Each project can tailor an appropriate standard process template to the needs of the project (this is some kind of ad-hoc static optimization, of course, with some reasonable limits). Since human participants (roles) perform mainly value-adding work (as well-defined small activities) and not the process administration per se, then the outcome of process instances becomes rather repeatable. Well-defined small activities are simpler to control, thus making the management of a process instance more active.

It is important to note that some level of flexibility should be anticipated to achieve such a tailoring to be carried out without causing any negative effects and without serious efforts. For example, artifacts should be easily versioned and models should be easy to understand.

9.5.2.4 Quantitatively Managed Process (Level 4)

A quantitatively managed process is a defined process that is controlled using statistical and other quantitative techniques. The product quality, service quality and process-performance attributes are measurable and controlled throughout the project.

Interpretation from a process management point of view: A normal executable process template is enriched to take into account the needs for proactive control of process instances. For example, the process template contains several checkpoints at which the performance of a particular process instance is measured to take an informed decision about the further execution of this process instance (see Samarin 2009). In some senses, a process instance interacts with the process execution engine. So, a process instance is systematically optimized without a change of its process template.

9.5.2.5 Optimizing Process (Level 5)

An optimizing process is a quantitatively managed process that is changed and adapted to meet relevant current and projected business objectives. An optimizing process focuses on continually improving process performance through both incremental and innovative technological improvements. Process improvements are selected on the basis of a quantitative understanding of their expected contribution to achieve the organization's process improvement objectives versus the cost and impact to the organization.

A critical distinction between a quantitatively managed process and an optimizing process is that the optimizing process is continuously improved by addressing common causes of process deficiency. A quantitatively managed process is concerned with addressing special causes of process deficiencies and providing statistical predictability of the results. Although the process may produce predictable results, the results may be insufficient to achieve the organization's process improvement objectives.

Interpretation from a process management point of view: A process template is optimized on the basis of performance analysis of many process instances and some enterprise-wide information that is external relative to this process template (e.g., a need to speed up all processes within the enterprise). This is a static (design-time) optimization. Some techniques for dynamic (run-time) modification of a process template may be considered as well.

9.5.2.6 Process Operations in CMMI Process Types

Table 9.3 summarizes the process operations that are involved in each CMMI process type. The nature of involvement is indicated as "Implicit" (informal), "Explicit" (formal), or "I/E" (in between "Implicit" and "Explicit").

9.5.3 Implication of the Pattern

Table 9.3 helps to illustrate that a tool for managing processes is desirable from (at least) the "defined process" (level 3) upwards to actually automate the management of processes. If such a tool can also provide objective analysis of process performance, then it may help to overcome the cultural barrier between imposed (levels 1–3) and institutionalized (levels 4–5) processes.

Table 9.3 Nature of involvement

Operation vs. type	Performed process	Managed process	Defined process	Quantitatively managed process	Optimizing process
Model	I/E (black box)	Explicit (locally)	Explicit	Explicit	Explicit
Implement	Implicit	I/E	Explicit	Explicit	Explicit
Execute	Implicit	I/E	Explicit	Explicit	Explicit
Control	Implicit	I/E	I/E	Explicit	Explicit
Measure	Implicit	Implicit	I/E	Explicit	Explicit
Optimize	Implicit	Implicit	Implicit	I/E	Explicit

9.6   Pattern: Structuring IT Organization (SITO)

9.6.1   Business Concern to Be Addressed by the Pattern

A complex organizational unit (referred to here as a "department") with several functions is to be restructured into a set of smaller units (say three to five, referred to here as "divisions"). This pattern addresses the question of what is the best way to achieve this and, at the same time, to take into account the necessary separation of duties and the potential synergy between functions.

As this pattern was originally developed for the re-structuring a particular IT department, it was decided to express this fact in the name of the pattern, although this pattern is applicable for various areas.

9.6.2   Logic of the Pattern

The following algorithm is proposed.

1. Specify all departmental functions: F1, F2, . . .
2. Define a set of "prohibition" rules: P1, P2, . . .
   Each prohibition rule justifies why two particular functions can't be in the same division. An example of such a rule is the "separation of duties" which is a key concept relating to internal control to protect an organization from fraud and errors.
3. Define a set of "synergy" rules: S1, S2, . . .
   Each synergy rule justifies why two functions should be in the same division. An example of such a rule is client coordination whereby there is a single point of contact for each client.
4. Draw a (symmetrical) matrix between all functions by assigning the prohibition and synergy rules for each relationship (see Table 9.4). For cases where neither rule exists, indicate "=" (neutral).
5. Identify clusters in the relationship matrix. For example, functions F1 and F2 form a cluster.
6. Use the clusters identified as guidelines for creating departmental divisions.

Table 9.4 Example of the relationship matrix

Function	F1	F2	. . .
F1		S1	=
F2			P2
. . .			

9.6.3 Implication of the Pattern

This pattern makes the decision logic for structuring an organizational unit explicit and thus an organizational design objectively validatable. Of course, this formal method offers only a first approximation that should be tailored to the specific enterprise (and the available level of talent) at hand.

9.6.4 Example of the Pattern

Suppose an IT department is growing and as a consequence needs to be restructured.

First, you should select all functions that will potentially be carried out by the IT department from the frameworks followed by the IT department (such as COBIT, ITIL, TOGAF, and PMBOK). For simplicity, all these functions are combined into the following groups:

- GOVERN (governance)—group leading and carrying out "administrative" coordination by setting and maintaining internal policies, controls, and processes;
- ARCH (architecture)—group translating a customer's requirements into a viable plan and guiding (only "technical" coordination) others in its execution;
- SECU (security)—group defining policies concerning the confidentiality, integrity, and availability of information services;
- PM (project management)—group supervising the building of core services and capabilities;
- OM (operations monitoring)—group supervising the operation of core services and capabilities;
- BUILD—group developing core services and capabilities including application services, information services, and infrastructure services;
- OPER (operations)—group operating core services and capabilities, including deployment, pilotage, and service desk;
- EVAL (evaluate)—group carrying out internal control;
- INTERN (internal)—group providing supporting services for the whole department.

Second, you should define the prohibition rules, which are specific to the enterprise:

- P1: separate doing and supervising/controlling (because of the separation of duties principle);
- P2: separate architecture/design and implementation (because of the separation of duties principle and early quality assurance or "quality at entry" principle);
- P3: separate implementation and operations (because of the separation of duties principle);
- P4: separate policy definition and policy implementation (similar to legislation vs. executive power separation);
- P5: deep specialization for provision of particular services.

Table 9.5 Exemplary relationship matrix

	GOVERN	ARCH	SECU	PM	OM	BUILD	OPER	EVAL	INTERN
GOVERN		=	=	S1	S1	P1	P1	P1	=
ARCH			=	S2	S2	P2	P1	P1	=
SECU				=	=	P4	P4	P1	=
PM					=	P1	P3	P1	=
OM						P3	P1	P1	=
BUILD							P3	P1	=
OPER								P1	=
EVAL									=
INTERN									

Third, you should define the synergy rules that are specific to the enterprise:

- S1: need for close collaboration;
- S2: architecture is guiding implementation, because an architect is a person who translates a customer's requirements into a viable plan and guides others in its execution;
- S3: there is a close relationship between technical and administrative activities, because in the evolution of social-technical systems (including enterprises) how you do something may be more important than what you do.

Fourth, you should prepare the relationship matrix using the defined prohibition and synergy rules (see Table 9.5).

Finally, you can identify the clusters, namely {GOVERN, ARCH, SECU, PM, OM}, {BUILD}, {OPER}, and {EVAL, INTERN}, and use these clusters to form the divisions.

In this example, the BUILD function was divided into three functions, specific to the needs of the organization: BUILD process-centric services, BUILD knowledge services, and BUILD infrastructure services. The EVAL and INTERN were put in the CIO front office. The final structure of the IT department was as shown in Fig. 9.3.

The divisions of the IT department can be considered as a functional layer which is used by a layer of end-to-end processes of projects (see Fig. 9.4).

The technical and business knowledge and experience gained in each project are preserved, enriched, and re-used through an additional layer of "competence forums." Each forum is oriented to support "generic" capabilities, e.g., business process management (BPM), enterprise content management (ECM), and business intelligence (BI), built "on top" of specific capabilities as shown in Fig. 9.5.

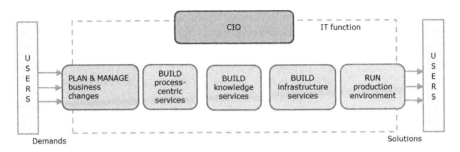

Fig. 9.3 The final structure of the IT department

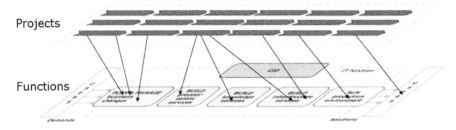

Fig. 9.4 Functions and projects in the IT department

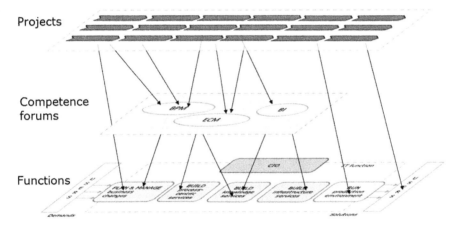

Fig. 9.5 Functions, projects, and competence forums in the IT department

9.7 Summary

This chapter has presented patterns for the execution level of the business architecture (see Chap. 1) to address specific business model choices in a reasonable way. These represent only a selection of possible patterns to share them, demonstrate their practical value, and to promote wider efforts for discovering and formalizing further business architecture patterns (including those at "higher-level" places in the business architecture). It should be noted that, since the presented patterns have been introduced as high-level solutions for common problems, the use of these patterns in a specific enterprise may require tailoring to the specific conditions at hand.

References

Campbell A (2010) Modelling behavior. http://ingenia.wordpress.com/2010/10/19/modelling-behaviour. Accessed 21 Sept 2014

Deming WE (1986) Out of the crisis. MIT Center for Advanced Engineering Study, Cambridge, MA

Olbrich T (2009) From coffee to changing the process perspective—a short illustration of the process experience. http://www.slideshare.net/Olbrich/process-experience-the-coffee-example-2103831. Accessed 21 Sept 2014

OMG (2011) Business Process Model and Notation (BPMN) v2.0 specification. Object Management Group, Needham, MA

Samarin A (2009) Improving enterprise business process management systems. Trafford Publishing, Bloomington, IN

Samarin A (2013a) Practical process patterns: Decision As A Process (DAAP). http://improving-bpm-systems.blogspot.ch/2013/10/practical-process-patterns-decision-as.html. Accessed 21 Sept 2014

Samarin A (2013b) Practical process patterns: LifeCycle As A Process (LCAAP). http://improving-bpm-systems.blogspot.ch/2013/11/practical-process-patterns-lifecycle-as.html. Accessed 21 Sept 2014

Samarin A (2014) Enterprise as a system of processes. http://improving-bpm-systems.blogspot.com/2014/03/enterprise-as-system-of-processes.html. Accessed 21 Sept 2014

SEI (2009) CMMI® for services, version 1.2. Technical report, CMU/SEI-2009-TR-001, Software Engineering Institute, Carnegie Mellon University, Pittsburgh, PA

Simon D, Fischbach K, Schoder D (2014) Enterprise architecture management and its role in corporate strategic management. Inf Syst e-Bus Manage 12(1):5–42

Business Architecture for Change Program Design and Planning

10

Adrian P. Apthorp

Abstract

It is an established practice of program and project management to plan based on product breakdown structures or rather to decompose the end product into individual deliverables. Following this common practice we consider how the key elements of our product (the changed business), described by the business architecture can and should be applied in designing and managing business change. In particular, we address the challenge of identifying and managing dependencies in large complex programs—something classical program management methodologies leave as an "exercise for the reader." The approach employs key business architecture deliverables that define the target architecture as well as those documenting the current architecture. In applying key aspects of the business architecture, such as capabilities, in program planning we seek to ensure alignment in various aspects of change across the organization and its resources, including IT systems. Our approach is a synthesis of project/program management and architecture practices. The approach described is based on the experience of taking an architecture-driven approach to a major business change program (Sprott 2008).

Always design a thing by considering it in its next larger context—a chair in a room, a room in a house, a house in an environment, an environment in a city plan.—Eliel Saarinen quoted by his son Eero, Time, 2 Jun 77.

A.P. Apthorp (✉)
DHL Express, Bonn, Germany
e-mail: aapthorp@theiet.org

© Springer International Publishing Switzerland 2015
D. Simon, C. Schmidt (eds.), *Business Architecture Management*, Management for
Professionals, DOI 10.1007/978-3-319-14571-6_10

10.1   Business Change Is a Complex Undertaking

Managing change to an established business can be likened to upgrading the parts on a "747" whilst it is flying. The business still needs to operate with no impact to service and at the same time make the necessary changes to deliver the benefits of the change to the business and its customers. The complexity and risks associated with business change are well documented. Many examples can be found of failure to execute change successfully, either with the change initiative being abandoned part way through with little benefit to show for it or worse. There are also many methodologies, often proprietary, which address business change either in whole or part (for example, the "soft" or human aspects of change).

The discipline of business architecture management, as part of the overall enterprise architecture management discipline, has gained increasing interest in the last few years due to the focus on making sense of the complexity within which large enterprises operate. Indeed, following the assertion that all businesses have an architecture explicit or not, then any business change must in some way reference the architecture of the business. However, this is often done implicitly and not considered holistically by many change or business transformation methodologies. A more complete methodology can be articulated for planning and managing business change where business architecture provides the common foundation throughout the life of a change initiative. Rather than describe a complete methodology here in detail, our focus is on using the business architecture to untangle some of the complexity of business change in order for the change problem to be made more manageable. The intention is to make the business architecture explicit and draw on its structure to partition the overall change in to (relatively) self-contained deliverables, as the basis for planning and subsequent operation. Indeed, the principles used for enabling the change can be applied to the target business architecture to enable future agility.

It goes without saying that in designing or building a program plan for business change there are many forces at play that give rise to complexity. These forces need to be balanced in order to mitigate risk and ensure that delivery is realized over the life of the program. Forces that need to be considered include:

- The natural and inbuilt dependencies of the target business architecture— Depending upon the scope of an initiative there are a wide range of dependencies in the target architecture that will drive the phasing of deliverables. For example, clearly a product cannot be sold (tell that to some sales people) unless the capability to market or deliver it is in place. An understanding of the dependencies in the target architecture will help identify an order of precedence for which areas of the business in scope can or should be tackled first.
- The existing environment—By definition, a business change program is not operating in a "green field" environment. Therefore, migration from the existing business environment (including processes, organizational structures, information technology [IT] systems, etc.) needs to be considered in the sequencing of program deliverables.

- Business priorities and benefits realization—With the high-profile nature of any business change program there is a significant expectation in maximizing the benefits to be gained and in a given (usually aggressive) time-frame. Certain priorities may already be attached to particular benefits; others may be seen as "low hanging fruits" and, therefore, anticipated earlier than others.
- Changing business conditions—Over the duration of a change program the conditions in which the business operates can change dramatically, for example, change of leadership, change of economic situation—positive or negative, etc. As a result, the scope or commitment to the program may change, including cancellation. Whatever the change, the business should be left in an operable condition.
- Other change initiatives—Typically, a large organization can have multiple change initiatives running at once, often in different functions. Clearly the portfolio of change initiatives should be complementary and not conflicting with each other.
- Trust and credibility—Any team charged with delivering a major business change has to establish trust and credibility from all of those affected by the change across the organization. This is in addition to the challenges associated with ensuring buy-in for the change in the first place (not tackled as part of this discussion). Establishing trust and credibility creates a "pull" effect within the organization for the subsequent realization of the change benefits.
- Resource needs—Resources of various types (e.g., people, equipment, financial) need to be identified and scheduled to work on program deliverables as efficiently as possible. Resource planning will not be discussed in detail; however, it is expected that the program plan developed through the approach described here will provide the basis for resource allocation. Indeed, the impact of resource constraints can be assessed against the plan, yielding, for example, an understanding of the trade-offs in addressing mandatory foundational changes vs. short-term benefits for realization.

A number of the forces clearly drive towards the need to establish and maintain confidence by delivering benefits early and regularly. Such drivers work against a "big bang" delivery. Incremental benefits-driven delivery is not wholly incompatible with needing to deliver the "building blocks" of the changed business. However, a balance is required between delivering foundational building blocks with no apparent immediate benefit and delivering direct visible benefits.

Indeed, as part of breaking down complexity, incremental delivery is one of the principles of our approach, resulting in benefits accrual and realization throughout the life of a change program. In this way we draw on some of the principles of agile software development (Beck et al. 2001) but applied to large-scale business change. Incremental delivery will support a future culture of change (or managed evolution). On the negative side, it may also increase costs in the short term, with tactical delivery. However, this can be considered a risk mitigation strategy with the additional benefit of future change readiness. It also has the risk and advantage that a change initiative can be stopped, if environmental factors dictate, with some benefits having already been realized.

In reviewing these forces, it is our contention that the business architecture provides the overall context to reconcile them, enabling mitigation of dependencies and complexity. This applies to both the final deliverable and the execution of change. We will explore this through discussing key elements of the business architecture and the experience of applying them in a major change initiative (Sprott 2008).

10.2 Planning a Europe-wide Business Change

An example of where the approach we describe has been successfully applied was in a business change program across the European region, involving 30 country business units. This program exemplifies all of the forces that we described in the previous section.

Having established a Europe-wide road transportation network, as the result of significant acquisitions (at least one per country), it became apparent that the overall value proposition and quality of service experienced by customers needed significant improvement. In order to address these needs it was determined that a standard product offering was required, supported by greater consistency in capabilities and integration of the core processes used across business units. Ultimately, this meant adopting standard processes and changing the operating model. Although not part of the original business objective, this solution also resulted in the adoption of standard IT systems by many country business units.

During the initial feasibility study, different options were explored in order to meet the required capabilities of the target value proposition. The two key ones being:

1. Enhancement of the current processes and IT systems to a common standard.
2. Adoption of existing proven standard processes and IT systems from another business line.

The second option, to adopt the proven standard processes, was ultimately selected to deliver the required capabilities. However, this still required some change to both the processes and IT systems to deal with transition and those specific capabilities not found in the other business line. The adoption of these processes and systems inevitably impacted other aspects of the business set-up in order to deliver the new and changed capabilities. Changes included which facilities and organization units would be used to fulfill certain capabilities. Also, as the processes in the two environments operated according to different information standards (e.g., account numbers, product coding, etc.) the foundations of many processes needed to change, even though the basic activities may have remained (at least superficially) the same or similar.

Also, as a networked business there was the need for coexistence during transition, in order to maintain at least the current level of service. Hence, the new had to interoperate with the old and vice versa. In addition, the individual country business units had to participate in planning and executing the change. This required a clear definition of what the target was and the constraints in which to operate, as well as the necessary coordination to ensure a smooth transition.

Therefore, even though many elements of the solution were available, the complexity of the actual change to the operating business was significant. This of course had to be achieved with the minimum of impact to customers or rather any impact experienced should be a positive one.

10.3   Foundations to the Approach

In our approach and this discussion we focus on the "hard" side of change (i.e., planning and delivery of tangible deliverables) by synthesizing the approaches of two disciplines: project/program management and business/enterprise architecture. In doing so, it is hoped that the complementary relationship between business (and enterprise) architecture and program management is reinforced. Of course, it should not be a surprise that these two disciplines are important if we consider the disciplines traditionally involved in the design, planning and delivery of new and changed buildings, cities or complex systems. However, there seems to be little established practice and training that brings the techniques and deliverables of both disciplines together in the domain of business change.

Although the emphasis is not on the "soft" side of change (i.e., the people aspects), this aspect is of course a significant consideration in ensuring success in a change management initiative. Indeed, business architecture can and should play a role in the "soft" side of change management.

10.3.1 Influences

Our approach draws on established architecture methodologies such as the "Architecture Development Method" from "The Open Group Architecture Framework" (TOGAF ADM)[1] (cf. The Open Group 2011) as well as techniques from information engineering (Finkelstein 1989), and standard project and program management practices [e.g., PRINCE2® (AXELOS 2014) and Managing Successful Programmes [MSP®] (Cabinet Office 2011)]. Indeed, our approach may be considered a realization of capability-based planning as per the TOGAF ADM, although our initiative predated its introduction in TOGAF 9.0. As previously noted, we also apply some of the principles of agile software development. In bringing these disciplines together for planning and managing business change, we focus on addressing the challenges previously outlined:

---

[1] The TOGAF ADM is specifically referenced; however, many of the concepts are common to "business systems planning" (BSP) and "enterprise architecture planning" (EAP).

1. Providing a technique for the key program planning step "now identify and manage your dependencies."
2. Incremental delivery and benefits realization.

By drawing on the practices and techniques of existing architecture methodologies and applying them in the context of business change, we seek to provide an approach that considers information systems/IT as components of the changed enterprise,[2] rather than the objective of it. This entails refocusing the emphasis of these methodologies towards the enterprise as a system, of which an IT system is a part, and hence addressing the significance attached to certain areas. This includes the emphasis on data rather than what the data represents, i.e., the "things" (tangible and intangible) that the business works with (e.g., shipments, vehicles, accounts, products) need to be understood in their own right, as distinct from the information about them.

With regards to project and program management methodologies it is not our intent to discuss established practices for estimation, monitoring, controls, etc. These are assumed. However, we highlight where architecture practices and deliverables play a role in designing both the expected outcome of a change program, and the structure and planning of the program itself.

10.3.2 Key Elements of the Business Architecture

Central to our approach for dealing with the challenges outlined above and as a basis for describing the target business architecture are *business capabilities:*

> A business capability is an [...] ability to execute a defined [...] pattern of activities and produce a desired outcome (e.g., product, service) by deploying specific resources and expertise and processing information in a defined organizational and cultural environment (Simon et al. 2014; also see Chap. 1).

Business capabilities are typically composed of a hierarchy of finer-grained business capabilities. The hierarchy can be established by exploring the processes that deliver a given capability. Capabilities that are common to more than one process or activity highlight the opportunity for aggregating resources into a specific functional unit within the business that realizes the given capability or set of capabilities. For example, a call center need not be specialized to the handling of one type of call or request (e.g., bookings or orders) but can have the ability to handle multiple types of request from a customer. Of course, some degree of specialization may be required depending upon the level of knowledge required for the range of call or request types to be handled.

By their nature, business capabilities are multi-dimensional (Malan et al. 2002–2006). Each dimension will shed light on various dependencies; however, the

---

[2] This type of approach has been referred to as concurrent business engineering (Leganza et al. 2009).

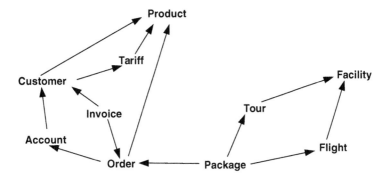

Fig. 10.1 Business object dependencies

first-order dependencies are found by exploring the business objects that realized capabilities act on.

Business objects are the "things" or entities (e.g., customer, account, order, product, etc.) that an enterprise acts on or deals with.[3] An understanding of the relationships between business objects provides insight into the natural dependencies within the enterprise. Indeed, the types of business objects handled by an enterprise are generally relatively stable; therefore, it can be assumed that if a key business object type or the way it is identified is impacted this will result in a major change to the business, e.g., a change to how a product or facility is identified can have major impact across the business. Many business object dependencies may be obvious (e.g., a product needs to be defined before selling it to a customer or an account needs to be opened before an order can be taken); however, by explicitly identifying them it is possible to identify what parts of the business architecture are tightly coupled and where dependencies can be broken (see Fig. 10.1).

Although business objects provide an understanding of the dependencies within the enterprise it is necessary to explore other elements of the business architecture to start identifying where dependencies can be mitigated. In particular, insight is provided by investigating how the capability usage of business objects is expected to change as a result of the envisaged business change.

By identifying and naming business objects, alignment on the terms and definitions associated with them serves to establish effective communication throughout a change initiative and the operation of the future business. These terms will appear in naming business capabilities, business processes, and associated key performance indicators (KPIs).

Business processes, or more specifically, the *end-to-end business processes* that flow through the organization to deliver value to customers and the business, are the

---

[3] As business objects are the types of things that the enterprise cares about, in many cases data about them needs to be stored and handled. However, it must be clear that they are not synonymous with the objects that are the focus of object-oriented programming, although they may be represented by them.

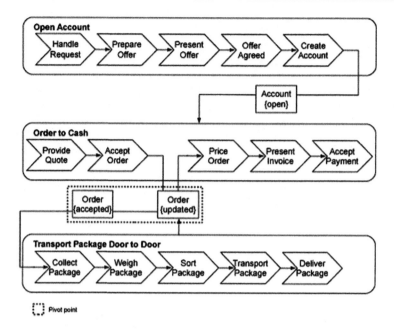

Fig. 10.2 End-to-end processes with pivot points

other key element of the business architecture that we draw on. Activities within a business process pass business objects between them, changing their state, as well as consuming or referencing other business objects. End-to-end business processes[4] (e.g., Order to Cash) operate or focus on a specific business object, transforming it in the context of a clearly defined customer and service/product provider.

By exploring end-to-end business processes and identifying the business objects passed between them, business object dependencies can be confirmed. Also, process interfaces, where business objects are passed in a given state, can be clearly identified, exposing natural places in the business architecture where dependencies can be mitigated. At such places pivot points may be established in the architecture (see Fig. 10.2). Pivot points are "axes" within an architecture around which change can be managed. We will say more on the value of pivot points in Sect. 10.5.3.

10.3.3 Target Business Scenario

Established program and project management practices tell us to plan based on product breakdown structures or rather to decompose the end product in to

---

[4] End-to-end business processes (Davis 2010) are similar to the concept of value streams (Brown 2009) described by Martin (1995). However, we place particular significance on the transformation or change in the state of the subject business object.

Table 10.1 Target business scenario table of contents

Section	Description
Vision	The overall vision for the changed business including the drivers for change. This section basically represents the business motivation layer as per this book's business architecture framework (see Chap. 1)[a]
Business environment	A description of the environment in which the target business is expected to operate. This includes the context for relationships to external parties such as customers, suppliers, and regulatory authorities, and therefore describes major parts of the business model (including the operating model) as per this book's business architecture framework (see Chap. 1)
Product definition	We identify the product definition separately here, as in our initiative the definition and standardization of the product was a major deliverable. For other initiatives, it may be considered part of the business environment (or, in other words, the business model [see above])
Principles	Principles make explicit the fundamental decisions and policies that constrain and guide the design of the changed business such as, for example, "standard business processes will be adopted." Where design decisions are unclear, the principles should be referred to for direction and, if necessary, further principles identified. Principles may be found embedded in various places, including the vision, business environment, or product definition, but should be made explicit
Business objects	Definition of the business objects in scope or impacted by the business change. This includes a description of the relationships between business objects and any attribute or structural changes.[b] For example, in our case different nomenclature was introduced for identifying accounts and facilities. The volume and distribution of business objects should also be provided. Business objects fit within the business execution part of this book's business architecture framework (see Chap. 1), but reflect all the entities of the business not just the information entities
Required capabilities and end-to-end processes	Description of all the major capabilities, highlighting the changes of the changed business at key touch points and the supporting end-to-end processes. Ideally, these should be described independent of the organizational model. The organizational model is expected as an outcome of the business design. Key performance indicators (KPIs) should be included as well. Again, this section basically maps onto the business execution part of the business architecture framework (see Chap. 1)

[a]The business architecture framework has initially been described by Simon et al. (2014) and, as indicated, is outlined in further detail in the introductory chapter of this book
[b]These may be formalized in a business object model, as an entity relationship model of business objects. The business object model is often referred to as a conceptual data model in texts discussing data models

Fig. 10.3 The architecture
framework, separating design
from the architecture
elements

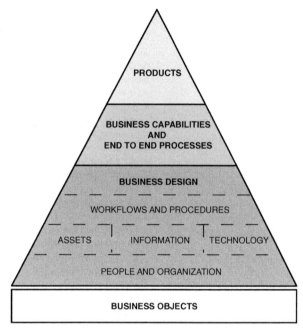

individual deliverables. In turn, the product break down structure should be transformed in to a work breakdown structure as the basis for costing and scheduling. Therefore, a description of the end product is critical for planning.

In the MSP® methodology the end product is described in a blueprint (which MSP® acknowledges to be delivered by a business or enterprise architecture activity). In our approach, the blueprint is described in a target business scenario document. This document describes the envisioned capabilities as well as other key aspects of the changed business. It is a high-level description of the desired business rather than a detailed specification or design of the future business processes, systems, organization, etc. This allows us to take an iterative (and "agile") approach to planning and managing the change. To support this approach, the target business scenario therefore needs to articulate the essential nature of the changed business, the target business architecture, from which key planning assumptions can be derived. The target business scenario then provides the overall context for the change and is the "anchor" or common reference that all subsequent deliverables relate back to. It is maintained under change control throughout the change program. Table 10.1 describes the table of contents for a target business scenario.

Although originally based on the TOGAF notion of a business scenario, the emphasis is fully on the required change in the business (as can be seen from the table of contents). As such, the target business scenario is a statement of requirements of the changed business and therefore does not detail the target business design, i.e., the physical processes (workflows and procedures), IT systems, facilities, and organizational setup. These are expected deliverables of the program itself.

The separation between the business architecture elements described in the target business scenario and the business design, that is a response to it, is summarized by the architecture framework illustrated in Fig. 10.3. Business objects are shown to provide the foundations of the architecture and the business itself.

10.4   Applying the Business Architecture

Having established the business architecture foundations, we will now explore their application in a business change initiative, based on our experience. In our initiative we considered three phases to a change program:

- Phase 1 (Program Definition)—This phase delivers the target business scenario and establishes the options and case for change.
- Phase 2 (Program Design)—Program design develops the overall structure and plan for the program to deliver the change, as well as the overall business case.
- Phase 3 (Program Delivery)—The delivery phase elaborates on the business architecture and initial business design developed during phase 1, and of course implements the change.

Our particular focus in applying the business architecture is phase 2, to design an effective approach and plan to deliver the changed business and associated benefits, i.e., the program design.

10.4.1   Phase 1: Program Definition

The target business scenario is the key business architecture deliverable from the definition phase of a change program and acts as the primary reference for program design and delivery. The program definition phase follows an iterative process of development and refinement of the target business scenario and testing it against various solution options.

A draft target business scenario (referred to as initial business scenario in Fig. 10.4) is developed based upon the overall aspiration of the change sponsors according to the outline in Table 10.1, identifying the vision, business environment, and key capabilities (new, changed, and existing) that support the vision. The draft target business scenario is then used as the basis of a feasibility study to establish the overall viability of the change. This is achieved by developing an initial view of the business design to meet the needs of the changed business articulated in the target business scenario. The assessment is necessarily a high-level one that will identify the major resources (across the organization) that will be impacted by the change, in order to provide an order-of-magnitude estimate of cost that can be rationalized against the anticipated benefits.

In our case the business design was the responsibility of each business unit to develop in response to the target business scenario, including guiding principles.

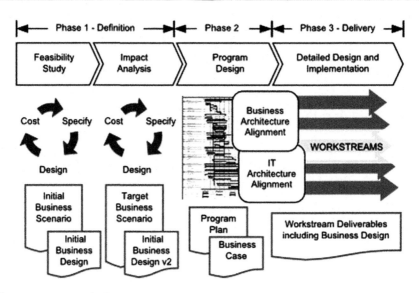

Fig. 10.4 Program phasing

Development of the draft business scenario was the responsibility of the senior enterprise architect assigned to the initiative with overall ownership transferred to the program executive by the end of phase 1.

The initial view of the business design will most likely identify a number of basic options to fulfill the target business scenario. Also, it is more than likely changes to the target business scenario will have been identified from the feasibility study that should be incorporated into a revised target business scenario. Assuming that the feasibility study provides a positive assessment, a more detailed impact analysis can now be conducted to assess the identified solution options in more detail and select the preferred one with associated costs. The results of the impact analysis then provides the basis for the business case, which is then finalized with the program design (phase 2). It can also be anticipated that further refinements will be made to the target business scenario as well as the business design as a result of the impact analysis.

It should also be clear that the activities and deliverables of this phase will provide an input to the phase 3 business design deliverables as well as to an assessment of the gaps to be closed between the current and changed businesses. In addition to this, they supplement the target business scenario with inputs for phase 2, where the change program itself is designed and the program plan is developed.

10.4.2 Phase 2: Program Design

In designing a change program the objective is to establish an overall structure and plan for the program that delivers benefits at key milestones in program execution. Core to the program design is the identification of a number of parallel workstreams with minimum dependency between them. A workstream may be a single project or be divided in to a series of projects that incrementally deliver benefits. Although there will of course remain dependencies between them, workstreams can be phased to ensure that critical path dependencies are followed.

In the same way that principles play a key role in the design of the target business scenario, they are also important to the program design. Therefore, key program design principles need to be established. In this discussion we are illustrating certain principles based upon the experience of what worked for us. These can potentially contribute to a catalog of business transformation patterns. Such principles may include:

- Change will be delivered incrementally.
- Workstreams deliver the complete change, including deployment in the field.
- Workstreams are scoped to end-to-end business processes, and can be cross-functional.
- Information exchanges/process interfaces are the key to interoperability and decoupling. Interfaces are more important than applications.
- Design for migration/transition to enable current and future change.

As we asserted earlier, the basis for identifying dependencies are the business objects in scope or impacted by the change program. Therefore, we start with developing the dependency map of business objects (see Fig. 10.1). The dependency map can be developed by simply exploring which objects have a creation dependency on other objects. For example, an order cannot be created without knowing the product or the customer. Alternatively, if a conceptual data model (or business object model) already exists for the business, the dependencies can be identified through the foreign keys of the entity relationships.

Separately, the business objects should be mapped to the capabilities that are in scope of the change program. Mapping is done by identifying which capabilities create or transform a business object. This yields to a matrix similar to a CRUD matrix,[5] except that the mappings are highlighted with an "X" (see Fig. 10.5). The information as to which business objects are referenced by capabilities to create or update another object is given by the business object dependency map. Inevitably, there will be a clustering (Veryard 1994) of capabilities around certain objects,

---

[5] CRUD or "Create," "Read" "Update" "Delete" matrices are an established technique in enterprise information architecture (cf. Cook 1996) and in database analysis and design for partitioning and optimizing systems and databases.

	Agreement Negotiation	Account Opening	Quote Provision	Order Acceptance	Order Invoicing	Package Tracking	Package Sorting	Package Loading	Network Planning	Pickup Scheduling	Flight Scheduling	Delivery Scheduling
Product												
Tariff												
Customer	X	X										
Account		X		X								
Invoice				X								
Order			X	X	X				X		X	
Package						X	X	X				
Tour								X	X	X		X
Flight								X	X		X	
Facility							X		X	X	X	X

Fig. 10.5 Example of capability to business object mapping

which gives an indication of which capabilities can be delivered together and, therefore, of how to divide the program into workstreams.

With the results of the business object dependency and business object/capability mapping activities, a capability dependency map (Veryard 2012) can be created and visualized. The result is a map of the natural dependencies between all the capabilities in scope for the change program, indicating the natural order of precedence and providing insight in to where dependencies can be broken. This map, once developed, can be subsequently reused in further change initiatives, as can many of the other business architecture artifacts that are developed in this phase. It can also help to identify capabilities that may be missing. For example, if there is a dependency on the "Product" business object, we may discover that there is not yet a planned capability to maintain the product catalog (see Fig. 10.6).

The insight gained from the capability dependency map can be further analyzed by reviewing the capability changes to be delivered by the program and how they affect the business objects they act on, i.e., if there is no change to a business object then that dependency link can be broken. If the object structure is changing, then this will have a bigger impact on dependent capabilities than if the object is simply extended. In our case, the method of identifying the "Product," "Account," and "Facility" business objects changed, placing dependencies on the associated capabilities. However, there was no change to the "Package" object, allowing us to decouple the associated capabilities from the order ones.

Of course this map does not take into account the critical to deliver requirements as seen by the business, but gives an idealized view of how a major change program

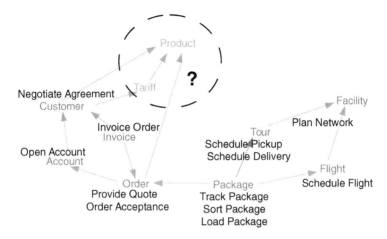

Fig. 10.6 Example of capabilities overlaid on business object dependencies

can be decomposed in to deliverable sets of capabilities and hence workstreams. In order to introduce a business-prioritized view, the business sponsors need to prioritize the capabilities identified in the target business scenario. By applying the priorities to the dependency map, key enablers (in terms of subsequent deliverables and business benefits) can be identified, and the scope, goals and, objectives of the program's workstreams/projects can be refined. Where conflicts are identified as a result of reviewing the priorities against the dependency map, the migration strategies discussed in Sect. 10.5 can be applied to mitigate the conflicts where possible.

Workstream scope can be further refined by ensuring alignment to the end-to-end business processes, which deliver the core capabilities of the business. Indeed, it is likely that the capabilities scoped within workstreams will already be broadly aligned to these processes. However, formalizing this alignment will have several benefits:

- Capabilities delivered together will realize or be realized by an end-to-end functioning process.
- The need to address the capabilities for the operational management of the end-to-end process will be highlighted.
- Process interfaces will be established or reinforced at critical points along the process chain providing decoupling and enabling future change.

The clustering of capabilities with the inherent responsibility for certain business objects also provides an idealized logical organizational structure as an input to the business design. This is only logical as it does not reflect the number of resources and their distribution required to deliver the capabilities.

Each identified workstream (see Table 10.2 for example of scoped workstreams) should now be scoped based upon the capability changes to be delivered along

Table 10.2 Business architecture scoped workstreams

Workstream	Objective—Capability changes to deliver	Dependencies
Product management	Product and tariff structure definition Product catalog publication and maintenance	
Account opening	Reduce time to open an account. Account maintenance Migrate existing accounts to new structure	Product and tariff structure definition
Order to cash	Standard Order to Cash processes	Account maintenance
Network design	Consistent facility identification Plan required facilities and reorganize Optimize flight schedules Optimize tour schedules	
Package transportation	Accurate and timely package tracking	Consistent facility identification

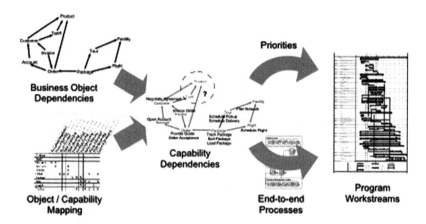

Fig. 10.7 Summary of steps to design the program

business object and end-to-end process lines, with the change requirements for each workstream linked to the original requirements, i.e., the target business scenario. Therefore, the relationships between workstreams will be based on business object dependencies (see Fig. 10.7). Each workstream should also be phased (in case of a long workstream) to deliver business benefits through changed capabilities at key milestones. In our case, this was clarified by identifying the capabilities required to enable specific product features. As a result, as specific workstream projects delivered a changed capability, the product feature was realized as a benefit.

Given the incremental and evolutionary approach, it can be anticipated that at various points during the change program some parts of the business will operate to the new model and other parts to the old model. Therefore, at significant milestones in program delivery interim "configurations" of the business will be established. These configurations form transitional architecture(s) of the program and are an essential part of the program design. They ensure that the business can continue to operate even though the overall change is partially complete and provide a firm footing for subsequent changes. Section 10.5 explores the migration strategies that can be used to identify the transitional architectures.

Typically, there is an additional cost associated with implementing such configurations; however, experience shows that the benefits outweigh the cost. The benefits result from incremental delivery of benefits, risk mitigation, and simply breaking the problem down into manageable chunks.

Our initiative benefited from a number of existing architecture models, such as business object and process models. The architecture team, comprising a senior enterprise architect and process architect, was responsible for ensuring review of the existing models and for development of the phase 2 architecture deliverables. This included the first draft of the program plan, which was subsequently transferred to the program manager. In addition to the review with subject matter experts, input to the deliverables came from the senior business function stakeholders and the program executive, especially in terms of establishing priorities and confirming dependencies.

10.4.3 Phase 3: Program Delivery

Having established the essential structure of the business architecture in the definition phase and the scoping of individual workstreams and projects based on it, this now sets the context for detailing the business design in each workstream. As each workstream progresses through the design of processes and associated resources and IT systems to deliver capabilities, the resulting design deliverables should be verified against the architecture. Any changes or additions identified can then be contributed to the revision and extension of the architecture (see Fig. 10.8).

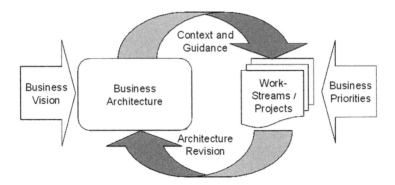

Fig. 10.8 Update of the business architecture through projects and programs

This clearly has implications for the governance of the program to ensure the alignment of deliverables from each workstream with the overall architecture. We will not explore the governance here in any detail, except to highlight the need to establish the accountability within each workstream/project for alignment with the target business scenario and through it the business architecture. This assurance role should typically be assigned to someone other than the workstream leader/project manager. This establishes a balance between project management time and cost drivers with ensuring overall architecture fit.

As in any other initiative, specific workstreams will identify issues that require mitigation and result in changes to scope. Given that the scope is set in the context of the business architecture, it is now more straightforward to establish impacts to other workstreams and adjust accordingly. Indeed, such changes should be reflected in an update to the target business scenario and all other related architecture deliverables. Indeed, the linkage of workstream scope to the target business scenario via capabilities enables requirements traceability throughout the program.

10.5 Migration Strategies and Patterns

As we are in the business of transforming a business from one state to another, we need to consider how the business will continue to operate as the program progresses, as well as how to effect the change as smoothly as possible. In addition to examining dependencies, as discussed earlier, certain migration strategies (informed by the business architecture) can be employed that enable coexistence, mitigate conflicts in priorities, and promote the change. These are important tools to consider in phase 2 when designing the program.

Therefore, once again, we return to the business object and capability dependencies and explore how to both exploit and mitigate them, through patterns and strategies for:

- Sequencing change,
- Decoupling change in different parts of the business, and
- Establishing pivot points (or "axes") around which change can be managed.

In making the organization change-ready, these strategies can be employed on an ongoing basis and not just in a one-off change program.

10.5.1 From Object Specification to Execution

The characteristics of certain types of business object and their lifecycle states provide insight into optimizing the sequence of change (Fig. 10.9). It should come as no surprise that the object dependency map highlights the fact that transactional business objects (high-volume, fast changing objects that result from delivering the products or services of the business, e.g., orders, packages) are dependent on

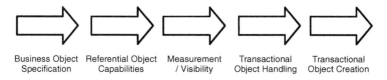

Business Object   Referential Object   Measurement   Transactional   Transactional
Specification   Capabilities   / Visibility   Object Handling   Object Creation

Fig. 10.9 Sequence of change—from object specification to execution

referential business objects (low-volume, relatively slow changing objects that define the business, e.g., products, facilities).

This insight implies a natural sequence for planning change, i.e., that referential business objects are foundational to the business and the capabilities associated with them need to be available before the capabilities associated with transactional business objects can be put in place or changed (see Fig. 10.6).

However, care should be taken to separate the definition or specification of a business object from the instances of it, otherwise it might appear that there are cyclic dependencies in the business. For example, the product specification is required to identify the capabilities to deliver the product, and presumably the capabilities to deliver the product need to be in place before it can be sold. Therefore, clarifying the state of the object (e.g., specified, designed, available) will help to resolve any cyclic dependencies that may be apparent from the business object dependency map.

Also, it is important to plan for and put in place the capabilities associated with providing visibility on and measuring the performance of business objects (for example, the "order" object) through their lifecycle. By putting these capabilities in place early in the change program, the ability to manage progress towards the desired operational processes and capabilities is established. This will also enable focus on quality in the data and the resulting processes. Establishing the monitoring and management capabilities is, of course, dependent upon the relevant business object specifications being developed and referenced.

10.5.2 Decoupling

In order to isolate change in one part of the business from another, we need to find ways to decouple it, or minimize the direct knowledge that one part of the business requires of another. By designing the program based upon the method we have described above, we have already established the foundations for decoupling. That is, by identifying the object dependencies around capabilities and by scoping workstreams by end-to-end processes, we establish a number of critical touch points or interfaces between workstreams and the changed business (e.g., product, tariff, account, and facility from Table 10.2). These interfaces will in effect encapsulate the responsibilities of one workstream from another. This reflects the fact that by identifying opportunities for decoupling in the target business architecture (the changed business) we can use these same interfaces for decoupling workstreams. This allows for evolution both in the business as the program delivers and in the changed business.

These interfaces therefore need to be put in place so that the changes can be managed either side of them. This first requires a common understanding of the object(s) being shared through the interface. Tactical implementations of the interface may then be required to enable the interface with a basic capability to fulfill or provide mapping between the new and the old until the target capability is delivered; this is in effect a facade.

Depending upon the nature of the interface, such facades may be implemented through IT systems or via physical process and organizational changes. Although this is not a discussion on IT integration, the following patterns have proved to be valuable in managing change and are highlighted here for illustration:

- integration broker
- shared database
- service-oriented interface

Within the realm of physical process and organizational approaches, a "clearing house" or broker function are strategies that may be used to achieve decoupling. Also, a degree of decoupling between parallel workstreams can be achieved by establishing the specification for an interface and then working to this (including testing). Only when the parts (of the business) being decoupled are ready, are they brought together then.

10.5.3 Pivot Points

In order to manage change effectively in any system, certain reference points need to be established so as to avoid chaos, i.e., everything changing at once. Indeed, it is likely that the target architecture is different from the current, and will have been partitioned in different ways, e.g., with changed organizational or system boundaries. Therefore, we need to find key reference points in the target architecture that we can relate to the current architecture and manage change around.

These reference points form the "axes" of the architecture and are typically at points where key elements of the architecture come together. These reference points, therefore, exhibit the highest dependencies in the architecture (not necessarily the change). However, having established these reference points, other elements of the business can change or develop independently of each other.

Depending upon the scope and nature of the change the specific reference points might vary; however, certain reference points should be identifiable for the business as a whole. The "Order" business object and associated capabilities might be seen as an obvious pivot point (see Figs. 10.2 and 10.6). On one side of it, you have the production processes that fulfill the order; on the other side, there are the billing processes; and finally, you have the customer requesting a service based upon a product offering.

Therefore, it is important to identify what the pivot points are and establish them as early as possible in the change program. Depending upon the change, mitigation of dependencies around the pivot points will be required. This can be achieved through decoupling as described in Sect. 10.5.2.

10.6 Conclusions and Further Work

We have explored how, starting with the foundations of the business architecture that are made explicit in a target business scenario, it is possible to design and execute a business change program. This is based upon the experience of employing such an approach in a large multi-national business change program. The principles and learnings have been abstracted with the intent to establish patterns and principles that can be applied in other change scenarios. These can be summarized as follows:

1. *Business object* dependencies are the starting point for identifying capability dependencies and scoping change deliverables.
2. Scope workstreams based on clustered *capabilities* and *end-to-end business processes*.
3. Seek to *decouple* parts of the business from each other enabling current and future change.
4. Establish *pivot points* around which change can be managed.
5. Use the flow of information in the business, exhibited by the types of business objects (*referential* and *transactional*) to promote change.

Underlying these principles are those of *incremental delivery* and *managed evolution*. There is clearly follow-on work required to validate and build on these principles in other change programs and apply them to other businesses and business models. Also, the role of other elements of the business architecture needs to be further explored.

10.6.1 Reusing the Approach

Although the approach described here has been used to plan change to a significant business line across multiple functions, it is anticipated that it can also be applied to different scopes of business change, in particular where the change affects several business capabilities or processes. This could be a new or enhanced service offering, or process optimization to reduce costs. Given the architecture elements and principles that this approach is based on, it is applicable to the realization of service-oriented architecture. However, it does not assume or indeed mandate that such an architecture style is employed.

Once explicitly established, the architecture can then be used as a reference for successive business changes through ongoing "managed evolution" as well as for running the business. Indeed, as illustrated in Fig. 10.8, other change initiatives should draw on and supplement the business architecture, enabling increased alignment and further embedding the business architecture. We will not explore in detail all the areas in which the business architecture can become embedded, except to point out that the terms and definitions based on business objects, capabilities, and processes should become part of the business language, and of course physical process descriptions can be used for training. As the practice and discipline of applying and updating the business architecture is established, we can expect that the organization's business transformation and change maturity will increase.

10.6.2 Exploring Other Elements of the Business Architecture

The approach we described here focuses on key elements of the business execution architecture (see Chap. 1) in order to design a program to deliver a changed operating business. As such, it draws on key elements of the other business architecture layers.

In developing the target business scenario we have assumed that the business model is a given and did not delve into its design. Indeed, the business model should be the basis for identifying required capabilities. Hence, if the business model changes, then this is reflected in the required capabilities.

Although organizational design is not directly addressed in the target business scenario, a change in the business' operating model (Ross et al. 2006) needs to be reflected in the target business scenario by establishing our target operating model—this can be articulated by principles, e.g., process standardization—and which capabilities can/are to be outsourced or delegated (e.g., subcontracted) to other parties. This necessarily has an impact on the capabilities required to manage the relationship with other parties that are different to managing internal resources. Indeed, the principles for defining KPI's and establishing compensation mechanisms are developed based upon the target operating model.

In our case, there was a change in recharge model between different business entities that illustrates the need for different capabilities to implement the recharge model. This is aside from the "soft" change management necessary to apply the new recharge model.

10.7   Final Word

We started out to design and deliver a business change program based upon an architecture-driven approach and program management best practices. This we did successfully. In developing an architecture-driven approach we drew on established architecture methods and practices from different areas (e.g., software and enterprise architecture) as well as our own experiences in managing change. Having done so, we have taken a systemic view of the business/enterprise, drawing on some of the general principles of systems thinking and practice. We also hope to have contributed to the development of business architecture practice by identifying and capturing key patterns and principles for enabling change in large organizations.

Acknowledgements Firstly, I would like to thank the many colleagues at DHL Express, past and present, who have influenced my approach to enterprise and business architecture, and provided the opportunity to put it into practice. Specific thanks go to Sten Larsson and Piotr Wójtowicz for taking the time to read the drafts of this chapter and for contributing their insights to the finished article.

References

AXELOS (2014) PRINCE 2. http://www.prince-officialsite.com/. Accessed 12 Feb 2014

Beck K et al (2001) Manifesto for agile software development. http://agilemanifesto.org/. Accessed 12 Feb 2014

Brown GW (2009) Value chains, value streams, value nets, and value delivery chains. BPTrends. http://www.bptrends.com/bpt/wp-content/publicationfiles/FOUR%2004-009-ART-Value%20Chains-Brown.pdf. Accessed 22 Sept 2014

Cabinet Office (2011) Managing successful programmes manual. TSO (The Stationery Office), London

Cook MA (1996) Building enterprise information architectures: reengineering information systems. Prentice Hall, Upper Saddle River, NJ

Davis R (2010) Processes in practice—thinking end-to-end: time for Cinderella to go to the ball? BPTrends. http://www.bptrends.com/publicationfiles/ONE%20DAVIS%2004-06-10-COL-Processes0in-Practice-Davis-final.pdf. Accessed 22 Sept 2014

Finkelstein C (1989) An introduction to information engineering: from strategic planning to information systems. Addison-Wesley, Reading, MA

Leganza G, Cullen A, Scott J, An M (2009) Case study: DHL express uses business architecture to design a new service offering. Forrester Research Inc, Cambridge, MA, USA

Malan R, Bredemeyer D, Krishnan R, Lafrenz R (2002–2006) Enterprise architecture as business capabilities architecture. Bredemeyer Consulting. http://www.bredemeyer.com/pdf_files/Presentations/EnterpriseArchitectureAsCapabilitiesArch.pdf. Accessed 22 Sep 2014

Martin J (1995) The great transition: using the seven disciplines of enterprise engineering to align people, technology, and strategy. Amacom, New York

Ross JW, Weill P, Robertson DC (2006) Enterprise architecture as strategy: creating a foundation for business execution. Harvard Business School Press, Boston

Simon D, Fischbach K, Schoder D (2014) Enterprise architecture management and its role in corporate strategic management. Information Systems and e-Business Management 12(1):5–42

Sprott D (2008) Enterprise architecture Europe - conference notebook. CBDI J (June):13–15

The Open Group (2011) TOGAF® version 9.1. Van Haren, The Netherlands

Veryard R (1994) Information coordination: the management of information models, systems and organizations. Prentice Hall, Upper Saddle River, NJ

Veryard R (2012) Organizing business capabilities. http://rvsoapbox.blogspot.de/2012/02/organizing-business-capabilities.html. Accessed 12 Feb 2014

Part IV

Modeling and Measuring

Building Agile Enterprises: A Model-Based Approach to Rapid Realization of Business Value

11

Marc M. Lankhorst and Bas van Gils

Abstract

Agility is a key ability of enterprises, but agility does not come for free. Organizations need to choose where to focus their efforts in becoming more agile. This chapter describes an integrated approach for the development of agile enterprises, based on sound engineering principles. This approach uses various types of models and analysis instruments from the business architecture field. Further, this chapter shows how virtualization techniques can contribute to business agility. This is against the background of an increased focus on "data as an asset"—independent of the systems that currently hold the data—that represents an important development for many organizations. As a matter of fact, many organizations also face increased reporting requirements (due to ever changing legislation, for example). Finally, having agility on a per-system basis is not enough, because you run the risk of building agile silos. The role of architecture in fostering enterprise-wide coherence and in bridging the gap between strategy and execution thus is the final topic of this chapter.

11.1 Introduction

Agility is a key property of enterprises. The pace at which customers demand changes, the pressure of new laws and regulations, and the ease with which competitors can copy their services leads to tremendous pressure on companies. Pressure to change, to adopt new technologies and practices, to scale up or to reduce cost are typical examples. In many organizations, being agile is therefore as crucial as being able to innovate. Innovation and agility are necessary competences for a sustainable business.

M.M. Lankhorst (✉) • B. van Gils
BiZZdesign, Enschede, The Netherlands
e-mail: m.lankhorst@bizzdesign.nl

© Springer International Publishing Switzerland 2015
D. Simon, C. Schmidt (eds.), *Business Architecture Management*, Management for Professionals, DOI 10.1007/978-3-319-14571-6_11

But agility does not come for free: organizations need to choose where to focus their efforts in becoming more agile and therefore need to think strategically about where agility is necessary, required, or unwanted.

There is a strong connection between the different technology-related competences of an enterprise: the digital options that modern technology creates, the structural agility resulting from these options, and the competitive actions the enterprise can take. And all of these crucially depend on what is called entrepreneurial alertness: strategic and systemic foresight.

11.2 Perspectives on Agility

To deal with various drivers for agility (see Sect. 11.5.2), organizations both need to address their development change processes, which need to be responsive to these drivers, and have existing business processes, structures, and information technology (IT) applications that are flexible enough to accommodate the required changes. For example, an insurer's introduction of a new online service for providing insurance products requires a rapid and responsive development process for such a service, while the existing Internet channel, back-end systems, and associated fulfillment processes must be flexible enough to easily incorporate this new service.

Thus, two kinds of agility are the foundation for the agile enterprise (Lankhorst 2012). First, we have *process agility*: using agile practices for design and development, focused on people, rapid value delivery and responsiveness to change. This is the most common use of the term "agility" in an IT context, with agile software development processes such as Scrum at the forefront, but the same agile processes apply in a business context as well. But agile development processes alone are not enough: you still run a risk of creating inflexible and fragmented systems.

This leads us to the need for *system agility*: having organizational and technical systems that are easy to reconfigure, adapt and extend when the need arises. We use the term "system" here in a broad, system-theoretic sense, including business processes, business services, organizational structure, etc., and not just IT applications and technical infrastructure.

Agile systems have five important properties (Lankhorst 2012):

1. Making changes to the system is easy. This is of course the primary issue.
2. These changes can easily be deployed, not only in a technical sense but also including, for example, the impact on business processes or human resources.
3. Side effects of these changes are easy to deal with, to minimize disruption of and risk to the day-to-day operations.
4. The system is easy to integrate with its environment, for example through the use of standards.
5. The system can easily be decoupled from its environment, either to replace or reuse it in another context.

Having agile processes and systems thus creates the foundation for true *business agility*: using your process and system agility as an essential part of your enterprise strategy, outmaneuvering competitors with shorter time-to-market, smarter partnering strategies, lower development costs, and higher customer satisfaction.

Whether it is useful or necessary to be agile in a specific domain depends, on the one hand, on the organization's environment (in particular on the events and changes in this context), and, on the other hand, on the organization's strategy, as we will describe in more detail later. In the remainder of this chapter, we will concentrate on system and business agility. The issues and opportunities of process agility are sufficiently known and described elsewhere.

11.3 Becoming More Agile

Taiichi Ohno, the founding father of Lean, reputedly said that "You cannot be Lean. You can only become Lean." To some extent, the same can be said about Agile: you cannot be agile, you can only become more agile [see, for example, Towill and Christopher (2002) for a good discussion on the relation between agility and lean]. A straightforward way of working for becoming more agile follows the next steps. In the next sections, we will describe each of these steps, and illustrate this approach with a practical example.

1. assessing the current agility of the organization (Sect. 11.4);
2. determine the business motivation for agility, i.e., which changes in the environment affect the organization (Sect. 11.5.2);
3. assess how agile the organization needs to be from the perspectives of business model and business execution (Sects. 11.5.3 and 11.5.4);
4. define a course of action to achieve this (Sect. 11.6).

Of course, this process is used iteratively in a plan-do-check-act fashion (Deming 1986), measuring the outcomes and possibly changing course, adapting your strategy, or dealing with this feedback in another fashion.

11.4 Assessing Agility

Creating truly agile enterprises is not an easy task, and something that may take several years. Where do you start? What are the quick wins and bottlenecks? How do we avoid going "only" for the low-hanging fruit, rather than making a strategic choice to let agility become part of the corporate DNA?

This section presents a two-part capability model based on common models from the literature, to help organizations assess their current and desired agility. It provides insight into the next steps that are useful to improve your agility. Note that we explicitly avoid the term "maturity" here: it is not our intention that all organizations should strive for the highest possible level in this capability model,

Table 11.1 Process agility capability levels

No	Name	Description
1	Initial	The organization is starting to recognize that it has issues with aspects of agility. However, no formalized roles, procedures, measurements, or instruments are used yet to address these issues
2	Managed	The organization has started explicitly to manage its agility, and agile ways of working are introduced at the project level
3	Defined	Management of enterprise agility progresses beyond the project level. Business drivers for agility are recognized and the organizational strategy appreciates agility as an enabling factor
4	Quantitatively Managed	Agility is addressed in the full service lifecycle, and the organization actively measures outcomes and guides its process and system agility using quantitative techniques
5	Optimizing	The organization's strategy is based on its agility; agile teams' performance has been highly optimized, based on the results of continuous improvement and sharing experiences within and outside the organization

but rather that they choose appropriate capabilities that fit their specific strategy and circumstances, and to strive for balanced capabilities in the several agility areas.

The capability model combines the process and system aspects of enterprise agility that together underpin its business agility. The process agility capabilities use the common capability maturity levels known from models such as the CMMI (SEI 2010), and include aspects from the Scrum maturity model of Yin et al. (2011), and the "Agility@Scale" model of Ambler (2010). We distinguish five capability levels, listed in Table 11.1.

For the capabilities concerning system agility, we use a scale based on the work of Ross et al. (2006), the "Service Integration Maturity Model" (OSIMM) (The Open Group 2009), and the "Business Decision Maturity Model" (BDMM) (von Halle and Goldberg 2009), again adapted to an agile context. Table 11.2 lists these levels.

11.4.1 Example

We illustrate this with an anonymized example from our own experience: the Agency for Quantity and Quality (AQQ), which is tasked with the provision of all kinds of statistical reports, financial analyses, and other information products to the Ministry of Policy and Governance[1] from an unnamed Western-European country. This organization is big (in terms of number of staff) and heavily compartmentalized. As with many organizations, there is increased regulatory pressure on financial and quality aspects. Public opinion about the (lack of)

---

[1] We are sorry we cannot be more explicit, but that would harm the anonymity of the organization presented here.

Table 11.2 System agility capability levels

No	Name	Description
1	Silos	System agility is unknown and possibly quite low. Individual parts of the organization are developing their own services independently, with no integration of data, processes, standards, or technologies
2	Standardized technology	System agility is addressed reactively, only at the level of individual systems, and focused on IT. Standardized technologies and platforms have been put in place to communicate between silos, and to integrate the data and interconnections
3	Optimized core	The IT systems in the silos have been analyzed and broken down into reusable component parts. Models are used for the design of the business and IT operations, and at the level of enterprise goals, drivers, and requirements
4	Business modularity	Business drivers for agility are monitored continuously. Models are used at three levels of abstraction: (1) for requirements and design purposes (2) to obtain management information; and (3) in suitable domains also for direct implementation Models are also used to identify and combine independent business modules and services. Business services to the environment can quickly be realized across the enterprise by combining and configuring internal and external business services
5	Dynamic venturing	The organization's strategy is based on its agility. Architecture is used as a core instrument to orchestrate business and IT as an integrated whole, not only for design purposes but also in close relation with the organizational strategy. The architecture extends beyond the borders of the individual organization and includes the networked enterprise level. It is used as a strategic instrument: strengths and weaknesses are measured using architecture models and used as input for strategic discussions, to spot business opportunities that may result from current and/or future business capabilities of the organization itself and of its partners. Thus, the agility of the organization is used as an asset with which it competes and collaborates in a networked environment. A continuous improvement cycle of the organization and its architecture ensures it stays ahead of the curve

performance of the organization is a key driver and is largely determined by interpretations of the published performance reports.

The AQQ's customers—cabinet members, policy makers, and regulators—require ever more reports that combine existing data sources in novel ways. For example, a newspaper article on injustice is picked up by a Member of Parliament who asks the Minister about the number of citizens affected by this specific problem, and the AQQ has to come up with the right numbers at short notice. Moreover, the Board of the Agency wants to be more pro-active and offer new kinds of analyses and reports to its clients, and possibly even expand into serving private-sector clients.

The structure and information systems of the organization are perceived as a barrier to agility. For example, building a new or extending an existing data mart for some query often takes up to 9 months. When we analyze the current capabilities of the organization, we see that it scores quite low. Its process agility is at the initial level: it recognizes the need for agility, but is not yet actively managing this, nor does it use agile ways of working. Likewise, its internal structure is siloed: the original tasks that were assigned to it by the Ministry have been translated into separate departments. These have their own IT systems and databases, which are often based on the same data sources. Integrating this wealth of data would provide many interesting opportunities, but is currently not feasible.

11.5 Desired Agility

Next to the general capabilities of an organization, as addressed in the previous sections, we need more detailed insights into the areas in which an organization wants to be agile. We thus present an instrument to identify the need for agility of an enterprise, based on its strategy and business drivers. This is combined with an analysis that identifies potential barriers to agility to find the "agility hotspots," areas in which the organization wants to be flexible but current agility is lacking. These are the areas on which you need to concentrate.

11.5.1 Assessment Instrument

The analysis instrument we present comprises a set of questionnaires that is intended for business managers, strategists, and architects. It contains questions about the organization's strategy, business drivers from its environment or context, and the potential barriers and limitations in adapting to these drivers. These questions address the frequency and impact of changes from the environment, and the time the organization needs to accommodate these changes. Some examples are listed in Table 11.3.

Based on the answers to these questions, the agility requirements for the organization can be determined by linking the strategic choice and drivers to the different aspects of process agility and system agility. For example, for an insurance company that has a customer intimacy strategy, differences in customer segments (their expectations, their value to the company, etc.) may be the driving factor for agility, requiring, for example, changes to channels and customer interaction based on these differences. The need for agility will then focus on the customer-facing business processes and IT systems, requiring flexibility in their design and a rapid design and realization process for such customer-oriented changes. Our agility analysis assesses which elements of an organization are most likely to be affected by strategic and situational factors and shows what the relative importance of these influences is. The next sections describe this instrument in more detail, first focusing on the "why," i.e., the business motivation perspective (strategy and

Table 11.3 Sample questions from agility questionnaire

Strategy
How would you classify your competitive strategy? (customer intimacy, product leadership, operational excellence)
Which value center approach do you use to manage your IT investments? (cost, service, profit, or investment center)
Business drivers
How often do you introduce new products or services?
How often do you change parameters, rules, processes of a service to match the customer's situation or demands?
How often do you involve different business partners in realizing or delivering your services?
How often do you change the internal organization, processes, and/or systems to improve efficiency or quality?
Barriers to change
How long does it take to add a new channel to an existing business service?
How long does it take to modify a business process because it has to use a different IT system?
How long does it take to change the number of people involved, if demand changes?
How long does it take to change the rules or parameters of products or services?

drivers; Sect. 11.5.2), then on the "what," i.e., the business model perspective (Sect. 11.5.3), and finally the "how," i.e., the business execution perspective (Sect. 11.5.4) (see Chap. 1 for an overview of these perspectives).

11.5.2 Desired Agility: Business Motivation Perspective

Whether it is useful or necessary to be agile depends on the organization's environment and, in particular, on the events and changes in this context. To assist organizations in assessing their current and desired agility, we must first address these business drivers for agility. Organizations need internal flexibility in several aspects to be able to respond in an agile manner to these external and internal drivers. Seven common business drivers for agility can be observed (Lankhorst 2012):

1. *Product/service dynamics*: market demands or new opportunities leading to introducing new services, phasing out services, or changing service parameters, rules, or other aspects;
2. *Revenue dynamics*: market and internal cost factors leading to changes in pricing strategies and other aspects that influence your revenue stream;
3. *Volume dynamics*: changes in demand and supply, requiring, for example, resource scaling;
4. *Channel flexibility*: changes in the use of different channels to deliver services, add new channels, drop expensive ones, move to new technologies;
5. *Supply chain flexibility*: involving different partners in realizing or delivering your services;

6. *Continuous compliance*: new rules and regulations that need to be complied with;
7. *Technology adoption*: availability of new technologies that can be used to lower costs or gain an advantage over competitors.

These drivers map onto the drivers and constraints concepts in the business motivation part of the architecture framework applied throughout this book (based on Simon et al. 2014; see Chap. 1). Each of these drivers has, when selected for implementation, its own impact on the organization and its information systems.

Next to this, the need for agility also depends on the organization's chosen competitive/value strategy (according to Treacy and Wiersema 1997) and IT investment strategy (Venkatraman 1997), as per the strategy element of this book's framework. Organizations that focus their strategy on operational excellence may decide to build very efficient, but perhaps less flexible processes and systems than organizations that choose to focus on customer intimacy or product leadership (see Chap. 4 for further details on these so-called value disciplines). Also, the parts and aspects of the organization that need to be most agile depend on the value strategy. For customer intimacy, for example, agility in customer-facing processes and channels will be highly important, whereas product leaders will stress the agility of their products and services.

To determine the focus of your agility efforts, you must be aware of these environmental drivers in order to find the "agility hotspots" of your organization.

11.5.3 Desired Agility: Business Model Perspective

For an analysis of system agility, we need to look at the "what" in relation to the "why" outlined in the previous section: what kind and level of agility does the organization need, from the perspective of the business and environment in which it operates? Different drivers have impact on different parts of the organization. For example, channel flexibility is strongly linked to the way channels and business functions are interconnected. In this way, the organizational target of any driver can be identified, given a certain choice of model. We use the *"Business Model Canvas"* (Osterwalder and Pigneur 2010) to describe the business model and link the seven drivers for agility identified in Sect. 11.5.2 to the nine concepts in the Canvas. All in all, the building blocks of the Canvas represent major parts of the business model constituent of the architecture framework used in this book (there are some reasonable additions in this framework though; see Chap. 1).

For our purposes, we have also extended the Canvas, in this case with a *"Risk and Compliance"* concept. This addresses the way the organization chooses to deal with various internal and external risks (addressing financial, operational, and other risks, e.g., in terms of its risk appetite) and what the influence of regulatory pressure is on their business model. For example, a bank will typically have a low risk appetite and is under high regulatory pressure, so it needs to respond quickly to policy changes but will have extensive decision-making processes on business

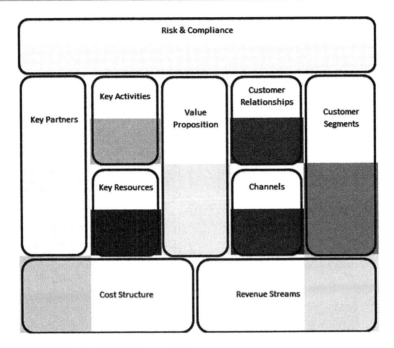

Fig. 11.1   Agility hotspots in business model

changes, in order to control risk. On the other hand, an Internet startup may take considerably higher risks and operates in a less regulated environment, making it more agile in its decision making on, for example, the products and services it offers or the IT infrastructure it uses.

We have analyzed our anonymized governmental organization AQQ using the agility questionnaires outlined in the previous section. The results are summarized in two "agility maps," as depicted in Figs. 11.1 and 11.2.

For this organization we see that the biggest mismatch in required and realized agility is in customer relationships, channels, and key resources. The background is that the Ministry is under pressure from politicians with respect to the ever rising costs in its domain, and the AQQ needs to provide management information to the Ministry to provide the insight needed to curb these costs. However, the "event-driven" nature of politics makes this need for information very dynamic; any article in a national newspaper on yet another incident of overspending will generate parliamentary questions to the responsible Minister, who in turn will ask for more or better management information, resulting in new information demands for the AQQ. And this is just one example; the AQQ provides this type of information to

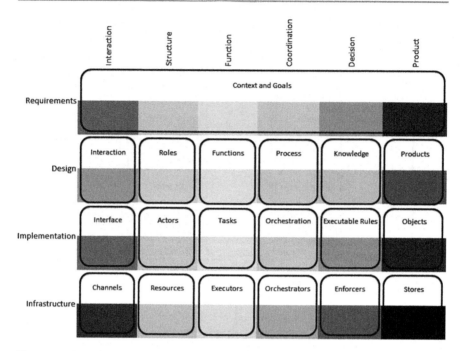

Fig. 11.2 Agility hotspots in realization

many organizations in the Ministry's domain. Further analysis shows that the agility hotspots signify:

- better relationships to customers in order to provide timely and accurate information that is adapted to their specific requirements;
- a need for more and higher-quality data sources and the means to combine different sources to create relevant reports, for example using a data warehouse (as a key resource);
- better channels to provide various institutions with access this information, including the delivery of "open data" to the general public.

Having this impression of the necessary system agility from a business model perspective, i.e., knowing the "what," we now zoom in on the "how," the realization of agile systems.

11.5.4 Desired Agility: Business Execution Perspective

To analyze system agility from a realization or business execution perspective, i.e., addressing the "how" of system agility, we use a two-dimensional framework structured along two axes: service aspects and abstraction levels. In our realization framework, we use four abstraction levels:

1. The *requirements level* deals with the motivation and rationale behind the service, and comprises the service requirements from a business perspective. This is of course closely linked to the business model and business motivation perspectives described before.
2. The *design level* contains the interactions, processes, functions, rules, and objects that are needed to realize the service.
3. The *implementation level* describes how the service will be implemented, in terms of both the people and the technology involved. Ideally, this level can be skipped, i.e., if the design models are directly executable on the infrastructure. More often than not this is not realistic, which makes it necessary to also look into the implementation facets.
4. The *infrastructure level* is where "the rubber meets the road": the people and technology actually delivering the service. On the one hand, there are people with suitable capabilities who deliver services to customers. To be able to deliver these services, they execute tasks, coordinate activities, manage other people, and enforce that rules are obeyed (or not). On the other hand, there is the IT infrastructure which delivers automated services and comprises both generic hard- and software infrastructure and specific applications on top of that.

An important architectural approach that can provide more system agility is the use of models and model-driven tools to facilitate the development and change process by solving agility (and other) concerns still at a relatively high, IT-independent abstraction level. These models can then be targeted to suitable IT infrastructure, either by transforming them to technology-oriented models or software code, or even by directly interpreting and executing these models. The latter improves both the innovation and the execution capabilities of the enterprise, because it shortens the path from "business idea" to "business execution" and it improves the business insight in the operational reality as well.

Furthermore, by dealing with each aspect of a product or service separately before dealing with the bigger picture, we can maintain a grip on the complexity and avoid that design concerns get mixed up. This supports agility by providing a single point of definition and change for each aspect. An important example in business design is the separation of the "know" from the "flow," i.e., managing the business rules separately from the business processes in which they are applied (von Halle and Goldberg 2009). This promotes reusability of rules and adaptability of processes. Another well-known example of this principle from application development is the use of a three-tier architecture, separating presentation, business logic, and data. Below, we describe the *six aspects* we distinguish (Lankhorst 2012).

11.5.4.1 Interaction

The interaction aspect concerns the way in which the enterprise interacts with its environment. It includes the enterprise's collaboration with its various partners and how its clients interact with the business services it provides. These services may be delivered through an online channel, but traditional, human-centric services, delivered, for example, via the telephone or over the counter, are also part of this. This interaction aspect can be viewed as an elaboration of the customer channels concept of the Business Model Canvas, and also comprises interactions with partners (e.g., the supplier channels in the business architecture framework used in this book).

11.5.4.2 Structure

The structure aspect concerns the way in which the enterprise organizes its human and technological resources. This includes the organizational structure, comprising the definition and allocation of roles, responsibilities, authorizations, reporting lines, et cetera, but also the information system structures, i.e., the technical and application architectures. This is basically an elaboration of the key resources part of the Business Model Canvas, and it corresponds to the organizational structures and resources elements (from the execution level) of this book's business architecture framework (see Chap. 1).

11.5.4.3 Function

The function aspect addresses the individual elements of business and application functionality that, orchestrated and coordinated together, deliver the actual substance of a service. This comprises both the (manual) tasks of employees and the (automated) service logic of applications. Individual functions (and the services they deliver) are coordinated via the coordination aspect, they use and produce information from the information aspect, and they employ rules and calculations from the decision aspect. This can be viewed as an elaboration of (parts of) the key activities concept of the Business Model Canvas, and to some extent it corresponds to the business process aspect at the execution level of this book's framework.

11.5.4.4 Coordination

The coordination aspect focuses on the various dependencies between the activities needed to deliver services. This includes, for example, the specification and (possibly automated) orchestration of business processes, workflow support, and so on. It comprises both the coordination within an individual organization and the coordination of activities with other organizations, which may be users of the service or partners in delivering it. This can be considered an extension and elaboration of the key activities area of the Business Model Canvas to incorporate the value chain coordination and cooperation aspects of this book's business architecture framework; at the execution level, it thus corresponds to the business process aspect.

11.5.4.5 Decision

The decision aspect captures the logic of reasoning used in the service domain to reach decisions, i.e., how decisions are (to be) made. For example, in the domain of insurance policies or banking products, this pertains to decisions based on calculations, and other (logical) derivations. Part of this logic may take the form of executable specifications, such as decision tables or executable business rules; other elements are typically used by people, both in delivering the service and in defining, checking, and enforcing an organization's rules of conduct. Again, this is an elaboration (of parts) of the key activities aspect of the Business Model Canvas, and as such it basically corresponds to the business process and the control aspects at the execution part of this book's framework.

11.5.4.6 Product

Finally, the product aspect is concerned with the things that the service produces and consumes, and the way in which these products are registered and managed. Products can refer both to tangible business objects, such as cars and pizzas, but also to intangible information items, such as insurance claims and pizza orders. This is where virtualization (for our running example) is an important example, as will be illustrated below. This is typically an elaboration of the value proposition part of the Business Model Canvas to detail the actual products and services behind a particular value proposition (as per the business architecture framework used throughout this book); at the execution level, this may primarily correspond to information entities.

11.5.5 Example

If we apply this analysis framework to our example organization, the Agency for Quantity and Quality, we can construct a heat map that shows you where the systems are less agile than needed (Fig. 11.2).

In this heat map, we see that the main issues are in the columns for the interaction and the product aspects. This stands to reason: the increasing demand for all kinds of policy data, delivered in various forms of reports, preferably online or even real-time, leads to issues in customer interaction.

Moreover, the information needed to create these reports has become a bottleneck; combining data sources in ever changing ways is a major challenge for the agency with its siloed organization structure and systems landscape. How can they become more agile in combining, integrating, refining, upgrading, and analyzing relevant data sources to create timely and relevant policy information? In the remainder of this chapter, we will concentrate on the latter aspect.

11.6 Improving Agility Through Data Virtualization

Data is an important theme for many organizations. Indeed, once could argue that this has been true since the rise of information technology in the 1970s. However, if we look at the literature over the last few decades, then it seems that there has been a gradual shift away from a focus on (information) systems towards managing data as an asset in its own right (Brooks 1995; Martin 1990a, b, 1995; Spewak and Hill 1993). As John Ladley (Ladley 2010) aptly summarizes it:

> The twenty-first century business features information as the fuel. We don't replace process; we enable operators in existing processes [. . .]. The bottom line is: if information is fuel—then improper treatment is risky. Fuel can be volatile. Fuel can explode.

In the light of this trend, we will show how data virtualization techniques can help organizations improve agility (Van der Lans 2012), not only at the level of their information systems but up to and including their business architectures, sometimes even up to the level of business models. We will first give an overview of what these techniques entail and subsequently illustrate how they improve agility in the organization. Note that the point is not to show off how "cool" this new technology is. Instead, we hope to illustrate that this type of technology can help organizations achieve improved agility.

11.6.1 Example

As we outlined in the previous sections, our example Agency for Quality and Quantity has been established through a series of tasks assigned to it by the Ministry, which has resulted in a number of organizational, informational, and technical silos. This is a common scenario: many organizations have grown either through an increased product portfolio with associated structures or via a series of acquisitions and mergers, and have ended up with various silos (Ross et al. 2006).

First of all, the AQQ organization also suffers from a siloed mentality: different departments find themselves really special and completely different from their peers in other departments. This has resulted on local ways of working and all manner of different IT systems.

To give an example of organizational issues hampering speed and agility: we discovered that, as part of different views on developing new information products for decision makers such as business intelligence reports, management had put an end to the debate and forced the standardization of a waterfall approach. This gave more grip, but agility was hampered, and the siloed landscape meant that data had to be pulled from many different sources. This reduced both development speed and confidence in the quality of the end product. Since the data was used for (strategic) decision making, this was a serious issue.

Numerous attempts have been made by the AQQ to standardize business processes and integrate IT systems. While these have fixed many (local) needs, the perception is that these efforts have been slow and expensive. Requests for new

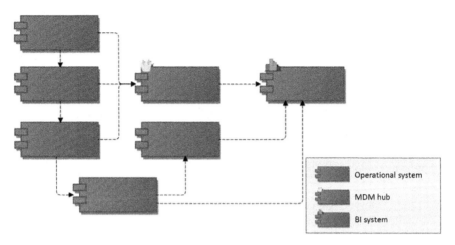

Fig. 11.3 Example application landscape and data flows

functionality as well as for reports have been piling up, and a business case for an enterprise data warehouse (EDW) has been in the making for a long time now. In fact, the idea of having a complete repository with all corporate data is appealing but, still, building it seems like a daunting task.

A typical abstraction of the issue is shown in Fig. 11.3. The diagram shows that there are many (logical) data flows between various systems which somehow seem to converge at the (planned) BI system. Some of these flows pass through the master data management (MDM) hub where some integration and standardization takes place. Even though some components, such as the MDM hub, are intended to improve (access to integrated) data, AQQ has learned that moving data across the landscape through each of these flows takes time and is a potential source of errors: there are minor differences between definitions in various systems, derivation rules and key calculations (for example, handling tax rates and discount schemes) differ, text fields are misused, etc. On top of that, there is also the widespread idea that semi- and unstructured data such as email and documents that are scattered across the organization potentially have a lot of value as well.

This is a situation where data virtualization techniques can help. Following the definition of data virtualization of Rick van der Lans (2012), we see data virtualization as a group of technologies that makes a heterogeneous set of databases and files look like one integrated database, which has some commonality with how many people see the concept of a federated database. As we will see shortly, though, data virtualization picks up where "traditional" data federation stops and provides organizations with a rich set of techniques for data integration issues.

Reusing the notation introduced by Van der Lans (2012), Fig. 11.4 illustrates the main idea. Working from the bottom up, we see a heterogeneous set of source systems, with all types of data (structured and unstructured). The data structures are replicated, wrapped, and—if so desired—cached in the virtualization server. From

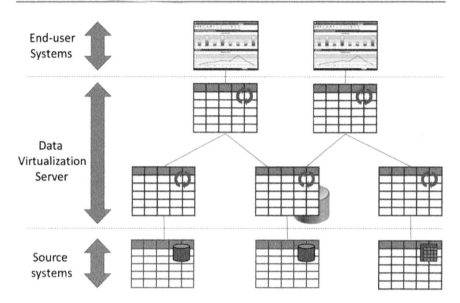

Fig. 11.4 Illustrating the principles of data virtualization

that point on, all data manipulations can be done in one virtualized environment, reducing the need for moving data through a landscape. Note that the type of access can also be configured: virtualized access can be "read only," or may include "write"-access as well. Transaction management functionality will make sure the data stays consistent.

One aspect of agility should be obvious from this discussion: development and data integration within the virtualized environment can be considerably more agile than in a traditional setting. Requirements and specification [for example, metadata management (Mosley et al. 2010)] could still be used, but rather than a long build-and-deploy time, we now have results available immediately in a virtual table structure. As a result, it is easy to learn-while-doing in quick and highly interactive cycles with end users: quick sprints will deliver a working prototype and later adjustments can easily be made without having wasted many valuable development hours.

This also demonstrates the fact that such a system itself is also considered to be agile. Referring to the properties of agile systems we mentioned in Sect. 11.2:

1. It will be fairly easy—and most of all: fast—to adapt to ever changing business needs for information.
2. Deploying changes to a virtualized data model is easier than changing the data structure of a physical database, which can entail all kinds of data conversion issues.
3. Dealing with the impact of changes is easier, since no software is adapted, lowering the risk of disruptions and keeping the impact localized.

4. Integration of the solution is simple, since existing interfaces remain stable.

Built-in features around security, auditing, logging, and monitoring (i.e., when things change in the source systems) provide the organization with the means to stay in control of their data. In short:

- Data virtualization decouples access to data from the source systems. This allows further manipulation of data without impacting the original systems.
- Virtualized access to structured and unstructured data allows for uniform querying. Caching avoids heavy work-loads on the original transaction systems.
- Data access can be optimized for various stakeholders with different needs, concept definitions, permissions etc.
- Virtualization allows for rapid, incremental development and delivery of information with minimal impact on source systems.

This mechanism can be considered a key source of agility that supports key activities in the organization. A virtual data warehouse with rapid and agile development of new data structures will make it easier to accommodate needs from management, who increasingly seek data-based, rationalized decision making to complement with creative strategic skill (De Wit and Meyer 2010).

Suppose, for example, that national newspapers are filled with stories about fraud: tax money is lost due to foreign and national criminals who have found legal loopholes. Parliament quickly needs the numbers to assess the impact. For validation purposes, data from other agencies must be incorporated into the analysis. Taking more than a week for such integration will not be acceptable. Also, when parliament takes decisive action, monitoring the effects of interventions will be an issue and requires an agile data landscape; as the debate in parliament evolves, AQQ will have to respond with near real-time data to facilitate further analysis and decision making.

The other obvious need for system agility in the field of data is in the realm of compliance and regulations. Many industries are heavily regulated, for example in finance or healthcare, and rules for compliance reporting change all the time. In and by itself this need not be an issue. However, we often see that concept definitions change slightly, derivations and key calculations become more complex, other types of information are required, and so on. Again, the rapid development cycles and flexibility offered by data virtualization helps to accommodate these changes.

11.7   Architecting Agility

Having agility on a per-system basis is not enough, because you run the risk of building agile silos. On top of this, a solid architecture approach is needed to ensure coherence between services, processes, systems and other constituents of the enterprise, avoiding local optimization and providing a clear link to the enterprise strategy.

To some it may seem that architecture is something static, confining everything within its rules and boundaries, and hampering agility and innovation. Many proponents of agile methods are opposed to the use of architecture, categorically classifying it as "Big Design Up-Front." They argue that stakeholders cannot know what they really need and the problem will change anyway before the project is completed, so you cannot provide any useful designs up-front.

This is a misconception about the role of architecture. A well-defined architecture helps you in positioning new developments within the context of the existing processes, IT systems, and other assets of an organization, and in identifying necessary changes. Thus, sound architectural practice helps an organization innovate and change by providing both stability and flexibility. The insights provided by a thoroughly documented architecture are needed to determine the needs and priorities for change from a business perspective, on the one hand, and to assess how the organization may benefit from technological and business innovations, on the other hand.

Agility is not the only concern of an enterprise. Many trade-offs have to be made. Cost efficiency versus flexibility, versus reliability, versus other "-ilities." A well-designed architecture helps in making such trade-offs, analyzing different change scenarios with respect to these different properties, and in assessing their impact across the enterprise.

Architecture thus serves several important roles in fostering agility:

- It bridges the gap between strategy and operations, by providing management with information to guide strategic and investment decisions, on the one hand, and giving concrete guidance for realization, on the other hand. Having such a clear "line-of-sight" between the strategic and operational level is essential both in defining a viable strategy, taking into account the possibilities and limitations of your enterprise, and in rapidly and effectively implementing this strategy, with an integral approach across all relevant aspects of that enterprise.
- It helps in focusing design efforts on those points of variability or uncertainty that are important from a business perspective: where do you expect future changes, and how can you facilitate these? Explicitly designing the necessary variation points in your architecture will help implement such future changes quickly.
- It provides a way of designing organization-level agility, for example by employing specific architecture principles (cf. Greefhorst and Proper 2011), creating reusable business-level building blocks, and, from an IT point of view, defining standardized interfaces, and using infrastructures that speed up development.
- It gives designers and developers the insight in the organization, its IT, and its environment that they need for making changes, assess their effects, and deal with these effects in a proactive manner, thus speeding up realization by finding the easiest route for implementation, reusing existing building blocks, and avoiding unnecessary rework.

The AQQ agency, for example, expects the most important points of variability in the many kinds of management reports they need to provide. This leads to

Fig. 11.5 Architecture in context

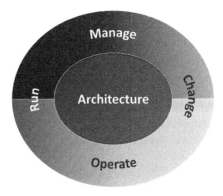

variability in the data sources they connect with in order to acquire the necessary input data, and in the analysis processes of these data sources. Hence, it needs an IT architecture that allows for rapidly connecting new data sources, for example by using standardized interfaces, data formats, etc., and, in particular, a business architecture that provides flexible business processes and business rules for aggregating and analyzing these sources to create the required management information.

An important architecture principle that fosters the flexibility needed by the AQQ is separating the "know" from the "flow" (as outlined earlier), i.e., separately managing the business rules used for data analysis and aggregation, and the business processes in which these rules are used. This facilitates changing only the computational part of the analysis without touching the workflow, which will often comprise a number of generic steps used across many different analyses.

Figure 11.5 illustrates this position of architecture as a way of interlinking the different perspectives outlined above. From top to bottom, we see that architecture serves as a bridge between strategic thinking and agile execution. It fosters coherence between the various elements of the enterprise and helps reduce management uncertainty, which is often a main obstacle to agile ways of working. On the one hand, architecture supports management in making business decisions. On the other hand, it is grounded in and provides guidance to the operational reality of the organization. This is the familiar strategic-tactical-operational distinction.

The "waterfall" or top-down style of strategy execution, however, does not work in an agile environment. Ponderous architectural processes that take many months to provide useful content will slow down organizational decision making and therefore hamper agility. Decision making should be as "local" as possible; only the high-risk, high-impact decisions need to be taken at the strategic level (see, e.g., Chap. 1). Architecture should be employed in a just-in-time and light-weight manner, especially when it gets closer to the operational level, and provide projects and operational teams with guidance when they need it, at the level of detail they need.

From left to right in the figure, architecture both provides insights that help run the enterprise as-is (the "going concern") and facilitates change to realize desired business outcomes. This distinction is less clear-cut than that of management vs. operations: disciplines such as Lean, Agile, and DevOps focus on continuous or incremental improvement in daily operations, and are therefore somewhere in the middle of this spectrum.

Agile thinking views the entire life cycle of business and IT artifacts and capabilities as a whole, largely doing away with the distinction between "running" and "changing." This implies that the business and IT landscape is seen as a portfolio of elements of different granularity, each with its own business value, life cycle, and rhythm. Allocating and reallocating budget to these elements based on expected and measured business value, matching the impedance of their life cycles, continuously creating new value, and reacting fluidly to external changes is the order of the day.

Related to this cyclical nature of agile processes is the use of feedback loops to respond to change (something sorely lacking in waterfall processes). Architecture should be used as a feedback mechanism as well, by incorporating useful local changes and, if necessary, feeding them back up the chain to the strategic level. Only then will it close the feedback loop and fruitfully contribute to enterprise agility.

References

Ambler SW (2010) IBM agility@scale™: become as agile as you can be. IBM Global Services, Somers, NY

Brooks FP (1995) The mythical man-month: essays on software engineering, Anniversaryth edn. Addison-Wesley, Boston, MA

De Wit B, Meyer R (2010) Strategy: process, content, context: an international perspective. Cengage Learning, Andover

Deming WE (1986) Out of the crisis. MIT Press, Cambridge, MA

Greefhorst D, Proper E (2011) Architecture principles: the cornerstones of enterprise architecture. Springer, Berlin

Ladley J (2010) Making enterprise information management (EIM) work for business: a guide to understanding information as an asset. Morgan Kaufmann, Burlington, MA

Lankhorst MM (ed) (2012) Agile service development: combining adaptive methods and flexible solutions. Springer, Berlin

Martin J (1990a) Information engineering book 1: introduction. Prentice-Hall, Upper Saddle River, NJ

Martin J (1990b) Information engineering book 2: planning & analysis. Prentice-Hall, Upper Saddle River, NJ

Martin J (1995) The great transition: using the seven disciplines of enterprise engineering to align people, technology, and strategy. Amacom, New York, NY

Mosley M, Brackett MH, Earley S, Henderson D (2010) DAMA guide to the data management body of knowledge. Technics Publications, Bradley Beach, NJ

Osterwalder A, Pigneur Y (2010) Business model generation: a handbook for visionaries, game changers, and challengers. Wiley, Hoboken, NJ

Ross JW, Weill P, Robertson DC (2006) Enterprise architecture as strategy: creating a foundation for business execution. Harvard Business School Press, Boston, MA

SEI (2010) Capability maturity model integration for services (CMMI-SVC), version 1.3. Software Engineering Institute, Carnegie Mellon University, Pittsburgh, PA

Simon D, Fischbach K, Schoder D (2014) Enterprise architecture management and its role in corporate strategic management. Inform Syst E Bus Manag 12(1):5–42

Spewak SH, Hill SC (1993) Enterprise architecture planning: developing a blueprint for data, applications and technology. QED Information Sciences, Wellesley, MA

The Open Group (2009) The open group service integration maturity model (OSIMM). The Open Group, Reading

Towill D, Christopher M (2002) The supply chain strategy conundrum: to be lean or agile or to be lean and agile? Int J Logist 5(3):299–309

Treacy M, Wiersema F (1997) The discipline of market leaders. Perseus Publishing, Reading, MA

Van der Lans R (2012) Data virtualization for business intelligence systems: revolutionizing data integration for data warehouses. Morgan Kaufmann, Waltham, MA

Venkatraman N (1997) Beyond outsourcing: managing IT resources as a value center. MIT Sloan Manag Rev 38(3):51–64

von Halle B, Goldberg L (2009) The decision model: a business logic framework linking business and technology. Auerbach Publications, Boca Raton, FL

Yin A, Figueiredo S, da Silva M (2011) Scrum maturity model. In: Proceedings of the 6th international conference on software engineering advances, Barcelona, Spain, 23–29 Oct 2011

Effectively Modeling Your Architecture

12

Gerben Wierda

Abstract

Enterprise architecture management is to a large extent about managing complexity; this holds for both the business and the IT architecture level. As a discipline, it has tended to focus on creating simplicity, such as embodied by principles, guidelines, and simplified models of what is or what is to be. This chapter is about the why and how of setting up a broader and deeper role of modeling in enterprise architecture management. In particular, it presents ways (specifically languages) to model the business architecture in its current state at a reasonable level of detail. It also discusses the role of modeling in future state planning.

12.1 Introduction: Managing Complexity in Enterprise Architecture Management

Though enterprise architecture management as a discipline has originally been established, in particular, to fight the intractable complexity of the information technology (IT) used by the business, the reason for any enterprise is its business goal and thus its business processes, and not the IT.

Enterprise architecture management has traditionally moved between a rather IT-oriented approach and a "start with the business" approach, e.g., the "business-IT-alignment" approach. In the extreme application of the first approach, the business is often ignored in practice. In the extreme application of the second approach, a (flawed) "waterfall" mechanism ensues, which generally has a limited effect on the problem that was to be solved: the intractable complexity of IT used by the business.

G. Wierda (✉)
APG, Heerlen, The Netherlands
e-mail: gerben.wierda@rna.nl

© Springer International Publishing Switzerland 2015
D. Simon, C. Schmidt (eds.), *Business Architecture Management*, Management for Professionals, DOI 10.1007/978-3-319-14571-6_12

Both approaches—the "IT-centric" and the "business-first" approach—are attempts to find a simplified starting point to manage the complexity of all the relations between IT and IT, business and IT, and business and business. The business-first approach, for instance, often at the start tries to establish a clear division of the business into business functions, so that these can be used to divide the landscape into—from the enterprise architecture perspective—manageable semi-isolated parts.

The problems with these approaches—starting in a specific "layer" (e.g., business, applications, infrastructure) leads to problem addressing the other layers—has led to another type of simplification: create a basic set of guidelines, often separately for each layer. This is the "principles approach." The Open Group Architecture Framework (TOGAF), for instance, starts with principles: clear and simple guidelines for design decisions that are taken later. TOGAF gives a series of examples (cf. The Open Group 2011), as exemplified in Table 12.1.

This sounds fine from a business perspective and it also is a truism: if there is no business case for a change, do not change. Now, given that changes in the IT landscape come by definition with continuity risks, as errors are all too human in these complex endeavors, business is generally not too keen on changes in the IT landscape such as infrastructure life cycle events,[1] such events being a detail that also escapes the attention of the abstraction-oriented enterprise architects. The

Table 12.1 Exemplary principle [adopted from The Open Group (2011)]

Principle	Requirements-based change
Statement	Only in response to business needs are changes to applications and technology made
Rationale	This principle will foster an atmosphere where the information environment changes in response to the needs of the business, rather than having the business change in response to IT changes. This is to ensure that the purpose of the information support—the transaction of business—is the basis for any proposed change. Unintended effects on business due to IT changes will be minimized. A change in technology may provide an opportunity to improve the business process and, hence, change business needs
Implications	Changes in implementation will follow full examination of the proposed changes using the enterprise architecture
	We don't fund a technical improvement or system development unless a documented business need exists
	Change management processes conforming to this principle will be developed and implemented
	This principle may bump up against the responsive change principle. We must ensure the requirements documentation process does not hinder responsive change to meet legitimate business needs. The purpose of this principle is to keep us focused on business, not technology needs—responsive change is also a business need

---

[1] Life cycle events are changes in the architecture that are driven by the evolution of used components. Good examples are operating systems that go out of maintenance, or updates of any type of software.

business may understand keeping up to date with security patches to operating system and updates to virus scanners, as this can be directly related to business demands with respect to security and continuity, but why update a SAN[2]-driver on a server (a server that uses the SAN, not one that provides it) if the old one works? The old adagium says: "If it ain't broken, don't fix it." Changes always carry risks and these risks are not welcome, especially when that change is happening in a period in which the business performs critical processes, like year-end reporting. So, all too easily, a business will ask for "freezes" in the IT landscape because of its continuity (business) need. Continuously, however, parts of the landscape change. That SAN environment at some point needs to be upgraded and at that time there is a clear business need. And then, unexpectedly, a while later, the business-critical SAN-using server fails, because the old driver and the new SAN turn out to have some hidden incompatibility. The SAN provider of course never tested its system with all the older driver versions of all operating systems. The data is corrupted and the IT department is blamed for the lack of continuity, while everybody forgets that it was the nasty little detail of the business demanding the freeze because of its own business needs that was the root cause of the problem. As the proverb says: "People trip over molehills, not over mountains."

Most existing approaches of enterprise architecture management have in common that they start out with trying to find a position where the world is clear and simple, so it can be managed from there. The example of the lowly SAN-driver (a small detail in the overall landscape, if there ever was one) is to show that principles and other simplification instruments may sound fine (especially when they are truisms), but that does not turn them into sufficiently reliable approaches to design/change decisions. And that is true for all the simplifications enterprise architects use to make their work as enterprise architects manageable and easier to communicate.

The bottom line in enterprise architecture is that there are a multitude of complex relations, both within the layers we recognize, but also between those layers. Looking at any layer in isolation carries large risks and so does ignoring details. Enterprise architecture is a holistic type of subject with a rather unlimited amount of complexity. There are approaches such as SIP (cf. Sessions 2008) that promise ways to minimize your architectural complexity by partitioning your business and IT. These may help a bit in fighting the "accidental" complexity of your architecture; they will, however, have no effect on its "fundamental" complexity. Such "object-oriented" approaches also generally tend to ignore the limits of the physical world: a nice layered architecture approach, with services and messaging between "functional partitions," or an architecture developed for flexibility, tends to suffer from performance issues and the limitations of the physical world. That is another part of the complexity that is often ignored in enterprise architecture management approaches: it is often assumed that everything is possible, technically, and that the

---

[2] SAN stands for "Storage Area Network"—a technology for offering network-based storage to systems.

world is not physical but logical. But when the whole architecturally beautiful setup leads to the risk department getting its numbers long after they are needed, pragmatic fixes (read: breaches of the ideal architectural picture) will be implemented. Business comes first, after all.

In other words: approaches to enterprise architecture management that try to establish a simplified model of reality to work from, be it functional divisions, principles, or other approaches, tend to operate in a world that lacks so much relevant detail that its decisions are brittle and of limited effect on the actual problem. Practicing enterprise architecture management, being a method to manage complexity, should not be based on ignoring that complexity, but on confronting it. This means three things:

1. If enterprise architecture management is to be successful, it has to be a collaborative effort in the company. The main reason for this is that nobody, not even an enterprise architecture department, has enough knowledge about relevant details to go at it alone. Setting up good enterprise architecture processes and organizing this collaborative use of the fragmented knowledge on all aspects of the enterprise is a key for success.
2. Enterprise architecture management needs a mechanism to assess the need for details. A good candidate is using the risk aspect. For example, instead of being based on ignoring details, abstraction in enterprise architecture must be based on "consciously leaving out irrelevant details." which assumes actually analyzing the potential effect of ignoring details before they are left out of the analysis.
3. Knowing your "current state architecture" (CSA) in enough detail is essential to improve the change-design-and-assessment process. The business architecture is an important aspect of that.[3]

12.2 Current State: Modeling Your Business

12.2.1 Why Model Your Business?

Businesses, especially complex ones, have a need to document themselves. Partly, this is for their own use: setting up standardized, reproducible behavior is essential for many an organization's success. There are, however, more reasons to document your business. Some of these are:

- Regulators demanding well-documented and auditable business processes and IT support. Note, this is the same one as the one mentioned above, just from another stakeholder.

---

[3] For more complete architectures, often the term "landscape" is a good replacement for the term "architecture" to make people aware that it is not about the guidelines but about the (to be created) reality.

- Less work finding out your start position at the beginning of a change initiative
- Identifying weak spots in your landscape and other uses for portfolio management

Such demands generally lead to initiatives to document the landscape. For primary business processes, many (but certainly not all) organizations have this as an established practice and they will have "business process manuals" that describe the processes that the business follows (though often not always at a reasonable quality). For IT, this is also an established practice, though certainly not always of a high quality either. Most larger organizations will have a "Configuration Management Database" (CMDB[4]) that is above all directed to IT infrastructure. Often, companies will have an IT service management system (e.g., to log incidents and calls) which implicitly also has an administration of available systems, sometimes roles (such a system owner), sometimes processes, the latter seldom coupled to the actual process documentation. Various business functions (service management, business continuity management, security, database management, operational risk management, etc.) generally keep their own administration, sometimes in dedicated systems, sometimes just in drawings, spreadsheets, and documents. Not surprisingly, these various administrations do not form a consistent whole. There might be simple differences, like an application named differently in different administrations and documentations, up to complete mismatches between the overlap of functions. The business continuity administration might be based on completely different process descriptions than those in the official business process manuals, for instance.

An essential property of these (fragmented) administrations is that they are very difficult to maintain. Look below the surface, and even those business process manuals will often have internal and external inconsistencies. The attempt to model some landscapes in drawings leads to impressive looking large posters on the wall, that, even if they are correct, are out of date within a few months.

There is only a single solution for this mess: modeling. A model is structured (as opposed to unstructured) information that allows automated coupling between models as well as automated analysis. There are many modeling environments for both domain-specific models (such as process models) and (integrated) enterprise architecture models, and there are a lot of tools available. Many of these are based on a proprietary modeling language. For the modeling to be robust under tool change (and given the fact that these models should exist for a long time), and for other reasons, using standard modeling languages is generally preferred. For business process modeling, the leading standard is *BPMN*® (OMG 2011), the "Business Process Model and Notation" (or, depending on where you read in the documentation, "Business Process Modeling Notation"), a standard managed by the Object

---

[4] A CMDB is a system to document the IT that is being maintained (at an instance level). It is often limited to hardware items such as computers, keyboards, monitors, and a rough sketch of software installs.

Management Group. For enterprise architecture modeling, the leading standard is *ArchiMate*® (The Open Group 2013), managed by The Open Group. Both standards overlap in several ways, e.g., processes are concepts that are modeled in both.

12.2.2 A Single Logical Model

Before describing the key parts of a current state modeling setup, we should clarify an important aspect of business modeling: it is unavoidable that there are multiple models of your organization in use in your organization. They are seldom recognized as models, but in practice they are. Examples, in line with the previously mentioned documentation efforts, are:

- A CMDB will effectively contain a "model" of your infrastructure, possibly with links to applications, business actors and business roles such as owners, etc.
- An operational risk management tool will have a "model" of your processes, roles and actors, maybe business functions.
- The IT service management ("help desk") tool will have a "model" of applications, maybe processes, owners, platforms.
- The business continuity management administration will have a "model" of processes, applications, maybe data.
- The security function will have a "model" of applications, maybe processes.
- The business will have a "model" of its processes (flow charts with documentation), applications used, roles, actors, data, etc.
- Information management will have a "model" of all applications, platforms, maybe business processes or business functions, etc.
- "Run" managers (those responsible for keeping IT running in day-to-day operations) may have their own "model" of what they are managing, e.g., an overview of databases, servers, software.
- Management may keep "balanced score cards," and strategists may work with business model canvases, both based on a structuring of the organization.
- HR maintains the "management structure" of the organization, generally in HR systems.

All these models describe a single reality (your business) from a particular point of view. The problem is that in most organizations, these models are separate and they may not tell the same story and sometimes they even contradict each other.

A good modeling approach therefore requires setting up the different physical models in such a way that:

- They form a single logical model.
- That single logical model can be maintained with limited effort.

12.2.3 Business Process Models: BPMN

Though many organizations still use unstructured approaches to modeling their business (word processing documents, including graphical representations such as flow charts), a standard process modeling grammar has established itself over the last decennium: BPMN, an open standard from the Object Management Group (OMG). BPMN looks like flow-charting (and as such is easily accepted by the business), but is based on a structured definition of the grammar (itself written in UML—the Universal Modeling Language, also from the OMG). It is also a grammar for which there is ample tool support, including free/open source solutions.

BPMN is not perfect. Even Bruce Silver—its leading teacher and author of a very good introduction to its use (Silver 2011)—admits that the grammar has its troublesome aspects.[5] These stem mainly from the fact that the language has been designed above all to model "executable" processes, that is, processes that can be directly executed by a computer. It is, in other words, a language that shows its technical heritage and that it was never initially intended as a documentation language for human processes to be understood by humans. Examples of peculiar aspects of BPMN are for instance the absence of a graphical representation of its core concept "Process," the ambiguity of a core element like "Pool/Participant," and the "bolted-on" nature of the (for humans important) "Lane" concept.

Though that sounds like a list of reasons not to use BPMN, this is not what is intended. BPMN is eminently usable for the purpose of structurally documenting your processes. What a list like the one above illustrates is that perfection is not necessary for usability.

BPMN is almost completely focused on modeling the behavior of an enterprise. It has structures for activities of all kinds, and has trigger- and flow-relations that can be used to create complex behavioral descriptions.

12.2.4 Enterprise Architecture Models: ArchiMate

Roughly of the same age as BPMN is ArchiMate, but it has grown in popularity beyond its initial following after its adoption by The Open Group as its standard for enterprise architecture modeling in 2009. ArchiMate is now a de facto "open standard" enterprise architecture modeling language, though it is not yet as wide-spread as BPMN.

ArchiMate was developed by a university-business collaboration in the Netherlands in the early 2000s. ArchiMate is fundamentally different from BPMN in a number of aspects, the main one being that it was not designed from a formal perspective but from a pragmatic perspective: the collaborators designed a language that fit their use of modeling. As such it is not based on a formal definition (as BPMN is), but on practical considerations. Where BPMN is more "early Wittgenstein"

---

[5] See Business Process Watch (2014) for several blog posts that address these issues.

(Wittgenstein 1984), ArchiMate is more "late Wittgenstein" (Wittgenstein 1958), and those who are familiar with the philosopher's work will understand that, while there is a common theme, the difference is rather fundamental.

ArchiMate is based on splitting the architecture in the usual enterprise architecture layers: business and information architecture, application and data architecture, and infrastructure architecture. Its internal structure in each layer is based on dividing into "active structure," that performs "behavior" which affects "passive structure," as in simple natural language like subject-verb-object patterns. Another special aspect is that relations between different elements in a model that are not directly connected (e.g., a business process and a server) may be derived from all the intermediate relations between the elements involved, thus offering standardized ways to summarize detailed models into simplified ones.[6]

12.2.5 Combining BPMN and ArchiMate to Create Models of Your Business

Table 12.2 summarizes the differences between BPMN and ArchiMate. These differences make the obvious idea of modeling process details in BPMN and the overall enterprise architecture in ArchiMate not straightforward.

Table 12.2 Comparison of ArchiMate and BPMN

ArchiMate	BPMN
Model the enterprise	Model (executable) processes
Split in layers: business, application, and infrastructure architecture	Not split in layers
Pragmatic metamodel	Formal metamodel
Fully graphical grammar	Graphical representations added to parts of the formal grammar
Strong on the structure, weak on the dynamics of the enterprise (i.e., triggers, flows)	Strong on the dynamics of processes, weak on the structure of the enterprise
Split in active structure, behavior (of active structure), and passive structure	Mostly behavior
Derived relations	No derived relations
Model/view separation common in tooling	Model/view separation not common in tooling

---

[6]This mechanism has various restrictions. For example, there are non-derivable relations that are clearly valid and derived relations that may not be valid. See Wierda (2014) for more information and, in general, a possible introduction into the language.

12.2.6 Patterns and Links

To call BPMN or ArchiMate a language is a bit of a misnomer, stemming from the
IT adoption of the word "language" for constructs like programming languages.
The elements that make up BPMN and ArchiMate are more elements of a *grammar*
than a *language*. What is said in the language depends not just on the grammar, but
what the elements are given as "name" (i.e., label). To make this clear with an
example, it is easy in ArchiMate to model that the Large Hadron Collider is being
managed using an Excel spreadsheet. Such a model is correct ArchiMate (correct
grammar), but the meaning is nonsense.

What ArchiMate and BPMN have in common with real languages is that there
are many ways to say the same thing. Not just in level of detail, but there is also a
certain freedom of choice on how to use the grammar and what elements to include.
Different modelers of a process or a piece of enterprise architecture will come up
with correct, but different models. This effect is stronger in ArchiMate than in
BPMN (as ArchiMate slightly more resembles the non-logical pragmatic nature of
ordinary language), but both grammars have this aspect.

The advantages of structured documentation of your business come from the
possibilities of manageable coupling of those different "models of reality" and
manageable maintenance of and reliable analysis based on those models. All these
advantages melt away when there is a total freedom of choice with respect to the
patterns[7] used. Because the languages themselves are limited in the structure they
force upon the modeler, using them effectively requires the disciplined use of fixed
patterns. Setting up and strictly following these patterns is a "conditio sine qua non"
for the effective and successful use of structured modeling of your business.

If these patterns are designed well and followed strictly, it enables the linking of
models in various grammars, creating that single logical model of your enterprise.
An example of a linkage between BPMN and ArchiMate models can be found in
Wierda (2014).

12.3 Future State and Change: Planning Your Changes

12.3.1 From Broad Strokes to Fine Detail: The Architecture of a Change

From Jan Hoogervorst comes the term "Columbus Management":

---

[7] As there are many ways to model each aspect (from business processes/functions to database
servers) each way can be considered a pattern (or a style). Using patterns means that one will
model the same aspect always exactly in the same structure, similar to using a very limited set of
grammatical constructs when writing text.

When we left, we did not know where we were going. When we arrived, we did not know where we were. And everything was paid for with other people's money.[8]

Interestingly enough, if you relate this to people, while most will understand that this means that starting a project without enough design is asking for trouble, some will argue that Columbus was successful. In reality, of course, Columbus was an exception. Most projects that were based on flawed or missing plans, then and now, failed (in Columbus' time often with deadly results). Going forward with a project, and hoping it will "strike lucky" like Columbus, does not seem like a rational strategy. That is why the idea of a "project architecture" to establish some guidance that makes the project more predictable is generally accepted.

Changes to our existing landscapes, certainly the more substantial ones, are generally the result of projects. These days, when working "under architecture," projects are generally required to create some sort of *"project start architecture"* (PSA). This deliverable is generally intended to guide the design work of the project.

The question of course is: what constitutes a good project architecture? Can we go ahead with allocating large sums of time, money, and people when we have only a vague idea what the outcome will be? Strangely enough, this is still what often happens. Projects often start with a dreamed up budget and plan, or they start in a phased approach that in the end eats up a multiple of the resources originally planned. The reason is that businesses are generally convinced that it is impossible to design everything in advance. They are right, of course, as the ultimate complexity overwhelms such an attempt.

The conviction that having all details in advance is impossible generally leads to an approach where there are no details in advance. Such an approach generally fails, as it are those details that derail the projects in the first place. What is needed, therefore, is a smarter approach to those details, and here modeling can help.

Without going into much detail: instead of trying to establish a well-defined level of detail to adhere to, it is much better to have a dynamic approach to details. It is clear that one has to end with all the details in place, at which time these details become part of your current state landscape. But the question which level of detail is appropriate for the start of your project requires a bit more intelligence.

From the field of "industrial safety" comes an approach that can be adapted to enterprise architecture management. In that field, risk is not seen as something to be avoided, as there is no such thing as "not taking risks." The key to safety is not "avoiding risks," but "consciously taking acceptable risks." This insight can be translated to enterprise architecture management's handling of—potentially risky—details. In our practice, we have adopted the definition (in enterprise architecture management): "Abstraction is consciously leaving out irrelevant details."

---

[8] Jan Hoogervorst is former Vice President Corporate Information Strategy of KLM Royal Dutch Airlines. He used this in a speech once, and told the author in private communication that he did not invent the term, but had also picked it up from someone else somewhere. The source is unknown.

It is clear that at the start of a project, not all details of the target state can be known. But leaving them out requires an assessment of the risk of leaving them out. There are two kinds of risk to contemplate: risk for the project's success (scope, cost, time) and risk for the ensuing landscape of the organization.

This translates to modeling as follows. A project start architecture should contain a model of what is to be delivered by the project: the target state. Details may be left out if it is estimated that leaving them out does not carry too much risk for neither the project nor the overall landscape. During the project, more and more details will be added until at the end the model is complete at the level of detail that is required for the current state architecture.

Next to modeling the current state architecture and target states for projects, planning of the overall future state can also be supported by modeling, though generally in a less detailed manner.

12.3.2 Future State: Multiple Models of a Single Reality and the BITMAP

A good *"future state architecture"* is more than just a sketch of the future and a roadmap to get there. This is not the place to delve into it deeply, but part of it can be supported by modeling.

And while current state models and project end state models need to be sufficiently detailed, future state models (such as domain target states, or plateaus[9]) may be more abstract and less detailed. Here too, the rule about details can help to decide on the required level of details.

When thinking about the future of the organization, architects need some sort of map of that organization. Enterprise architects often use a pattern where they divide the business into "business functions" and model part of their design patterns on the basis of such divisions. Now, the concepts of enterprise architecture—and "business function" is not an exception—are not universally defined. In some approaches, the function is an abstraction that looks like an "acting element" as in "the payments function makes sure that all payments are executed before they are late." In other approaches, such as in ArchiMate, the business function is behavior *of* an "acting element," so the active element may be "payments department" and its behavior the "paying invoices" business function. Such different uses of words lead to a lot of confusion in the enterprise architecture world. In this chapter, we will follow ArchiMate's definitions of these concepts.

---

[9] A plateau is a situation in the development of your landscape that will be in production. Projects deliver results, and when these results are used, the actual landscape changes. As there are many changes and many projects, or even phases of delivery in projects, working with the concept of a plateau gives you the possibility to view the interrelations between various change initiatives to make sure beforehand that the landscape in production will be acceptable and catch conflicts between change initiatives before they can become a problem.

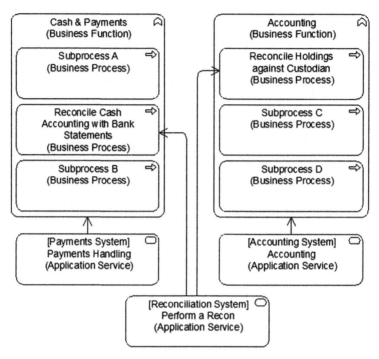

Fig. 12.1 The "Cash & Payments" business function and the "Accounting" business function with the applications they use (Wierda 2012)

Now, suppose we want to make a functional division of our company. As an example, suppose we have two aspects: handling our holdings (stock, bonds, etc.), and handling our cash. Both types of activities require a different set of skills, work with different external parties, use (partly) different administrations, etc. An example ArchiMate view can be seen in Fig. 12.1.

Here we see two ArchiMate business functions with some internal processes modeled. The arrows represent the ArchiMate "Used-By" relation, which tells us that the business uses a couple of systems (the "service" the application provides for the business). These services may be provided by one or more systems; in our labeling standard we label the application service generally with the name of the system that provides it, so in this example there is a 1:1 relationship between application and realized service.

Both functions need to reconcile their internal administration with the outside world. For "Cash & Payments" this means reconciling what is in the payments system with what is in the bank statements. For "Accounting" this means reconciling what is in the accounting system with the statements from the custodians (parties that keep assets for the actual owners, just like a bank keeps cash for its real owner).

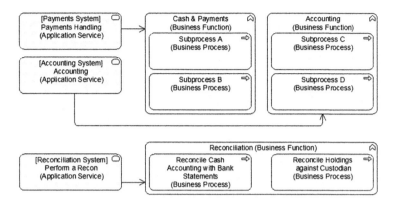

Fig. 12.2 Introducing the "Reconciliation" function (Wierda 2012)

Enterprise architects may end up in heated discussions about dividing the business into functions. This is because, from a different perspective, we may not have two functions, but three.

Figure 12.2 shows this different way of looking at the business. Enterprise (IT) architects are drawn to this way of looking, because they know that one of the problems they have to address is that the same kind of IT support may be implemented twice if you look purely at the business process. If you do not watch out, "Cash & Payments" sets up quite a different reconciliation system than "Accounting" and suddenly our landscape has two different systems for what is in effect the same functionality. Exactly this is something that working with enterprise architecture management is meant to prevent. In other words, simply dividing the business into functions and working from there towards the IT landscape may lead to suboptimal results from an enterprise (IT) architecture point of view. This example may be easily recognized, but when such divisions are coupled with design principles based on that division (e.g., "each function 'owns' its data" or "data communication between functions is message-based") it may quickly lead to unintended complexities or problems (e.g., performance of the eventual resulting setup).

ArchiMate's definition of a business function says it is a grouping of activities— a grouping that is based on aspects such as skills, resources, location, etc. The architect is in fact free to decide on which basis the division is to be made. But how should we solve the heated argument? The answer may be to "let go." If the choice of aspect leads to a different division, and both aspects make sense, then we can accept that there are multiple concurrent valid divisions. From a business perspective, a "Reconciliation" function may not make sense, but from an IT perspective it does, and such a perspective is also useful.

The idea is not to have an endless number of different functional landscapes; this would defeat the object of creating structure in these discussions in the first place. But there is nothing wrong with having more than one perspective. From a management perspective, one division may be needed; from a business-IT-

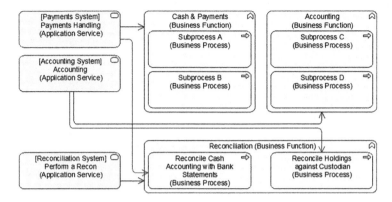

Fig. 12.3 Adding "Break Resolution" to the mix (Wierda 2012)

alignment perspective, another may be useful. The name we use for the one that is used for enterprise IT architecture (business-IT-alignment) planning is "BITMAP," which stands for "Business-IT Mapping."

The division in Fig. 12.2 above looks cleaner from the business-IT-alignment perspective: every function uses its own IT; a popular architectural principle is being followed. But our picture above hides details that show the opposite.

As Fig. 12.3 displays, if we add "Break Resolution"[10] as part of the reconciliation processes to the mix, the situation becomes more realistic and instead of a single reconciliation system being used by two business functions, the "Reconciliation" function now uses three systems (as shown by the additional "Used-By" arrows). It is still useful to have a BITMAP though, as it helps in keeping the IT landscape as simple as possible.

12.4 Introducing and Sustaining a "Modeling-Supported" Architecture Management Approach

Introducing a modeling-based approach in an organization is not easy. There are a couple of obvious requirements that need to be fulfilled:

- The appropriate skills (e.g., ArchiMate and BPMN modeling) need to be established in the organization.
- A serious initial investment needs to be made in setting up the current state models of (at least) the enterprise architecture and (more detailed) business processes.
- There must be an effective governance to keep the models up to date.

---

[10] Break Resolution is solving the found discrepancies between internal and external administrations, hence handling the exceptions that come out of the (automated) reconciliation process.

This is not all. To fulfill these requirements, other prerequisites are necessary. The most important is that the organization understands both the need and the feasibility of the approach. This is not easy, because many people in the enterprise architecture field do not believe the approach is possible. There is a widespread and deeply felt belief that doing this is either impossible (because of the overwhelming real complexity of organizations) or unnecessary (because other approaches like setting up design principles and abstract future state landscapes are expected to be sufficiently effective). Not having the shared belief makes the approach very difficult (if not impossible) to realize. It will probably take quite some time before using models more extensively in enterprise architecture management has established itself.

The fact that you cannot model everything in enterprise architecture has led to a practice where almost nothing is really modeled. But a smarter, risk-based approach to modeling may change that in the coming years.

References

Business Process Watch (2014) Blog. http://brsilver.com/blog/
OMG (2011) Business process model and notation (BPMN) v2.0 specification. Object Management Group, Needham, MA
Sessions R (2008) Simple architectures for complex enterprises. Microsoft Press, Redmond, WA
Silver B (2011) BPMN method & style, 2nd edn. Cody-Cassidy Press, Aptos, CA
The Open Group (2011) TOGAF® version 9.1. Van Haren Publishing, Zaltbommel
The Open Group (2013) ArchiMate® 2.1 specification. Van Haren Publishing, Zaltbommel
Wierda G (2012) Mastering ArchiMate, Ist edn. R&A, Heerlen
Wierda G (2014) Mastering ArchiMate, IInd edn. R&A, Heerlen
Wittgenstein L (1958) Philosophical investigations. Blackwell, Oxford
Wittgenstein L (1984) Tractatus Logico-Philosophicus. Suhrkamp, Frankfurt

Business Architecture Quantified: How to Measure Business Complexity

13

Christian Schmidt

Abstract

Complexity of both business and IT is one of the most frequently discussed topics in strategic management and enterprise architecture today. For many business leaders, complexity is of central concern due to its assumed impacts on operating costs, organizational agility, and operational risks. In fact, complexity growth may be considered one of the major drivers for misalignment. As a consequence, organizations are increasingly forced to manage the complexity of their business and IT actively. However, existing qualitative methods fall short of supporting this on a larger scale. Quantitative measures may be considered a promising means to assess and manage the complexity of business and IT architectures in a systematic and universal way. This chapter presents a generic framework for conceptualizing and measuring enterprise architecture complexity and applies it to the domain of business architecture. Using this book's business architecture framework as a reference, it is shown how business complexity can be operationalized and quantified using well-defined and practice-proven measures.

13.1 Why Complexity Matters

Complexity is blamed for many things. Many business leaders seem to think of it as a general source of evil. Complexity is held responsible for rising coordination efforts and operating costs. Complexity is said to drive up change efforts, thereby constraining agility and swelling the time-to-market. And complexity is perceived a major source of failures, poor quality, and increasing operational risks. But there is also another side to the story. Against the backdrop of growing market dynamics,

C. Schmidt (✉)
Scape Consulting GmbH, Frankfurt, Germany
e-mail: christian.schmidt@scape-consulting.de

© Springer International Publishing Switzerland 2015   243
D. Simon, C. Schmidt (eds.), *Business Architecture Management*, Management for Professionals, DOI 10.1007/978-3-319-14571-6_13

competition, and legal regulation, organizations are facing a permanent need to develop new and innovative solutions. Often, this comes at the price of expanding business and information technology (IT) complexity only. US mutual insurer USAA, for example, has been reported to deliberately take up higher levels of complexity in order to create a high-quality customer experience (Mocker and Ross 2012). As it stands, complexity is a burden, but it may also be a necessity. This *Janus face* of complexity together with the lack of a commonly agreed definition is a major source of confusion, making complexity management a rather controversial and challenging subject. It is the purpose of this chapter to add some more clarity to the discussion and show how the concept can be applied to the domain of business architecture.

Generally speaking, complexity may be considered a quality of a system (or architecture) referring to the *quantity* and *variety* of system *elements* and the *relationships* between these (cf. Schütz et al. 2013; Schneberger and McLean 2003). Per se, complexity is neither a good nor a bad thing. But as a matter of fact, it has various implications for the development, change, and operation of the system. Therefore, complexity should be regulated to an appropriate level. But what exactly does that mean?

Fundamentally, each system/architecture needs to fulfill the requirements imposed to it by the environment.[1] Fulfilling these requirements will call for a certain *minimum level of complexity* that cannot be reduced without causing dysfunctional behaviour.[2] Any complexity exceeding this minimum level may in turn be considered *architectural waste*. Waste elements and relationships are problematic in the sense that they will increase operations, change, and maintenance efforts. In the following, architectural waste is also referred to as the *complexity surplus* of an architecture or parts thereof. According to this terminology, approaching the optimal level of complexity equates to minimizing the complexity surplus.[3] However, in order to identify the minimum complexity, the requirements must be known. This may be straightforward for a certain software application. But how does this concept relate to enterprise and business architecture?

In enterprise architecture management (EAM), architecture layers have emerged as a good practice to structure and decouple the main parts of the overall architecture. The ArchiMate standard, for instance, distinguishes between a business, application, and technology layer and uses the concepts of business, application, and technology services to decouple these (The Open Group 2013).

---

[1] In line with the classic dichotomy coined by Drucker (1974), an architecture that fulfills all environmental requirements may be called effective (it "does the right thing").

[2] Referring to the classic dichotomy again, an architecture with minimal complexity may be called efficient (it "does the things right", i.e., with minimal effort) (Drucker 1974).

[3] It should be noted though that the strategic impact of the complexity surplus will be contingent on the role of depending variables like agility and efficiency within the organization. For example, a quality leader operating in a stable market environment may have less incentives to control the complexity surplus than a cost leader in a rapidly developing marketplace.

Following this conception, the requirements of a given layer are defined by the layer above. The application architecture, for example, needs to fulfill the requirements of the business architecture by providing appropriate application services. Taking a closer look into the business architecture as conceptualized in Chap. 1, the business execution layer needs to satisfy the requirements imposed by the business model, and in turn, the business motivation. Therefore, to determine the complexity surplus of a given architecture layer or domain, the complexity requirements of the overarching layer need to be evaluated. Successful complexity management will hence be characterized by minimizing the complexity of each architecture layer taking into account the layers above. This may be considered a major strategy to achieve architectural consistency and alignment.[4] As each architecture layer inherits complexity requirements from the layer above, the management of complexity will be most effective if layers are addressed in a top-down order.

However, it should be noted that requirements (and thus the optimal level of complexity) may vary across vertical domains or capabilities (Schmidt 2013). For differentiating front-end domains, for instance, a higher level of complexity may be appropriate than for non-differentiating back-end domains. Therefore, effective complexity management is not simply about reducing complexity throughout the landscape but rather about creating the right level of complexity in the right place, that is, finding the right positioning in the *complexity continuum* as symbolized in Fig. 13.1.

What makes an active management of business and IT complexity even more important is the underlying dynamics known as the *law of rising complexity* (Schmidt and Buxmann 2011; Lehmann 1997; see Fig. 13.2). In order to survive, organizations constantly need to adapt to changing environmental conditions.

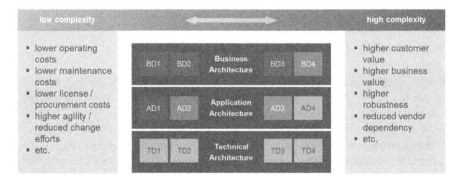

Fig. 13.1 The complexity continuum

---

[4] From an architectural perspective, alignment may be defined as the degree of consistency between the components of an architecture given by their properties and collocation. An architecture is well aligned if it is both effective (fulfills all requirements imposed by the environment) and efficient (does not contain any waste components or relationships).

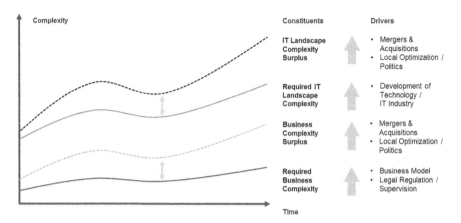

Fig. 13.2 The law of rising complexity (see also Rutz 2012)

In practice, this generally follows an evolutionary process mediated by internal and external stakeholders. This evolutionary process tends to favor local and short-term solutions, mirroring the need for swift implementation and the balancing of stakeholder power (Schmidt and Buxmann 2011). The managers of certain business lines, for example, often strive to create local solutions that they can control and shield from the rest of the organization. Also, mergers and acquisitions usually add to business and IT complexity. If not managed actively, complexity will hence rise continuously. Given the negative implications outlined above, an effective management of business and IT complexity may be considered a strategic capability that may even be turned into a source of sustained competitive advantage.

13.2 The Need for Quantitative Models

Given the importance of complexity in both business and IT architecture, methods are needed to actively manage and control the complexity within the various architectural domains. Until recently, complexity decisions have been mostly based on *qualitative reasoning*. Employing architectural repositories, enterprise architects usually engage in capturing and maintaining a structured model of the architecture (including components and their interrelationships). Traditionally, this data is primarily used for qualitative analyses. For example, graphical views and matrices may be created to demonstrate that certain capabilities have multiple (redundant) implementations or that key strategies are poorly supported by IT applications.

While this approach is working fine at the level of individual applications or even small landscapes, it has its limitations when it comes to very large business or IT landscapes as commonplace in today's multinational corporations. Practically, such architectures cannot be visualized graphically anymore. Also, the efforts required for a qualitative analysis may easily rise beyond the level feasible. Even more importantly, there are no proven mechanisms to aggregate the results of such qualitative analyses to a higher abstraction level (e.g., from domain to enterprise scale) and thus create a condensed high-level view.

To overcome these drawbacks, qualitative methods may be complemented by *quantitative methods* using dedicated *complexity measures*. Such measures could be calculated and aggregated across whole landscapes and integrated into a high-level reporting on the fundamental properties of an architecture.[5] The next section presents a generic framework that can be used to derive complexity measures in a systematic way. This is then applied to the domain of business architecture.

13.3   A Generic Framework for Measuring Complexity

Until today, no specific methods have been proposed to quantify the complexity of business architectures. However, measuring the complexity of enterprise architectures in general and IT architecture in particular has been approached by researchers more recently (see Mocker 2009; Widjaja et al. 2012; Schütz et al. 2013; Schmidt et al. 2013; Lagerström et al. 2013; Schneider et al. 2014a, b). In particular, a generic framework for conceptualizing and measuring enterprise architecture complexity has been proposed by Schütz et al. (2013) and further operationalized by Schmidt et al. (2013). In the following, the approach is presented and then extended to meet the requirements of a holistic complexity analysis.

13.3.1 The Heterogeneity-Based Complexity Model

According to the approach proposed by Schütz et al. (2013), the (structural) complexity of a system is defined along four dimensions: the *number* (or *quantity*) and *heterogeneity* (or *variety*) of system *elements* and *relations*. This approach is generic in the sense that it can be applied to any type of system and architecture including technical architecture, application architecture, and business architecture (cf. Fig. 13.3).

Following this approach, the problem of quantifying complexity is reduced to quantifying *heterogeneity*. In this context, heterogeneity (also referred to as *variety* or *concentration*) is defined as the diversity of elements or relationships of a system with respect to certain *characteristics* (attribute values). Heterogeneity can be captured as a statistical property and be described by means of empirical frequency distributions. For example, the distribution of database management systems within an IT landscape may be captured as shown in Fig. 13.4.

Based on such frequency distributions, statistical concentration measures may be applied (Widjaja et al. 2012). In particular, the *entropy measure* as introduced by

---

[5] In contrast to prevalent methods in the EAM field, this could be a key constituent of what may be called "*Quantitative EAM.*"

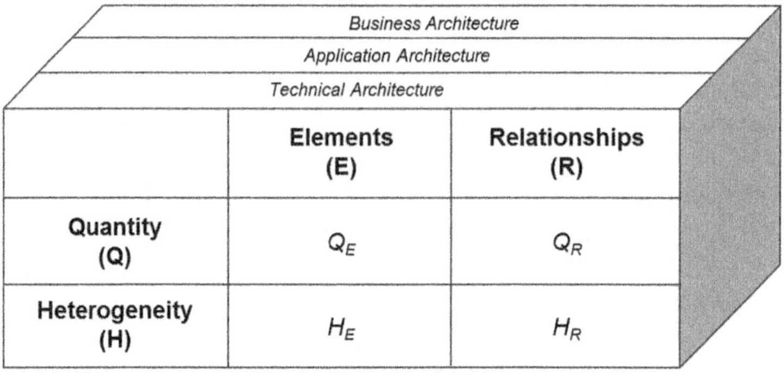

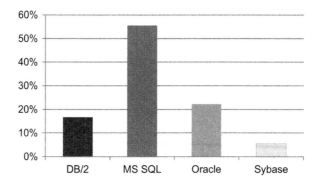

Fig. 13.3 Complexity dimensions (Schmidt 2013; see also Schütz et al. 2013)

Fig. 13.4 Frequency distribution of database management systems by type

Shannon (1948) has been shown to be well suited to measure heterogeneity within enterprise architectures (Schütz et al. 2013). Formally, the entropy measure is defined as

$$EM = \sum_{i=1}^{n} f_i \ln\left(\frac{1}{f_i}\right)$$

with f_i denoting the relative frequency of the respective attribute values (characteristics). As shown in Fig. 13.5, the entropy measure increases with the number of different characteristics and with approaching an equal distribution. In contrast to similar measures, it is also sensitive with respect to characteristics with small shares. Yet, proportional changes of absolute frequencies have no impact on the measure.

The entropy measure takes its minimal value if all elements share a single characteristic. The maximum value is reached at equal distribution to different

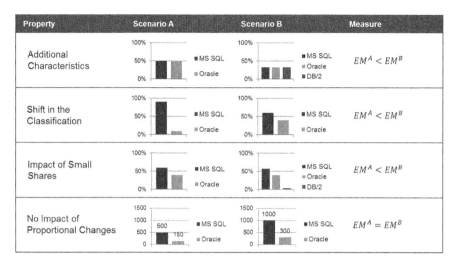

Fig. 13.5 Properties of the entropy measure (cf. Schütz et al. 2013)

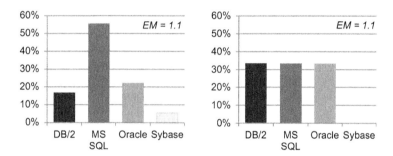

Fig. 13.6 Original distribution and equivalent equal distribution $\left(EM^* = exp(1.1) = 3\right)$

characteristics. Interpretation of the entropy measure is facilitated by the so-called *numbers equivalent entropy measure* $EM^* = exp(EM)$, which denotes the equivalent number of characteristics at equal distribution (see Fig. 13.6).

As shown in Schmidt et al. (2013), the generic heterogeneity-based approach may be used flexibly with any particular architecture framework and metamodel. In doing so, it may not only be applied to architecture elements but also to direct and indirect relationships between these (see Fig. 13.7). For example, the distribution of application systems along the underlying technology platforms or the concentration of business functions on applications may be analyzed (see Schmidt et al. 2013).

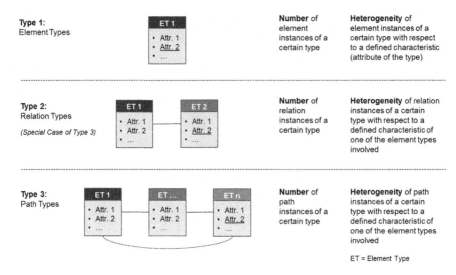

Fig. 13.7 Complexity aspects in metamodels (Schmidt 2013)

13.3.2 Extending the Basic Approach

While the existing heterogeneity-based approach has proven to be very versatile and powerful, it also has revealed some limitations (Schmidt 2013). In particular, it does not fully capture the internal *structure* of an architecture. The interfaces within an application landscape, for instance, may be analyzed for a concentration on applications or interface technologies. However, this does not account for the degree of *modularity* within the landscape. Yet, any experienced architect will agree that a modular application landscape divided into a set of loosely coupled application domains with interfaces predominantly within domains and only few interfaces crossing the domain boundaries will be much easier to manage than a landscape with interfaces placed at random. This is mainly due to a limitation in *change propagation* as the effects of changes can be contained within the respective domains. It may hence be argued that a complexity analysis should also address an evaluation of the architecture's modularity.

As shown by Aier and Schönherr (2007) and Simon and Fischbach (2013), architectural modularity may be assessed using the measure introduced by Newman (2006). For this purpose, the architecture (or parts hereof) needs to be transformed into a plain network consisting of nodes (e.g., applications) and edges (e.g., application interfaces). Modularity can then be calculated as the number of edges that fall into a set of given groups (modules, clusters) minus the expected number in an equivalent network with random edges (Newman 2006). It takes a value in the range between -0.5 and 1 with positive values indicating a *concentration* of edges within modules above the level expected for a random distribution.[6] Modularity can be determined with respect to a predefined clustering structure (e.g., an existing domain model). Alternatively, it may be looked for a previously unknown (inherent) clustering structure using dedicated search algorithms (see Newman 2006).

Another shortcoming of the basic approach is its focus on absolute figures. As shown in Sect. 13.1, the complexity of certain architectural domains or layers cannot be assessed in isolation. It rather needs to be put into relation with the requirements of superimposed domains. Therefore, *relative measures* capturing the quantity or variety of elements and relationships in relation to each other may be more appropriate. For example, the number of applications (from the application architecture) may be related to the number of business functions (in the business architecture). Similarly, the variety of platform technology may be put into relation with the variety of application systems.

Integrating these extensions with the basic approach results in an extended set of generic complexity measures that can be applied to arbitrary domains and at varying levels of detail. This is summarized in the *framework of complexity measures* depicted in Table 13.1. In the next section, the framework is applied to the domain of business architecture.

13.4 Measures for Business Architecture Complexity

Few authors have so far addressed the topic of business architecture complexity (e.g., Gottfredson and Aspinall 2005; Mocker and Ross 2013). Up to now, no systematic approach has been proposed to measure business complexity in its various aspects. Therefore, in this section, the generic framework presented in Sect.13.3 is applied to the *business architecture framework* introduced in Chap. 1. Starting with the business execution layer and progressing to business model and business motivation, the main concepts of business architecture are examined from a complexity perspective using the four complexity dimensions as a reference. Based on this, specific business complexity measures are proposed. This is illustrated by means of some examples.

13.4.1 Business Execution

According to Chap. 1, the business execution layer describes the business capabilities required by an organization and the way they are implemented in terms of processes, organization units, information objects, and so on. Obviously, complexity plays an important role in this area. Large organizations, for example,

---

[6] Referring to the four complexity dimensions of the basic approach as shown in Fig. 13.3, modularity may hence be interpreted as a special instance of relation variety (see Table 13.1).

Table 13.1 Framework of generic complexity measures

		Elements (E)	Relationships (R)
Quantity (Q)	Absolute	N_E: number of element instances (e.g., number of applications)	N_R: number of relation instances (e.g., number of business function implementations)
	Relative	$\frac{N_{E1}}{N_{E2}}$: number of element instances relative to each other (e.g., number of applications per number of business functions, irrespective of existing relationships)	$\frac{N_R}{N_E}$: number of relation instances relative to element instances (e.g., number of business function implementations per number of business functions)
Heterogeneity/ Variety/ Concentration (C)	Absolute	$EM_{E;A}$: entropy measure of element instances of type E by certain attribute A (e.g., concentration of applications by vendor)	$EM_{R;E;A}$: entropy measure of relation instances of type R (or path instances of type P) by certain attribute A of related element instances of type E (e.g., concentration of business function implementations by application names) $M_{R;E;A}$: modularity of relation instances of type R (or path instances of type P) with respect to attribute A of instances of type E (e.g., modularity of application interfaces along business domain names)
	Relative	$\frac{EM_{E1;A1}}{EM_{E2;A2}}$: entropy measure of element instances of type E_1 by attribute A_1 relative to entropy measure of element instances of type E_2 by attribute A_2 (e.g., concentration of technical platforms by vendors in relation to concentration of applications by vendors)	$\frac{M_{R1;E1;A1}}{M_{R2;E2;A2}}$: modularity of relation instances of type R_1 (or path instances of type P_1) with respect to attribute A_1 of instances of type E_1 relative to modularity of relation instances of type R_2 (or path instances of type P_2) with respect to attribute A_2 of instances of type E_2 (e.g., modularity of application interfaces in relation to modularity of business services)

often comprise hundreds of legal entities, processes, or sites, with major functional overlaps and redundancies. This type of complexity is well known in practice and various management methods like business process reengineering or lean management have been proposed do deal with it. But how can business execution complexity be formally described and measured?

Commencing with the *business capabilities*, a complexity assessment may start by looking at the *number* of (logical) capabilities in scope of the organization. Assuming that all capabilities are about equal in functional size, organizations with a larger number of capabilities may be considered more complex.[7] A fashion group, for instance, that maintains internal capabilities for the whole value chain from product design and marketing to manufacturing and sales, may be attributed a higher functional complexity than a competitor that is focusing on product design, marketing, and sales while relying on low-wage contractors for the manufacturing part.

In addition to that, the relationships between the business capabilities may be seen as important determinants of business execution complexity as well. In general, organizations with a higher *number* of *interdependencies* between capabilities (cf. Chap. 10) may be considered more complex than such with few relationships. As an example, a strongly integrated military forces organization comprising different highly interrelated capabilities like missile, missile-defense, and airborne surveillance may be attributed a higher functional complexity than a less integrated manufacturer of consumer goods.

Beyond that, complexity may be assessed along the *variety* or *concentration* of *dependencies* between capabilities. In particular, organizations with a higher degree of capability *reuse* (as expressed in a larger dependency concentration) may— ceteris paribus—be considered less complex than organizations with a lower degree of capability reuse. Similarly, capability networks with a higher level of *modularity* may be considered less complex as they will mitigate change propagation, making it easier to manage change and preserve organizational agility.

Even more than at the logical level, business execution complexity is determined at the physical level, i.e., the level of *capability realization*. It is here that duplication occurs and waste is created. In practice, most larger organizations comprise multiple (and at least partially redundant) implementations of the same capabilities. The procurement capability of a pharmaceutical group, for instance, may be implemented multiple times across different countries and deploying different variations of the same process type.[8]

Capability realization complexity can be captured in two ways. First, functional *redundancy* may be determined by relating the *number* of capability realizations or configurations[9] to the overall number of (logical) capabilities. The more such configurations exist per logical capability, the more duplication of work and the

---

[7] It should be noted that the actual complexity figures are strongly dependent on the used capability model and the associated level of detail. As a consequence, comparisons over time or between peers need to be based on the same reference model (or at least modeling guidelines) to be of any meaning.

[8] While there is good reason for the emergence of such architectures (e.g., historical evolution based on mergers and acquisitions), it is clearly in conflict with the goal of architectural efficiency as defined in Sect. 13.1.

[9] Capability configurations may be defined as existing combinations of business processes, organization units, information objects, resources, people, and culture in an organization realizing a certain business capability.

Table 13.2 Complexity measures for the business execution layer

Elements	Type		Measure	Interpretation
Business capability	E	Q	*Number* of (logical) business capabilities	Measures the "functional breadth" of the organization
	R	Q	*Number* of *relations* between (logical) business capabilities	Measures the degree of "functional interdependency" within the organization
		C	*Concentration* of capability dependencies by (re-) used capabilities	Measures the degree of "functional reuse" (logical level) within the organization
			Modularity of the business capability network	Measures the "functional decoupling" (logical level) within the organization (may serve as an indicator for change propagation and agility)
Capability realization (combination of process, organization unit, etc.)	E	Q	*Number* of business capability realizations per number of (logical) business capabilities	Measures the "functional redundancy" of the organization
	R	C	*Variety* of business capability implementations with respect to business processes, organization units, etc.	Measures the variety in capability implementation with respect to processes, organization units, etc.

more waste of resources will occur. Second, the *variety* of the implementation may be assessed with respect to processes, locations, etc. A manufacturing group, for example, whose capability implementations have been concentrated on 3 sites, may be considered less complex than a peer operating 30 sites across 20 countries (with differing legal frameworks, etc.). The same applies to the concentration of locations, processes, and so on.

The complexity aspects presented to assess the complexity of the business execution layer are summarized in Table 13.2. Their application is illustrated in Fig. 13.8.

The proposed measures are universal in the sense that they can be applied to different parts of an organization and at varying levels of detail. However, it should be noted that the optimal level of complexity may vary across different parts of the organization. Commodity services (like procurement, finance, IT, etc.), for example, may be assigned more ambitious complexity targets, because they can be standardized across business lines or regions. Capabilities required to differentiate in the marketplace, on the other hand, may make higher levels of complexity inevitable (e.g., to improve customer experience and satisfaction). To account for this, the complexity analysis needs to be extended to the overarching business model.

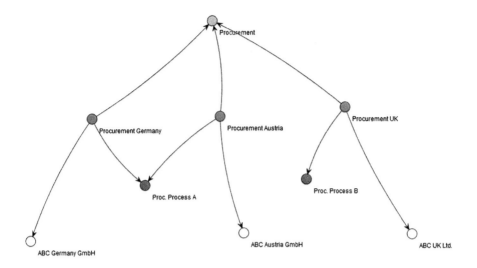

Capability Realization

$$\frac{N_{Capability\ Realization}}{N_{Capability}} = \frac{3}{1} = 3$$

$$EM^{*}_{Cap.\ Realization;\ Org.\ Unit} = 3.00$$
$$EM^{*}_{Cap.\ Realization;\ Process} = 1.89$$

Capability Realization by Organization Units

Capability Realization by Processes

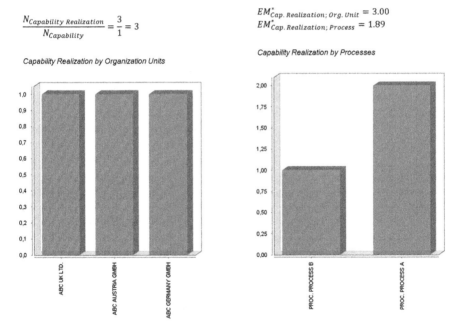

Fig. 13.8 Example for business execution complexity (procurement capability)

13.4.2 Business Model

While the concept of complexity is often used in relation to the business execution layer, it is less frequently applied to the business model.[10] Yet, it is the business model that sets the scene and the requirements for the business execution. An assessment of business complexity hence cannot be complete without a reference to the business model. What may be a perfect level of business execution complexity for an integrated technology group offering a variety of interrelated producer goods and related services (e.g., medical technology) may be completely inappropriate for a manufacturer of physical consumer goods (e.g., household appliances). But again, how can the complexity of the business model be formally described and measured?

First and foremost, business model complexity may be assessed along the *number* of core elements constituting the *network of value creation*. Depending on the industry, these elements will generally include customer segments, products/ services, distribution channels, supplier segments and supplier channels as well as the key activities taken up in the overall value chain.[11] The more of these elements exist, the more complex the network of value creation will be—given that all other parameters are left unchanged. As an example, the business model of a universal bank that serves many different customer segments including retail, high networth individuals, small businesses, and large multinational corporations may be considered more complex than that of a private bank serving only a small segment of wealthy individuals. Similarly, the business model of a direct bank using the Internet and call centers as the only distribution channel may be considered less complex than that of a traditional commercial bank serving a larger number of distribution channels including physical branches, agents, call centers, and online channels. The same applies to the number of products and supplier segments.

Second, business model complexity is impacted by the *variety* of the core elements. An organization with a highly heterogeneous set of products and services like Samsung, for example, including mobile devices, household appliances, and power plants, may be considered more complex than a company like Apple with a very focused offering. The same applies to customer segments, distribution channels, key activities, and supplier segments.

In addition to the number and variety of core elements, the *number* of *relationships* between these are important determinants of the business model complexity as well. The more such relationships are in place, the more variants (or configurations) of value creation exist within the business model. Obviously, a bank that serves its retail clients only through online channels and its high-

---

[10] The few authors who have addressed this include Gottfredson and Aspinall (2005) and Mocker and Ross (2013).

[11] In addition to the core elements of the value creation network, complementing elements like revenue streams and pricing models, cost structures, value chain coordination mechanisms, or assets (see Chap. 1) could be analyzed in a similar way.

networth-individual clients exclusively through private banking branches (two relations) will have less variation in value creation than a bank that serves both customer groups through both channels (four relations).

Also, the *variety* of the relations may be assessed with respect to different dimensions. A business model with a higher level of concentration of the value creation configurations with regard to certain distribution channels or customer groups may be considered less complex than a business model that employs all these elements at equal weight.

Taking a closer look at the *product/service offering*, business model complexity may also arise from the dependencies between individual products/services. An organization with a large *number* of product/service *dependencies* may be said to be more complex from a product/service portfolio perspective than an organization with only few such dependencies. However, given a certain number of dependencies, complexity may be considered lower if products and services are based on a small set of reusable base products/services. In a commercial bank, for example, various different checking account products (e.g., with/without branch service, for students/adults, with/without savings account) may be based on a common base product. Therefore, the *concentration* of product/service *dependencies* may be an additional indicator for product/service complexity.

In larger organizations, *common business services* are often centralized within dedicated service units. These service units then act as internal service providers to a number of consumers (e.g., country-specific entities) within the group (*service-oriented architecture*). In such settings, business models can be described for each service provider. Beyond that, the interactions taking place between service providers and service consumers may be analyzed. This is of particular relevance from a group complexity perspective. For this purpose, the *structure* of service *dependencies* between legal entities/service units may be evaluated. Groups with a higher degree of service *reuse* (as reflected in a larger service usage concentration) may—ceteris paribus—be considered less complex than organizations with a lower degree of service reuse. Similarly, service networks with a higher level of *modularity* may be judged less complex, as they will mitigate change propagation and make it easier to manage change and preserve organizational agility.

The complexity measures presented to assess the complexity of the business model layer are summarized in Table 13.3. Their application is illustrated in Fig. 13.9.

The proposed measures can be applied to different parts of an organization and at varying levels of detail. Large organizations often employ different business models for their main business lines. Conglomerates like Siemens or General Electric, for example, may follow completely different business models for power, transportation, and health technology. In such organizations, the business model complexity may be assessed separately for each business line. In addition to that, the *number* of business models and the *number* of *relationships* between these may be regarded as further determinants of the overall business model complexity of the group.

Table 13.3 Complexity measures for the business model layer

Elements	Type		Measure	Interpretation
Customer segment	E	Q	*Number* of customer segments	Measures the "customer breadth" of the business model
		C	*Variety* of customer segments according to certain attributes (e.g., customer segment type)	Measures the heterogeneity of the customer segments
	R	Q	*Number* of *relations* between customer segments and products/services, distribution channels, supplier segments/channels, key activities, etc.	Measures the dependency between the customer segment dimension and other dimensions of the business model
		C	*Concentration* of customer segments along products/services, distribution channels, supplier segments/channels, key activities, etc.	Measures the "customer segment concentration" along other dimensions of the business model
Product/service	E	Q	*Number* of products/services	Measures the "breadth" of the product/service portfolio
		C	*Variety* of products/services according to certain attributes (e.g., product class)	Measures the heterogeneity of the product/service portfolio
	R	Q	*Number* of *relations* between products/services and customer segments, distribution channels, supplier segments/channels, key activities, etc.	Measures the dependency between the product/service dimension and other dimensions of the business model
		C	*Concentration* of products/services along customer segments, distribution channels, supplier segments/channels, key activities, etc.	Measures the "product/service concentration" along other dimensions of the business model
		Q	*Number* of dependencies between products/services	Measures the degree of "product/service interdependency" of the business model
		C	*Concentration* of product/service dependencies	Measures the degree of "product/service reuse"
			Modularity of product/service dependencies	Measures the degree of "product/service decoupling"

(continued)

Table 13.3 (continued)

Elements	Type		Measure	Interpretation
Distribution channel	E	Q	*Number* of distribution channels	Measures the "distribution channel breadth" of the business model
		C	*Variety* of distribution channels according to certain attributes (e.g., channel type)	Measures the "distribution channel variety"
	R	Q	*Number* of *relations* between distribution channels and customer segments, products/ services, supplier segments/ channels, key activities, etc.	Measures the dependency between the distribution channels and other dimensions of the business model
		C	*Concentration* of distribution channels along customer segments, products/services, supplier segments/channels, key activities, etc.	Measures the "distribution channel concentration" along other dimensions of the business model
Supplier segment	E	Q	*Number* of supplier segments	Measures the "supplier breadth" of the business model
		C	*Variety* of supplier segments according to certain attributes (e.g., supplier segment type)	Measures the "supplier segment variety"
	R	Q	*Number* of *relations* between supplier segments and customer segments, products/services, distribution channels, key activities, etc.	Measures the dependency between supplier segments and other dimensions of the business model
		C	*Concentration* of supplier segments along customer segments, products/services, distribution channels, key activities, etc.	Measures the "supplier segment concentration" along other dimensions of the business model
Key activity	E	Q	*Number* of key activities	Measures the "activity breadth" of the business model
		C	*Variety* of key activities according to certain attributes (e.g., activity type)	Measures the variety of key activities
	R	Q	*Number* of *relations* between key activities and customer segments, products/services, distribution channels, supplier segments, etc.	Measures the dependency between key activities and other dimensions of the business model
		C	*Concentration* of key activities along customer segments, products/services, distribution channels, supplier segments, etc.	Measures the concentration of key activities along other dimensions of the business model

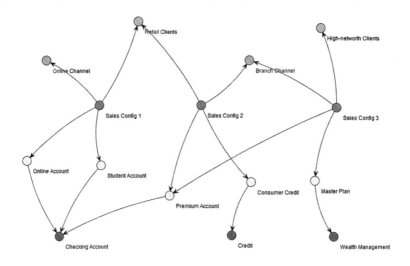

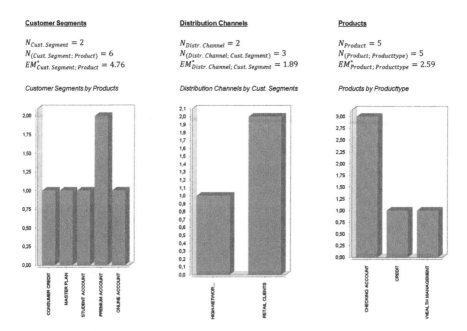

Fig. 13.9 Example for business model complexity (commercial bank)

As with the business execution, the optimal level of complexity may vary depending on the complexity of the business environment and the goals and objectives of the organization. A strongly regulated market environment like the pharmaceutical industry, for example, may impose special requirements to the business model (e.g., distribution to the end consumer via licenced pharmacies based on medical prescription only), hence setting limits to the minimum complexity possible. Therefore, an assessment of the business model complexity needs to take into account the underlying business motivation.

13.4.3 Business Motivation

As shown in the previous sections, the concept of complexity applies well to the domains of business execution and business model. But how about the business motivation? Clearly, the business model followed by an organization should be in line with the overarching system of environmental/boundary conditions and organizational objectives.[12] To achieve an optimal alignment, all these factors must be addressed while maintaining a minimal level of complexity. An insurance company, for example, with ambitious profitability objectives, operating in a strongly regulated and highly competitive environment, may need to adopt a more sophisticated business model that leverages the expertise of independent agencies to grow into a set of profitable niche markets. The same business model may be far too complex (and risky) for an organization operating in a much more simple business environment. But how can the complexity of the business motivation be formally described and measured?

According to Chap. 1, the business motivation layer is comprised of business influencers (internal and external drivers and constraints), business ends (esp. mission, goals, objectives), and business means (strategies, business directives/principles). Just like with the business execution and business model layer, these may be described as a network of elements and relationships. A strategy, for example, may be related to a number of objectives that it is supporting. The objectives may, in turn, be linked to the business goals that they are based on. Finally, the business goals may be associated with certain internal and external drivers. Based on such a network of business influencers, business ends, and business means, complexity may be analyzed as follows.

At the top level, business motivation complexity may be assessed along the *number* of *business influencers*. Depending on the industry, business influencers will generally include shareholder requirements (e.g., regarding minimum dividends), regulatory requirements (e.g., applicable laws and accounting standards), market conditions (e.g., degree of competition), technological developments (e.g., new materials or production methods), and so on. The more such drivers and/or constraints exist, the more complex the business motivation may be considered. A bank operating under the Basel III regime, for example, will have to comply with a larger number of (frequently changing) regulatory constraints than a retailer for consumer electronics. Where business influencers can be categorized into certain classes, the *variety* may be taken into account as well.

---

[12] This corresponds with the EA school of "Enterprise Ecological Adaption" as introduced by Lapalme (2012).

At the second level, business motivation complexity may be assessed along the *number* of *business ends*. These generally include the mission, goals, and objectives followed by the organization. The more of these exist, the more complex the business motivation may be considered.[13] A utility firm, for example, may notice an increase in motivational complexity if environmental goals (e.g., CO_2 reduction) are added to financial and organizational goals. If business means are categorized into certain dimensions (e.g., using a "Balanced Scorecard"), the *variety* may be analyzed as well.

In addition to that, business motivation complexity may be assessed along the *number* of *dependencies* between business ends, but also with respect to business influencers. The more such dependencies are in place, the more complex the business motivation may be considered.

Also, the *variety* of the *relations* may be evaluated. A business motivation with a higher level of concentration of dependencies on a small set of common goals and objectives may be considered less complex than a business motivation that connects to all goals and objectives in an equal way.

Finally, business motivation complexity may be analyzed along the *number* of *business means*. These typically include strategies and directives. The more of these elements, the more complex the business motivation may be considered. A reinsurer, for example, that follows different strategies for the "Life & Health" and the "Property & Casualty" business may be considered more complex from a strategic perspective than a competitor that attempts to address these lines of businesses with the same general strategy.[14]

Beyond that, the *number* of *relationships* between the individual business means need to be taken into account. The more such dependencies are in place, the more complex the business motivation may be considered. Google, for example, with its large number of interrelated strategies for different segments from online advertising, mobile device ecosystems to household appliances—each one serving the others—may be attributed a higher level of strategic complexity than a traditional manufacturer of mobile devices. Again, the *variety* of the *relations* may be assessed. A business motivation with a higher level of concentration of dependencies on a small set of strategies and directives may be considered less complex than a business motivation where all business means are of equal importance.

The complexity measures presented to assess the complexity of the business model layer are summarized in Table 13.4. Their application is illustrated in Fig. 13.10.

---

[13] Like with other element types, measures will be strongly dependent on the actual modeling of goals and the chosen level of detail. As demonstrated in Chap. 2, goals should be defined in an atomic way with each goal addressing only one aspect.

[14] However, such a differentiation may be a strategic necessity given varying market conditions.

Table 13.4 Complexity measures for the business motivation layer

Elements	Type		Measure	Interpretation
Business influencer (driver, constraint)	E	Q	*Number* of business influencers	Measures the degree of internal and external influence in the business motivation
		C	*Variety* of business influencers according to certain attributes (e.g., internal, regulatory)	Measures the variety of the internal and external influence
Business end (mission, goal, objective)	E	Q	*Number* of business ends	Measures the "size" of the organizations' system of business ends
		C	*Variety* of business ends according to certain attributes (e.g., Balanced Scorecard)	Measures the variety of business ends by type
	R	Q	*Number* of dependencies between business ends and business influencers	Measures the degree of dependency between business influencers and business ends
		C	*Variety* of dependencies between business ends and business influencers	Measures the concentration of business influencers along business ends
		Q	*Number* of dependencies between business ends	Measures the degree of dependency between business ends
		C	*Variety* of dependencies between business ends	Measures the concentration of relationships between business ends
Business means (strategy, directive, principle)	E	Q	*Number* of business means	Measures the range of business means
	R	Q	*Number* of *dependencies* between business means (e.g., strategies affecting each other)	Measures the degree of strategic dependency
		C	*Variety* of *dependencies* between business ends and business means	Measures the concentration of business ends on business means

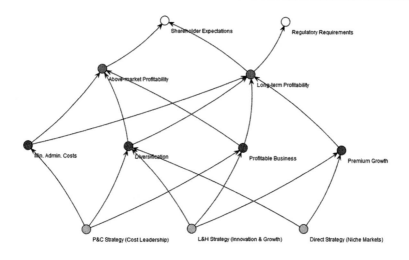

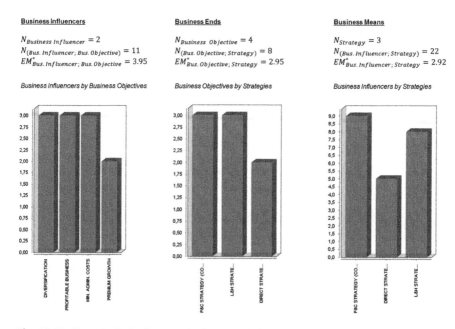

Fig. 13.10 Example for business motivation complexity (reinsurer)

13.5   Putting Business Complexity Measures to Practice

In the previous section, a broad range of possible measures for assessing the complexity of business architectures has been presented. To put these into practice successfully, some additional steps need to be taken. Most importantly, the concept of complexity measures needs to be introduced to the target organization and the required measures and reports need to be implemented.

13.5.1 Introducing Complexity Measures

Implementing a complexity reporting in a given organization may be a difficult task. In order to create maximum value for the organization and its stakeholders, the particular context and requirements of the organization need to be taken into account. This is of special importance, as implementing a complexity reporting will generally lead to additional efforts in the short run. Beyond that, there is a risk that complexity measures are misunderstood or misused. By some stakeholders, they may even be perceived as a threat. For these reasons, and in line with the method proposed in Chap. 15, the introduction of a business complexity reporting should be based on a thorough analysis of stakeholder needs. During such an analysis, the main application scenarios should be reviewed and prioritized.[15] In general, complexity measures may be employed for the scenario types shown in Table 13.5.

In addition to these general scenarios, complexity management may be focused on certain architecture layers or domains depending on the given situation and context of the organization (cf. Chap. 15). For example, a company with a well-defined and lean business model but a large extent of redundancy in operations may

Table 13.5 Application scenario types

Application scenario	Description
Decision support/ simulation	Calculation (and comparison) of complexity impacts for major decision variants (e.g., target architecture scenarios)
Comparative analysis	Calculation (and comparison) of complexity measures for different parts of the overall landscape (e.g., between domains, business lines, etc.) and identification of hot spots
Benchmarking	Calculation (and comparison) of complexity measures for different organizations in search for best-in-class complexity figures
Architectural controlling	Systematic planning of target complexity figures as part of a continuous architecture management (e.g., differentiated by architecture layers and domains)
Risk management	Calculation of complexity measures as part of the internal management of operational risks

---

[15] This may be strongly facilitated by using a detailed catalog of typical application scenarios as a reference.

concentrate on business execution complexity in the first place. Similarly, the scope may also be set to certain domains that need special attention (e.g., harmonization of procurement, accounting, etc.). Based on such a priorization, the measures of primary relevance may be selected for implementation.

13.5.2 Technical Implementation

After the application scenarios and required measures have been identified, methods must be implemented to calculate the actual figures based on available data and to create appropriate reports. Generally, the calculation of measures should be based on the data captured in the architecture repository. This way, the calculation of measures can be automated and fully integrated with existing architecture data management processes. Data elements that are not yet available in the repository should be added first. The calculation of measures may then either be implemented within the architecture management tool or based on specialized tool support for complexity management.[16]

13.6 Conclusion and Outlook

In this chapter, a generic approach for measuring complexity was presented and applied to the domain of business architecture. It was shown that the notion of complexity is of relevance not only to the business execution but also to the business model and business motivation layer. A more complex system of business drivers, goals, and objectives is more likely to require a more complex business model. This is turn will generally call for a more sophisticated (and thus complex) business execution layer. For all these layers, a number of measures were proposed and illustrated by examples. Using these measures may be supportive in minimizing the complexity surplus and optimizing the overall architectural alignment.

However, assessing and managing business architecture complexity remains a difficult task. First of all, broad stakeholder buy-in is required in order to gain visibility and acceptance for such an initiative. Second, data needs to be captured and maintained in an appropriate form. This will generally require an extension of existing architecture repositories and the respective data maintenance processes. Also, measures need to be adjusted to the organization-specific metamodel. As the actual figures are strongly dependent on the modeling approach and associated level of detail, care must be taken to ensure that appropriate reference models and modeling guidelines are used consistently. Beyond that, appropriate methods need to be defined to handle missing data elements. Last but not least, it must be

---

[16] An example for such a specialized tool kit is the Plexity Analyzer™, which supports a flexible configuration and calculation of all relevant complexity measures based on arbitrary data/metamodel structures.

emphasized that complexity assessments often require thorough analyses that can only by carried out by skilled and experienced architects. Such analyses will comprise drill-down operations and supplemental research. The results should hence always be commented and interpreted qualitatively.

Further research is required to determine the relevance of the proposed measures in more detail and to evaluate their practical use. Beyond that, methods for aggregating the complexity measures and relating the figures of different layers to each other need to be developed. Generally, more research is required on how to actually manage complexity given that appropriate complexity measures are in place. As initial results from the IT architecture domain indicate, complexity is not a one-dimensional variable that can easily be reduced across all its facettes (Schmidt 2013; Schmidt et al. 2013). Instead, it appears that reducing the complexity of a certain aspect (e.g., number of applications, vendor variety) will often lead to an increase of complexity in another aspect (e.g., number of application usage). Also, the impact may vary between a local and a global perspective. Application consolidation, for example, will typically lead to a reduced number of applications and a reduced vendor variety. However, the dependencies of the particular target application will generally rise (in terms of interfaces with other system, usage relations, country/languages, etc.). From a local perspective, the complexity will hence increase. It may be concluded that similar mechanisms apply to the consolidation and centralization of business capabilities or the streamlining of business models, for example. Additional research is required to evaluate this in more detail and to give business architects appropriate methods at hand.[17]

References

Aier S, Schönherr M (2007) Integrating an enterprise architecture using domain clustering. In: Lankhorst M, Johnson P (eds) Proceedings of the Second Workshop on Trends in Enterprise Architecture Research (TEAR 2007), St. Gallen, Switzerland, 6 June 2007, pp 23–30

Drucker PF (1974) Management: tasks, responsibilities, practices. Harper & Row, New York

Gottfredson M, Aspinall K (2005) Innovation versus complexity. What is too much of a good thing? Harv Bus Rev 83(11):62–71

Lagerström R, Baldwin CY, Maccormack AD, Aier S (2013) Visualizing and measuring enterprise application architecture: an exploratory telecom case. School working paper 13-103. Harvard Business, Cambridge, MA

Lapalme J (2012) Three schools of thought on enterprise architecture. ITPro, November/December 2012, IEEE Computer Society, pp 37–43

Lehmann MM (1997) Laws of software evolution revisited. In: Montangero C (ed) Software process technology—proceedings of the 5th European workshop on software process technology, Nancy, Oct 1996 (Lecture notes in computer science), vol 1149. Springer, Berlin, pp 108–124

---

[17] In addition to the framework presented in this chapter, centrality measures from the domain of network analysis may be used to assess local complexity and counteract global "over-optimization" (cf. Simon and Fischbach 2013).

Mocker M (2009) What is complex about 273 applications? Untangling application architecture complexity in a case of European investment banking. In: Proceedings of the 42nd Hawaii international conference on system sciences (HICSS), IEEE Computer Society, Washington, DC

Mocker M, Ross JW (2012) USAA: capturing value from complexity. CISR working paper No. 389, MIT Sloan School of Management, Cambridge, MA

Mocker M, Ross JW (2013) Rethinking business complexity. CISR Research Briefing XIII(2), MIT Sloan School of Management, Cambridge, MA

Newman MEJ (2006) Modularity and community structure in networks. Proc Natl Acad Sci USA 103(23):8577–8582

Rutz U (2012) IT complexity management @ Commerzbank—overview on Commerzbank initiative. Presentation at EAMKON conference, Stuttgart, Apr 2012

Schmidt C (2013) How to measure enterprise architecture complexity: a generic approach, practical applications and lessons learned. Presentation at The Open Group conference, London, Oct 2013. www.scape-consulting.com/index.php/schmidt-2013d.html. Accessed 25 Oct 2014

Schmidt C, Buxmann P (2011) Outcomes and success factors of enterprise IT architecture management: empirical insight from the international financial services industry. Eur J Inf Syst 20(2):168–185

Schmidt C, Widjaja T, Schütz A (2013) Messung der Komplexität von IT-Landschaften auf der Basis von Architektur-Metamodellen: Ein generischer Ansatz und dessen Anwendung im Rahmen der Architektur-Transformation. In: Horbach M (ed) INFORMATIK 2013, GI-Edition (Lecture notes in informatics (LNI) P-220). Köllen Verlag, Bonn, pp 1261–1275

Schneberger SL, McLean ER (2003) The complexity cross: implications for practice. Commun ACM 46(9):216–225

Schneider AW, Zec M, Matthes F (2014a) Adopting notions of complexity for enterprise architecture management. In: Proceedings of the 20th Americas conference on information systems (AMCIS), Savannah, GA

Schneider AW, Reschenhofer T, Schütz A, Matthes F (2014b) Empirical results for application landscape complexity measures. In: Proceedings of the 48th Hawaii international conference on system science (HICSS), Kauai, HI

Schütz A, Widjaja T, Kaiser J (2013) Complexity in enterprise architectures—conceptualization and introduction of a measure from a system theoretic perspective. In: Proceedings of the 21st European conference on information systems (ECIS), Utrecht, The Netherlands

Shannon CE (1948) A mathematical theory of communication. Bell Syst Tech J 27:379–423, pp 623–656

Simon D, Fischbach K (2013) IT landscape management using network analysis. In: Poels G (ed) Enterprise information systems of the future, CONFENIS 2012, Ghent, Belgium. LNBIP, vol 139. Springer, Berlin, pp 18–34

The Open Group (2013) ArchiMate 2.1 specification. Van Haren Publishing, Zaltbommel

Widjaja T, Kaiser J, Tepel D, Buxmann P (2012) Heterogeneity in IT landscapes and monopoly power of firms: a model to quantify heterogeneity. In: Proceedings of the 33rd international conference on information systems (ICIS), Orlando, FL

Part V
Guidelines for Successful Implementation

Business Architectures for Niche-Market Enterprises

14

Tom S. Graves

Abstract

Much of the current focus of attention for business architecture has been on new startups or on existing large enterprises, but there is also a great deal that can be usefully learnt in applying the same principles to the needs of smaller niche-market businesses and organizations. This chapter describes a real-life case study with a small restaurant chain in Central America that wanted to expand outward into other cities in its region. The brief engagement covered a broad scope from high-level strategy all the way down to day-to-day operations, and, working with the principals of the business, delivered explicit action plans that gave detailed guidance for a broad range of themes such as business models, business alliances, marketing, advertising, building layout, workflows, performance metrics, recruitment, and training. The chapter ends with some lessons learned about what does and does not work in this type of business architecture engagement, what to do about these in further real-world practice, and some suggestions on how to apply these techniques in other forms of business architecture work.

14.1 Introduction

This chapter describes a brief, real-life consulting engagement, applying business architecture techniques to the needs of a small business in Central America. In contrast to a more conventional formal style, the chapter has been written in an intentionally story-like format, so as to emphasize the immediacy of the nature of this type of work.

T.S. Graves (✉)
Tetradian Consulting, Unit 215, 9 St John's Street, Colchester, UK
e-mail: tom@tetradian.com

© Springer International Publishing Switzerland 2015   271
D. Simon, C. Schmidt (eds.), *Business Architecture Management*, Management for
Professionals, DOI 10.1007/978-3-319-14571-6_14

14.1.1 Background

Sitting out on the deck at breakfast with our clients, the sound of birdsong in the warm morning air of Central America, and that glorious view out over the rainforest, all came together to give an easy sense that all was well with the world. But as indicated by the volcano that could be seen quietly simmering again in the far distance, and the cracks from the recent earthquake still visible in the road as we came here, we were well aware that surface appearances could be deceiving—and the same could be true of this company, too.

Our purpose here was twofold. Our clients here—we will call them Juan and Edward—ran a small yet very successful restaurant and food-business in the local region, but their recent attempt at expansion into new outlets in the capital city had fallen flat. They had asked my colleague Michael—a close friend of many years—for his views on what had gone wrong, and what they could do about it.

On our side, we had long wanted to test our hypothesis that business architecture techniques were not solely for startups or large organizations: they could also be used for small-to-medium-sized existing organizations.

Also—and importantly—we had to be able to prove that our approach to business architecture could deliver real business value fast: all within this one morning session, in fact.

This session gave us all an opportunity to address each of these concerns.

14.1.2 What Is Business Architecture?

In our own work, we position business architecture as a support for managing business strategy, and as a component of enterprise architecture—the latter in a rather broader sense than is usual at present, stretching far beyond information technology (IT) alone.

At its simplest, and in line with the foundations provided in the introductory chapter of this book (Chap. 1), we define a business architecture as *the set of structures and stories that underpin "the business of the business."* More generally, we regard the core theme of all architectures as "things work better when they work together, on purpose." The process of business architecture development and, in turn, business architecture management, is therefore the application of various models and techniques to identify and apply that architectural content in a business context, and better support "things working together" in that organization's business. Importantly, it is not solely about strategy: as per the framework used throughout this book, the emphasis throughout is on linking all the way through from business motivation to business model to business execution, and all the way back again.

The *structures* in scope for this business architecture might include higher-level concerns such as business models, organizational structures, brand architectures, and financial structures, but may also cover more detail-oriented concerns such as logistics, short-term business cycles, and even staff training. The limits are not predefined, but follow a dynamic focus on "just enough detail."

The *stories* in scope for this business architecture would encompass concerns such as enterprise vision, values, and culture and, perhaps most importantly, how these interact in practice to support trust from customers and other stakeholders, and to enhance overall effectiveness—without which the enterprise cannot thrive. In this sense, "story" is that which supports the human elements of the architecture, much as structure supports its technical elements—*"Architecture [as] a vehicle for the telling of stories, a canvas for relaying societal myths, a stage for the theatre of everyday life"* (Frederick 2007). Again, the emphasis here is on practical means to link every step between strategy and execution—but in this case, more for the human context for the business.

In recent years, most of the focus for business architecture seems to have been on for-profit business models—particularly for startups, as in the "Business Model Canvas" (Osterwalder and Pigneur 2010) or the "Lean Startup" method (Ries 2011)—or organizational structures and high-level maps such as the "Business Motivation Model" (OMG 2010) and Porter's "Five Forces" context map (e.g., Porter 1979).

However, our understanding is that the same principles should apply to the business of all types of organizations: for-profit, government, non-profit, or whatever. In this case, we needed to apply those models and techniques to the business needs and concerns of a relatively small for-profit organization.

14.1.3 Client Context

The client's company—which, for reasons of commercial confidentiality, we will rename as "Sabor"—consisted of five tightly integrated business units:

– delicatessen
– chocolaterie/patisserie
– cafe
– restaurant
– catering

Their main location, in the business district of a popular tourist town, was structured as follows:

– front: delicatessen and covered part of the cafe
– mid: chocolaterie and open-air part of the cafe
– rear: restaurant

In this location, the cafe area provided approximately 20 places, and the restaurant—much of it partially covered or open-air—some 50 places. The kitchen area and walkway provided a strong visual and functional boundary between the restaurant area and the rest of the operation. This location operates 7 days a week, with public opening hours of around 14 h per day.

Catering, food delivery, and bulk food preparation—primarily for the delicatessen—were run from other sites elsewhere in the town and the surrounding district.

Staffing was not discussed, but we did know that the main location has around ten front-of-house or waiting staff working at any one time, and probably at least as many in the main kitchens at that location.

Financials were likewise not discussed, but the business is known to be successful and profitable, and is not in any financial difficulty. It also has a strong reputation, both locally and in the region, and strong repeat business both from the town and from national and international visitors.

Some 6 months previously, Juan and Edward had opened another smaller location in the capital city, capitalizing on the company's considerable reputation, and with the intent of using it as a springboard for major growth. However, it had not been a success, and had been closed down after only a few months' operation. We did not know the reasons for the failure, but we did know that Juan and Edward wanted our help in assessing its causes, and identify options to address those issues, so that they could try again with better chance of success.

14.2 Consultation: Architecture Development

14.2.1 Initial Discussion

Meeting together for a shared breakfast at the clients' house was typical for that country's business culture, and provided a means via which clients and consultants could get to know each other and build a practical rapport.

This preliminary stage also helped us to address a number of practical language issues. Edward and my colleague Michael are fully bilingual in Spanish and English, but Juan's English was more limited, and my own Spanish more limited again. In practice, most of the discussion was in English; occasionally Juan would have to switch to Spanish, which I could mostly follow but could only reply in English; but Edward or Michael could provide additional translation where required.

The translation difficulties would on occasion also extend beyond natural-language to culture and idiom. For example, in our work for Latin America, we have yet to find an exact equivalent word for the English term "enterprise" in Spanish or Portuguese, that extends beyond the notion of "commercial organization," to include and encompass the much broader multi-stakeholder concept used in enterprise architecture.[1] These kinds of challenges are common when working across cultural and/or linguistic boundaries.

---

[1] The nearest-available Spanish term—"ecosistema"—does imply the required broader scope, but does not fully include the overlay of purpose that underpins a human enterprise.

Careful questions elicited further information about the failed venture in the capital city. This had been based on just one of the business themes, as a stand-alone delicatessen. Business had been quite good, with significant return-custom, but not sufficient even as a new venture to cover its costs. Interestingly, one of the repeated complaints from customers had been that there was no seating area at which to consume purchases from the delicatessen—a complaint perhaps in part arising from the fact that eating in public is somewhat frowned upon in that country's culture.

We were also able to ascertain more about the company's history. It had been started by Edward as a family venture almost 20 years earlier; Juan had joined the team some 5 years ago, as a working-partner, and at the time was also studying for an MBA. For both principals, a core personal driver for the business had been around food and health: Juan said that in his previous business—selling pre-made sandwiches to retail stores—he had found that he had been unable to eat his own company's product, due to allergic reactions to some of the ingredients. Edward commented that it was not uncommon for Sabor's clients to say that it was the only place in town where they considered they could safely eat everything on offer. This theme of health and food was therefore clearly important as a core reason both for the company's existence, and for its continuing success.

By this point, it was time to move into the main room, to do the in-depth exploration.

14.2.2 Context Map

The meeting was in a private house, so there were no whiteboards available. Instead, we used a large drawing-pad (36 × 24 in.) and various other props laid out on the central table.

We had determined beforehand that the company's basic business model was not a primary concern, so there was no immediate need to use a business model framework such as the Business Model Canvas (Osterwalder and Pigneur 2010). Likewise, although the concerns were strategic, they did not seem to be much about competitive positioning, and hence were not the kind of themes for which classic competition-oriented strategy tools such as Five Forces were a good fit. Instead, since the discussion had indicated that the core concerns were around clarity on overall direction, and relationships with stakeholder groups, we had decided to guide this part of the session with a *context map* or stakeholder map, based on the service context component of the "Enterprise Canvas" suite of models, as described in Graves (2010). In his own consultancy work, Michael describes this context map as the "*holomap*"—the term we will use here. For the same reasons, we had also expected to do some work via values-based enterprise narrative or story, as per Graves (2012).

The holomap describes the context for an organization in terms of four distinct types of relationships, or four layers of an "enterprise":

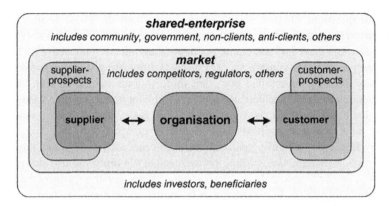

Fig. 14.1 Context map

- no interaction ("organization-as-enterprise"): the organization centered on itself, without external context
- direct transactional interactions ("supply chain"): suppliers, customers, and others in the direct value network
- indirect transactional interactions ("market"): analysts, recruiters, regulators, standards bodies, and others (including competitors) in the overall marketplace for this type of enterprise
- non-transactional interactions ("enterprise ecosystem"): investors, families, communities, non-clients, anti-clients, and others that can be impacted by and impact upon the organization and its business

We can summarize this set of relationships visually in a context-space map (Fig. 14.1).

Although this context map diagram is available in pre-printed form, at various scales, we have often found that for live exploratory sessions with clients it can be more useful to draw the diagram by hand, to enhance engagement and create stronger personal ownership of the resultant outcomes. Doing so also makes it easier to support free-form amendment and customization—such as in this case, where Juan and Edward wanted a stronger initial emphasis on competitors, and, later, on potential allies (see Fig. 14.2).

We spent perhaps 15–20 min moving around in the conceptual space described by the service context map, asking Juan and Edward to identify and describe the various groups of stakeholders and relationships in each of the enterprise layers, as above—and also including internal stakeholder relationships such as with employees.

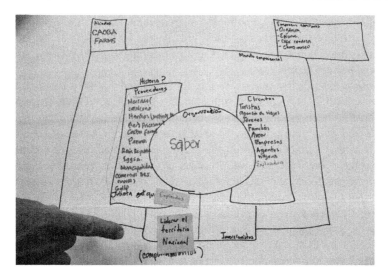

Fig. 14.2 Sabor holomap

14.2.3 Vision and Values

We then explained that a shared enterprise of this type—one that encompasses many different stakeholder groups, each with their own interests and concerns—is held together and, in effect, defined by a unifying "vision" or "promise." The vision identifies the "why," "how," and "what" of the overall shared enterprise, and, via concomitant values, the effective definitions of success within the shared enterprise (note that these values in turn provide the context for an organization's value propositions, as will be seen later). Importantly, the scope of the vision extends *beyond* the organization itself: it is not about the organization, but about the purpose and success criteria for the organization's relations with all of those stakeholders in the shared enterprise.

Given this, we asked Juan and Edward for their vision for the organization and enterprise. Juan replied that he had recently done this as part of his MBA course, and had decided on a vision of "to be the national leaders in the restaurant business."

Michael wrote this vision statement onto a small sticky-note, and placed it in various positions on the context-map, each position representing a different stakeholder group: customer, supplier, trade journalist, employee, investor, non-client, family member, and others. At each place, he asked Juan to take on the role of the respective stakeholder; he then read the existing vision statement to Juan, and asked him for his response as that stakeholder—how he felt as that stakeholder in response to the vision statement.

Through this simple role-play process, Juan quickly understood that that type of vision—"to be the national leaders in the restaurant business"—was essentially meaningless, or worse, to anyone but himself. It had seemed right, in terms of his own ambitions and the MBA textbook: but from the stakeholders' perspectives it would, at best, be interpreted as pointless grandiosity, whilst some of the responses were frankly unprintable. It was clear that, for a meaningful vision, they would need to start again, from scratch.

As a guide towards that revised vision, we suggested that they could start from their own stories about food and health, that they had told us earlier. This immediately led to the understanding that, for both of them, health was their most important concern: food was more a means to achieve and support that health. Extending onward from that, further questioning and further stories built towards a clear set of values for their enterprise, and prioritization of those values: for them, the enterprise was about food, and the sharing of food, that was healthy, tasty, well-presented, of the place, and of the time.

Michael then repeated the previous process, writing that summary of values onto a small sticky note, and placing it in various positions on the context map. This time the connection for each stakeholder group was clear—and also the differentiation in the marketplace, too, since there were no others amongst the 80-odd cafes and restaurants in the town with an identical mix of values, or with such a strong emphasis on health above all.

At this point, further stories started to emerge. One of the more important was that they had consciously structured the main restaurant around the style of a *finca*—a traditional country estate somewhat equivalent to a winery in Europe, Australia, or the US, and also traditionally a place both for more open family gatherings but also with quiet corners for discreet business dealings on the side. Hence, for this tourist-oriented town, the very successful mix of relatively small cafe area at the front, versus the much larger restaurant area out the back.

Yet the finca concept would not match up so well with a city-type culture: in terms of the values, it would not be "of the place." To put it at its simplest, family and business both took place in significantly different ways in the city, compared to how it would be done on an upmarket country estate—even though the people involved were the same. It became clear that the attempt to recreate the finca formula outside of its appropriate context was a key reason why the attempt to expand into the city had failed: too much of a formulaic reiteration of content, without appropriate adaptation to context.

To address the needs of the same type of clientele, but in that different place, a different emphasis would be needed: we suggested, for example, a close parallel with the role of the coffee houses of seventeenth century London, which became key hubs for business, law, science, and much else besides. For the faster-paced city context, those relationships between cafe and restaurant area would need to be reversed: a larger and more overt cafe area, with fast-paced service yet still focused on health and presentation, versus a smaller yet perhaps even-more-discreet booth-type space out the back for the serious and private business deals.

The other theme that arose from this part of the discussion was that it also clarified the elements that would be needed for any expansion. The crucial factors for success became outlined as follows:

- emphasis on values first, starting with health and food
- recreating the overall finca concept, yet adapted to and implemented as the equivalent in the respective context
- a minimum of two or more of the five service themes (cafe, restaurant, delicatessen, chocolaterie/patisserie, catering) at any given location—because the interplay and interdependence between each of the service themes was understood to be a key part of the overall business story

Although we ourselves would probably not be involved in that future work, Juan and Edward earmarked each of those points as key guides for a revision of their expansion strategy.

Finally, we looked at some illustrations of the values in practice right down to operations level—the actual processes carried out at the organization's sites. For example, the value theme "looks good" needed to apply not only to presentation of food on the plate, in the kitchen, but also how the plate itself was presented and introduced at the diner's table. Edward understood straight away how their table staff training would need to change somewhat to emphasize this point—the organization's values as expressed in practice, right down to the smallest details.

We also assessed the impacts of prioritization of values-in-practice. One example here was the value pair "of the place" and "of the time." This could be interpreted, for example, as an emphasis on food that was specific to the region, and following the seasons. On discussion, it became clear that although these were relevant values for the enterprise, they were not the highest priority—as they would be for a gourmet restaurant, for example. Instead, suitable engagement with those values might extend to including a "Regional and Seasonal" page in the restaurant menu, somewhat akin to the existing "Specials" page, but changing weekly or monthly in tune with the local seasons. The key point, though, was that Sabor needed to emphasize health in food above all others of its values.

14.2.4 Allies and Stories

We then explored how to use the vision and values more broadly, for other business issues beyond direct business strategy. The first part of this was to address a concern or challenge that Edward had mentioned earlier at the breakfast: a real sense of isolation or aloneness in the market. The values map had shown that they did indeed have no direct competitors in the town, yet it also meant that they seemed to have no allies, either—no one with whom to compare notes, to do cross-marketing, and suchlike. At first glance, their nearest direct allies seemed to be not just in another city, but in another country entirely. Hence, in turn, that very real sense of isolation that Edward had described.

To identify potential allies in other industries or business domains, we suggested using a simple substitution tactic adapted from the engineering problem-solving toolkit TRIZ (Mind Tools 2014). In this case, substitution would be applied to the enterprise values—or, specifically, to any of the enterprise values other than the highest-priority value of health. Examples that arose from such substitution included:

- retain "looks good," change "tastes good" (food) to "feels good" (to the touch): clothing retailer with emphasis on health, natural fibres, comfort, "of the place," etc.
- retain "smells good" and "looks good," change "tastes good" (food) to "feels good" (on the body): cosmetics retailer with emphasis on health, natural materials, "of the place," "of the time," etc.
- change "tastes good" to "sounds good": music creator and/or retailer with an emphasis on how music supports health

A mere few minutes' worth of brainstorming and checking of address books turned up at least a dozen such potential allies in the immediate region alone, where before there had seemed to be none. For Edward in particular, this was a real eye-opener: almost before we had finished the session, he was already making plans for possible co-marketing with some of the people whose names had come up as potential allies.

Our focus then shifted to story—the role of story in business, as an anchor for personal meaning and shared meaning. By this, we did not mean any kind of grandiose "big story," but more the little stories and anecdotes that expressed the vision and values in real-world practice: practical illustrations of what it looked like and what happened when there was alignment to the vision and values, and when there was not.

Some examples we discussed included Edward and Juan's own stories of food and health—the *why* behind the company. These could be included as pages in menus, for example, or small in-store placards, somewhat equivalent to the building histories and event histories on various sites around the tourist areas of the town. Those stories would also become part of recruitment and on-boarding, as part of the selection and self-selection criteria for potential new staff, and for induction of new staff into the organization—an explicit description of "the way we do things round here."

Another concrete example was the small statue of the Virgin Mary, mounted on the wall at the far end of the delicatessen at the main site. "It was already there when we moved in," said Juan. In brief discussion, we all agreed that it not only "felt right" that it should be there, but also reflected the enterprise value of "of the place"—and, for many clients in this Catholic country, the enterprise value of health, too. We suggested that that too would be a useful place for a small story-placard, to engage people in the history of the place, and in the company's continuing engagement with place. We also recommended that similar small "of the place" features should be retained and emphasized in any sites where the company operated in future.

14.2.5 Summary of Architecture Development Outcomes

After 2 h of discussion, exploration, story-based enquiry, and work on the context map, it was time to bring the process to an end. This gave us an opportunity to assess what had been achieved in that time:

- identify and review stakeholders and overall business context
- review existing enterprise vision, indicating where and why it did not work as intended
- identify and concept-test revised enterprise vision and values
- review causes of lack of success for previous attempted expansion into another city, and identify key actions, attributes, and success criteria for redesign and relaunch
- use of vision and prioritization of values to guide strategy and design choices
- use of vision and prioritization of values to identify potential allies for co-marketing
- use of vision and values to guide selection and training of staff
- use of key values (particularly, "of the place" and "of the time") to guide site selection, site design, and interior design, adapting to place and context whilst still retaining consistent identity
- use of story to identify and illustrate alignment with vision and values
- use of story to identify and illustrate non-alignment with vision and values (for use particularly in staff training and suchlike)
- clear guidelines and roadmaps on how to apply all of these, and more

In summary, that is a lot of concrete, practical outcomes to have achieved in just one morning's work.

14.3   Consultation: Follow-up and Review

As a follow-up, Michael met briefly with Juan late the following week, a day or two after Juan's regular MBA tutorial in the city.

At first, Juan was somewhat dismissive of much of the work that we had done: "it's nothing new," he said, "I saw it all on my MBA course this week." After some gentle questioning, it became clear that some of what we had discussed in the business architecture session (such as the role of vision and values, and the importance of stakeholder mapping across a broader scope than just the immediate business model) had indeed been present in somewhat fragmented fashion in the content for his MBA course—but in fact several weeks earlier, when he had barely noticed it at all. He agreed, eventually, that it was only because we had shown him, during our discussion, how those fragments could be pulled together and applied to his own business context, that he had then been able to make sense of what his MBA course had supposedly been showing him. The respective content had been there in the course, after a fashion, but not the means or context to put it to practical *use*.

Juan then switched his objections into another direction: "you just made it all up on the spot," he said, "it was nothing more than a bunch of lucky guesses!" It was an unfair comment and he knew it: he had said it with a smile, and admitted later that he had felt he "should have known" everything that we had shown him, that in a way the fact that he had not known it beforehand was an affront to his pride as a businessman. Yet it's the kind of objection we would expect to see anyway in this kind of context: and there is a clear answer to it, too, in that "if a process is consistently 'lucky' in this way, it ain't luck!"

Although it was true that some of the techniques we had used were our own developments or adaptations, all of them had been publicly available in documented form for quite a while. And the technique that he had most dismissed as "luck"—the switching-around of values to derive suggestions for co-marketing partners—was, as mentioned above, a business-oriented equivalent of TRIZ and similar long-proven systematic methods for innovation in engineering.

Two of his other critiques were rather more fair: he would have preferred, he said, if we had explained more of what we were going to do, before we did it; and he had wanted concise examples of what kind of outcomes would be expected to be reached.

Those critiques would indeed have been valid if our aim had been to reproduce some kind of business framework or business model that had been created else-where—a so-called "best practice." Yet the explicit aim of the exercise here was to not copy other's work, but instead to build on the organization's own unique strengths and context—for which, by definition, the intent was that these should not be reproducible from or by others—and to search out for the new, the not-already-known—which, again by definition, could not be known beforehand.

Hence, by the nature of the work itself, it was inherently difficult to give a precise description beforehand of what we would do, and the outcomes that would or could be achieved. There was a definite structure and sequence that we had expected to use in the work, a definite aim for the work, and a distinct toolkit from which we could select appropriate tools as the session went along, so in that sense some of it was sort of known beforehand; but again by definition, there would always, and necessarily, be a certain amount of "flying by the seat of the pants" in this type of work, and demanding too much certainty beforehand would inherently hinder rather than help that work.

The way out of this trap, as we had explained, was to use metaframeworks and metamethods: frameworks to create context-specific frameworks, and methods to create context-specific methods. In this engagement, for example, the standard holomap and its associated methods were used as a base—i.e., a metaframework and metamethods—from which Juan and Edward could build their own customized holomap framework with its additional emphasis on competitors, and the modified methods that were used to identify potential allies. Yet the problem here is that metaframeworks and the like are built around patterns and principles rather than step-by-step instructions. And their outcomes or instantiations are context-specific frameworks and methods, which can use step-by-step instructions—but it is proba-ble that we will not and cannot know what those instructions and overall potential are until we create the respective frameworks and methods. By their very nature, there is always a sizeable amount of uncertainty about the whole process—and that is as it should be, since the explicit aim of the process is a guided dive into the unknown, in search of the previously unknowable.

The catch, of course, is that these can be very difficult concepts to explain—perhaps especially to those who have been schooled in MBA-style assumptions about certainty, predictability, and control, hence the kind of conceptual clashes evidenced in Juan's remarks.

On the more positive side, Juan did say that the work on vision and values had changed his thinking about how to tackle marketing and business growth, and was starting to re-work all of his previous ideas and plans along the lines that we—and they—had suggested during the session. A separate phone call with Edward also indicated that he too was starting to apply the outcomes of the session, particularly in identifying and building relationships with potential co-marketing partners from other types of business domains. Overall, then, quite a lot more of a success than Juan's somewhat dismissive remarks had at first implied it had been.

14.4 Conclusions

14.4.1 Hypothesis and Test

We had initially set out to test:

(a) whether business architecture techniques could be used appropriately for the needs of small to medium enterprises; and
(b) whether real business value could be delivered even in as short a time as a single morning, using those techniques.

We also needed to verify that the client was satisfied with the outcomes of the use of those techniques.

For (a), it was clear that the techniques we had used in larger scale engagements—in particular, the work with the holomap, with values and values mapping, and with business-oriented story—did apply just as well in this smaller scale context.

For (b), the business value delivered is summarized in Sect. 14.2.5 above, and its applicability and use by the client verified as per Sect. 14.3. The overall engagement encompassed a total of just under four hours: some three and half hours, start to finish, for the morning session; and a half-hour for the follow-up. Although there may be some situations—even for small enterprises—where it might not be practicable to deliver some form of real business value within that kind of timescale, we believe that our intent and expectation should always be to do so wherever possible.

Despite Juan's initial response during the follow-up, it became clear that both clients *were* satisfied with the outcomes of the process.

14.4.2 Lessons Learned and Benefits Realization

Although metaframeworks and metamethods are essential for this type of work, most business-folk are unfamiliar with such tools and techniques, and the lack of predefined prescription for their processes and outcomes may place those participants too far outside of their comfort-zone. As evidenced in Juan's response in the later follow-up, resistance to both process and outcomes may occur if these concerns are not addressed. Rather than launch straight into the process, we needed to take more care to introduce the techniques, and explain how they worked. This remained true despite the tight time-constraints that applied in this context.

To also address the same problem, we needed to do much better expectation-management, and make it clearer how the methods to be used would lead towards the desired outcomes. We could, for example, have pointed beforehand to TRIZ (Mind Tools 2014), as a long-proven technique that provides structured methods to guide inherently unstructured exploration and innovation.

Between us, Michael and I have more than 50 years' consultancy experience in at least 20 different industries, across many different business-cultures within a wide variety of countries across four distinct continents. As a result, it is perhaps too easy for us to forget that many things that are "obvious" to us are not necessarily "obvious" at all to others—especially to our clients. This was particularly evident when Michael and I, almost on reflex, came up with story after story, and example after example, from many different industries, to illustrate different points: the clients struggled to keep up, or to see or make the same connections that we did to their own industry. We needed to be more aware of this constraint, and tone down the rapid-fire cross-connections, to give more space for the clients to find their own way through the maze of possibilities.[2]

Overall, though, the processes and the overall experiment did lead to desired outcomes—benefits realization—both for the clients, and for ourselves. The clients ended up with a much clearer idea of strategy, and vision and values to guide that strategy right the way through to business model and business execution. For us, we were able to prove that the frameworks and techniques were indeed applicable to the business context of the small-to-medium enterprise, and could deliver real business value within the required very short timeframes.

References

Frederick M (2007) 101 things I learned in architecture school. MIT Press, Cambridge, MA
Graves T (2010) Mapping the enterprise: modeling the enterprise as services with the enterprise canvas. Tetradian Books, Colchester
Graves T (2012) The enterprise as story: the role of narrative in enterprise-architecture. Tetradian Books, Colchester

---

[2] We are not alone in this, of course: many architects, strategists, and others are likewise prone to this mistake, sometimes known as "the curse of knowledge."

Mind Tools (2014) TRIZ: a powerful methodology for creative problem solving. http://www.mindtools.com/pages/article/newCT_92.htm

OMG (2010) The business motivation model, version 1.1. OMG document number: formal/2010-05-01

Osterwalder A, Pigneur Y (2010) Business model generation—a handbook for visionaries, game changers, and challengers. Wiley, Hoboken, NJ

Porter ME (1979) How competitive forces shape strategy. Harv Bus Rev 57(2):137–145

Ries E (2011) Lean startup: how today's entrepreneurs use continuous innovation to create radically successful businesses. Crown Business, New York

Bringing Business Architecture to Life: How to Establish Business Architecture Practices in Your Organization

15

Christian Schmidt and Daniel Simon

Abstract

Today, business architecture management (BAM) is widely acknowledged as an effective means for organizations to cope with rapidly changing business environments and increasing levels of competition. However, establishing BAM practices in an organization represents a major organizational and cultural change that needs to be carefully planned and implemented. This chapter presents a method for introducing BAM practices and illustrates it by some examples. The method is based on BAM concepts itself. As such, it basically follows the business architecture framework described in the introductory chapter. The method may be used as a guideline by organizations wishing to exploit the full potential of BAM for the sake of sustained value creation.

15.1 Introduction

In the previous chapters, the value potential of business architecture management (BAM) has been demonstrated through various application scenarios and case studies. However, to realize these benefits in a particular organization, BAM practices need to be established first. Given that BAM is still an immature and less well-known discipline, this may be a difficult task in itself. As a matter of fact, only few organizations have successfully mastered the implementation of BAM practices thus far. Therefore, this chapter proposes a method for implementing business architecture management in a systematic way.

C. Schmidt (✉)
Scape Consulting GmbH, Frankfurt, Germany
e-mail: christian.schmidt@scape-consulting.de

D. Simon
Scape Consulting GmbH, Cologne, Germany
e-mail: daniel.simon@scape-consulting.de

© Springer International Publishing Switzerland 2015
D. Simon, C. Schmidt (eds.), *Business Architecture Management*, Management for Professionals, DOI 10.1007/978-3-319-14571-6_15

15.2   Applying Business Architecture to Business Architecture

Implementing business architecture management represents a major organizational change that needs to be consistently managed across the whole enterprise. In order to create value for its stakeholders, the BAM function must fit the particular context and requirements of the enterprise. This is of special importance as implementing BAM will generally lead to additional coordination efforts. In economic terms, implementing BAM can therefore only be justified if these additional efforts are offset by the long-term value created. Moreover, BAM needs to be properly positioned and anchored within the organization in order to become fully effective and reach the attained goals. Naturally, this will relate to processes and decision rules as well as the appropriate information technology (IT) support.

To achieve all this, the method proposed in this chapter is based on business architecture concepts itself. Central to the method is a process model describing the steps required to implement BAM in a given organization. This process model may be considered an extension of existing good practices for implementing enterprise IT architecture management functions as described in "The Open Group Architecture Framework" (TOGAF) (The Open Group 2011), for example. It is complemented by some special techniques to address typical challenges during the implementation process (see Sect. 15.6).

A high-level view of the process model is depicted in Fig. 15.1. It is comprised of two main stages. In stage 1, the BAM function is architected according to the needs of the organization. This broadly follows the structure of the BAM framework as presented in Chap. 1. Stage 2 then addresses the stepwise implementation of the required BAM capabilities. The following sections describe each stage in some more detail and outline the main steps to be taken.

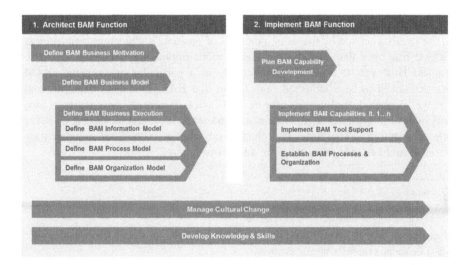

Fig. 15.1 Process model (high-level view)

15.3   Architecting the Business Architecture Management Function

In stage 1, the business architecture of the BAM function is developed. According to this book's BAM framework, this needs to start with the business motivation. In the context of BAM this means answering the question of why to do BAM at all and which objectives to follow. Based on that, the business model of BAM can be derived. In particular, this will ask for the potential consumers of BAM services, the value to be created, and the parties to be involved in the process of value creation. Finally, the business model is to be translated into a business execution architecture. This is to answer which capabilities are required and how they are to be implemented in terms of roles, processes, and information technology.

The approach followed is in line with lean management principles, since only those capabilities are planned and implemented that are actually needed to attain the defined objectives. The following sections describe the individual phases in some more detail.

15.3.1 Business Motivation: Setting Mission and Objectives for BAM

Every organization is different. Such differences may be due to the specific industry, management, and culture, but also to the maturity of the organization and the achieved level of strategy implementation. Hence, before applying the full range of business architecture concepts and tools, the specific context and needs of the particular organization should be identified and analyzed. For example, a company subject to a radically changing business environment may have a substantial need for continually advancing its business model and translating it into new organizational capabilities. An organization operating under stable market conditions, on the other hand, might put more emphasis on achieving and maintaining operational excellence. Therefore, in this case, BAM might be more focused on capability management and business process optimization, in particular.

It is the purpose of the first phase to set the right scope for BAM and identify the mission and objectives. To attain this, the internal (e.g., existing capabilities) and external drivers (e.g., market forces) and constraints need to be analyzed. This step should include a thorough *analysis of the possible stakeholders* of the BAM function and their respective concerns. Stakeholders are any individuals or groups within (or even outside) the organization that may have an interest in business architecture management or that might be affected by its operation. Typical stakeholders to be considered include board members, top-level business line managers, strategy and corporate development teams, chief financial officers (CFO), controllers, and chief information officers (CIO). In addition to these formal roles, individuals with strong influence but no formal power should be included as well.

Once the relevant stakeholders have been identified, they may be categorized by their level of influence within the organization and the level of interest they are expected to show with respect to business architecture management. This may most easily be visualized by means of a stakeholder portfolio (cf. The Open Group 2011). Based on this analysis, individual stakeholders should be approached in the order of relevance.

For each stakeholder or stakeholder group, specific interests and concerns should then be identified (cf. Kurpjuweit and Winter 2009). This may be achieved by asking for current topics of interest, personal incentives, and ideas on how the organization could improve. Such information may be collected most effectively in the form of small workshops and interviews. As part of these, stakeholders should first be introduced to the main concepts and general value proposition of business architecture management. This marks an important first step towards a successful adoption and proliferation of business architecture concepts and a corresponding architectural mindset (see Sect. 15.5). For this purpose, typical use cases/services of BAM should be presented, including possible deliverables (in terms of views of the architecture) and the questions to be answered by these (see, e.g., Fig. 15.4). This may be used to stimulate ideas and and give stakeholders a better understanding of what business architecture management can actually deliver to them and, at the same time, identify and discharge use cases that are perceived to be of less relevance. At this stage, a catalog of typical use cases/services and viewpoints to pick from may prove to be a valuable asset.[1]

Based on the results of the analysis, the mission of the BAM function can be defined (see Fig. 15.2 for an example). The scope of this may vary considerably ranging from a complete coverage of the business architecture framework to a more narrow approach focusing on certain areas (e.g., capability management).

In addition, the goals and objectives of business architecture management should be described based on the prioritized concerns. Typical goals may be to maximize strategic consistency, and to minimize the resulting business complexity. The role of complexity, in particular, may vary depending on the business environment and the general strategy (see Chap. 13). The high-level goals should then be translated into more operational and measurable objectives (e.g., minimize functional redundancy) and business architecture principles to help realize these objectives (see, e.g., Fig. 15.3). Principles are an important instrument to guide decision making and support architectural governance. However, they should be defined carefully and, as indicated earlier in this book (see Chap. 2), clearly related back to goals and objectives; this means there should be, among others, a clear statement of the (strategic) motivation in addition to the description of the principle's meaning and implications (cf. The Open Group 2011; Greefhorst and Proper 2011).

Finally, as a second means to help realize goals and objectives, appropriate strategies can be identified and evaluated (e.g., launch of a specific service offering, the implementation of a multi-channel communication to provide transparency of

---

[1] This is similar to what Buckl et al. (2008) provide for the enterprise IT architecture space.

> **Example: BAM Mission**
>
> The mission of business architecture management is to support the development of the business strategies within the entire group based on internal and external conditions, to integrate these strategies into consistent business models,and to translate these into the required business capabilities.

Fig. 15.2 BAM mission (example)

> **Example: BAM Principle**
>
> Non-strategic business capabilities are globally unique and implemented only once throughout the whole organization.

Fig. 15.3 BAM principle (example)

the architecture, etc.). This is likely to go hand in hand with the design of the business model as outlined in the following (as the business model reflects the strategic choices made to meet certain targets).

15.3.2 Business Model: Translating Stakeholder Needs into BAM Services

Once the general scope of mission and objectives has been set, the business model of BAM can be defined. That is, the *fundamental logic of value creation* is to be outlined. Again, a stakeholder-oriented approach should be followed, this time focusing on the actual consumers of BAM services though, including the value proposition to be offered. Therefore, the identified results of the stakeholder analysis may need to be revisited and translated into decisive service requirements. This may make additional workshops on a more detailed level necessary (to include lower-level hierarchies, for example). Based on a prioritization of the identified service requirements, the service portfolio of business architecture management and the associated deliverables can be derived. This is of particular relevance as business architecture comprises a broad range of concepts which may have different levels of relevance and value for different organizations. In this sense, tailoring the service portfolio to the specific needs of the organization is key in keeping business architecture management lean and focused.

After the services have been defined, the parties to be involved in the processes of service delivery (see below) and the general operating model of the BAM function can be determined. In many cases, a group-wide approach will be the first choice, integrating all relevant business units in a unified model. In this setting, the business managers of different lines of businesses participate in a group-wide effort to manage the business architecture holistically. However, this may be unfeasible in a more decentralized type of organization; this is where a replication model employing separate instances of BAM functions may be more viable (at least to start with).

Configuring business architecture management's overall chain of value creation also involves a proper design of the supply side. This is essentially about identifying the roles and organizational units who need to be involved as providers of architectural information required to create views and thus deliver the envisioned services. To some extent, these suppliers may also need to become consumers of BAM services to make them take the effort. It is thus essential to have clearly defined value propositions for all stakeholders involved. Finally, for both the supply and demand side of business architecture management, there should be proper communication channels that allow for a straightforward exchange of information and consumption of services. Channels such as wikis, blogs, and document management tools may hence be identified as essential parts of the business model (to be detailed in terms of software products etc. in later stages).

Finally, business model design should also involve a discussion of the core assets of the BAM function. For example, to fulfil the exemplary mission provided in Fig. 15.2 and thus take over an active part in strategy development, multiple core assets are required. These include the architecture model/descriptions as a unique knowledge base that can be used to evaluate choices, a strong network within the enterprise that allows to interconnect different stakeholders (see Sect. 15.6.4), but also dedicated capabilities related to strategy development. This leads over to the definition of the overall set of required BAM capabilities as outlined in the following section.

15.3.3 Business Execution: Architecting the BAM Capabilities

After the service portfolio has been defined, the *capabilities* needed to provide the services have to be identified and their implementation has to be architected. For instance, a base capability "manage business architecture model" may be identified. In addition, core capabilities such as "lead strategy development" or, according to the use case presented in Fig. 15.4, "perform strategic evaluation of project portfolio," need to be defined. These are then translated into the necessary *processes*, *organizational structures*, and *information objects* (the latter of which need to be eventually implemented in an adequate tool environment).

15.3.3.1 Defining the BAM Information Model

An important aspect of business architecture management is to describe the different architectural components and their interrelations in a structured way (i.e., in a content metamodel). This is a prerequisite for identifying and eliminating inconsistencies. As with IT architecture, a formal model will be beneficial, as it allows for a systematic capturing and stringent analysis of the architectural information. Although the number of entities and artifacts especially in the higher-level domains of the business architecture may be limited, a shared repository will strongly increase transparency and efficiency in managing the data.

Example: BAM Use Case / Service

- Use Case: Ensure Strategic Alignment of the Project Portfolio
- Deliverables: Architecture Review of Project Portfolio
- Viewpoints: Investment Heat Map, Portfolio Map
- Stakeholders: Portfolio Manager, LoB Manager, Executive BoardMembers, etc.
- Value Contribution: Optimize Investments Based on Strategic Priority

---

Fig. 15.4 BAM use case (example)

Therefore, in this phase, the required information objects (and related tool support) need to be defined. Following lean management principles, these should be derived from the relevant services and viewpoints as identified in the previous step (cf. Kurpjuweit and Winter 2009). For example, the delivery of the service "ensure strategic alignment of the project portfolio"—and hence the creation of views such as an "investment heat map" (see Fig. 15.4)—requires "project" and "business capability" objects as well as a relationship like "project operates on business capability" to be part of the information model (cf. Aier et al. 2008). Rather than crafting the information model from scratch, a reference model should be used and tailored by eliminating the elements and relationships that are not required. In the absence of a fully defined reference model, the business architecture framework presented in Chap. 1 may be used as a starting point.

15.3.3.2 Defining the BAM Process Model

In this step, the processes needed to implement the business architecture management capabilities are designed. Typically, this will include both planning- and governance-related tasks. Planning processes describe the activities and participating roles in defining a consistent future state of the business architecture or parts thereof (e.g., "target business model planning"). Governance processes, on the other hand, are used to ensure that the defined target architectures are actually implemented. For example, a process for architectural reviews of projects and initiatives may be defined, including the required process interfaces and involved roles. Beyond that, support processes like capturing and maintaining the architecture information and delivering views and analyses are generally required.

When defining the process model, special emphasis should be put on the interactions between the BAM core processes and any related business processes. Even more like with IT architecture management, BAM cannot be carried out in isolation, but must be fully embedded into any "plan and build" processes. A process for reviewing the project portfolio and individual project ideas, for example, needs to interface with project portfolio and project management processes (cf. Simon et al. 2013). Special care should also be taken to ensure that business architecture management is properly integrated with IT architecture management.

15.3.3.3 Defining the BAM Organization Model

In parallel to the processes, appropriate roles and organizational units need to be defined for taking over BAM-related tasks. This typically includes a core team (or competence center) for managing the core processes and maintaining the related methodology and tool sets. However, as with processes, it is of high relevance that existing roles and organizational units are properly integrated so that BAM actually reaches into the whole organization (and is not turned into an "ivory tower"—a phenomenon that is well known from the IT architecture management field). To that end, a collaborative approach using local business architects in the various business functions may be appropriate. Key to this, however, is to develop a culture that is characterized by open-mindedness and mutual trust and in which BAM is understood as a joint endeavor. In addition, existing committees should be reviewed in terms of whether there should be any BAM participation. For example, it may be reasonable for a representative of the BAM function to become a member of the project portfolio board (if existing) to realize the service "ensure strategic alignment of the project portfolio." Of course, also incentives need to be set and appropriate controls be implemented. This may include the definition of appropriate key performance indicators.

It is important to note that, to account for the wide spectrum of business architecture content (from business motivation to execution), different BAM roles may be required. Again, this depends on the services to be provided by the BAM function. For example, in case of a comprehensive approach that operates on the business architecture as a whole, it may be reasonable to distinguish between a "strategy architect" for the higher-level domains and a "capability architect" for the lower-level domains of the business architecture. With the defined roles and organizational structures, the BAM organization finally needs to be adequately sized. This is a crucial prerequisite for the BAM function to be appropriately staffed as part of the second stage.

15.4   Implementing Business Architecture Capabilities

In stage 2, the required business architecture capabilities are actually implemented. As described earlier, this needs to address at least the information, the process, and the organizational dimension.

15.4.1 Planning Capability Development

When it comes to capability implementation, there is no need for a big bang approach. To mitigate risks, capabilities should rather be implemented in iterations, with each iteration addressing a defined set of capabilities or capability levels. However, capability implementation should be carried out according to the priorities identified within the previous steps. Hence, a *roadmap for capability implementation* should be defined as part of this activity. A capability radar that spans the relevant capability dimensions can be used to plan and track the development of a capability along various increments towards full implementation (cf. The Open Group 2011).

15.4.2 Implementing a Tool Set

As pointed out in Sect. 15.3.3.1, a structured model of the architecture is also recommended for the domain of business architecture. Tool support in form of a *repository* will be of great value for managing the model, collecting the required data, and creating the relevant views. Beyond that, it may be used to plan the future architecture, to analyze gaps, and to plan the transition.

While business and IT architectures may be managed separately using only inputs from each other, an integrated approach is generally preferrable due to the large number of dependencies. Therefore, when introducing business architecture management, existing tool sets from the domain of enterprise IT architecture should be analyzed first. If there are no major constraints, the existing solution may best be adapted and enhanced to comprise the business architecture layer as well. Only in cases in which this is unfeasible, a new tool selection process should be initiated.

Both the assessment of existing tools and the selection of a new tool should be based on the requirements defined with respect to information, process, and organization model. However, special emphasis will usually be on the tool's capabilities to implement the information model and to provide the required views. Beyond that, non-functional requirements like usability, flexibility, complexity, and cost should be taken into consideration as well.

In line with the capability implementation roadmap, the tool implementation may be carried out in multiple iterations. In particular, the information model may be refined stepwise starting from a very much focused model that is further detailed in later stages of BAM implementation.

15.4.3 Establishing BAM Processes and Organization

Hand in hand with the tool implementation, the required processes and elements of primary and secondary organization need to be created according to the architecture blueprint defined in stage 1. This will generally include the roll-out of planning, governance, and support processes. Beyond that, roles and decision-making bodies need to be established and staffed. Again, an incremental approach may be followed, as defined in the capability development roadmap.

Information workshops are a proven instrument to ensure that all relevant stakeholders are informed about the changes taking place. This may be combined with a demonstration of the tool and the deliverables that can be created based on this. In general, the roll-out of the BAM processes and organization should be carefully planned and supported by a thorough change management as described in the following section.

15.5   Managing Change and Developing Skills

Implementing business architecture management represents a major organizational change. As such, it needs to be supported by an overarching *change management*. Generally, this includes measures to "unfreeze" the existing organization, make the required changes, and then "freeze" the new state. Change management should be addressed right from the start and accompany the full implementation process. From a change management perspective, the stakeholder interviews and workshops conducted in stage 1 provide a good opportunity to activate stakeholders and to set expectations for the steps to follow. Similarly, the roll-out workshops of stage 2 may be used to demonstrate results and collect feedback. After all, the stakeholders' acceptance of the new processes and tools will be key to BAM implementation success.

Change management should be complemented by dedicated *training courses*. Such courses may form an essential element to promote business architecture methodology throughout the organization and to develop the required skills. In addition, these courses may be used as a reasonable starting point for initiating and establishing a business architecture community within the organization. This may include regular meetings, in which any individuals interested in business architecture may participate and may have the chance to be informed about new deliverables, discuss, ask particular questions, contribute ideas, communicate desires, and increase their general understanding of business architecture management. Finally, in addition to training courses, on-the-job training and hospitations (e.g., in certain business domains) should be taken into consideration for skill development; in particular, this is not only to learn the methodology but also to obtain the required knowledge of the architecture.

15.6   Dealing with Specific Challenges

In this section, some of the typical challenges encountered when introducing business architecture management are presented and hints are given how they may be overcome.

15.6.1 Finding the Right Level of Formalization

One particular problem when discussing business architecture concepts derives from the different mindsets of the stakeholders involved. While IT managers are used to a formalization of problems and solutions, business line manager may be more "hands-on" in nature (cf. van Gils 2009; Simon et al. 2014). In addition, some stakeholders may even be afraid of the transparency and traceability created by BAM practices and the formal models behind. For example, there may be fears of weaknesses being disclosed to the public (see below) or of losing power due to an elimination of personal knowledge advantages. Beyond that, there may also be

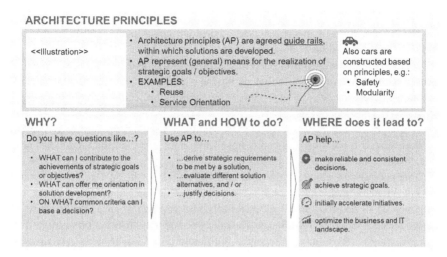

Fig. 15.5 Communication template (example)

worries about individual solutions (and the degrees of freedom associated with these) being removed or at least questioned from an enterprise-wide point of view.

While some formalization is required to reap the benefits of an architectural approach and facilitate decision making, overformalization should be avoided, especially when it comes to discussions with non-architects. This entails the use of communication means that are of a less formal character (than "classical" architectural views). Above all, target-group specific communication is essential to gain the required understanding and acceptance.

An initial part of this are easy-to-understand depictions of what certain architectural constructs are about and what they may be used for. One-pagers incorporating visuals and ideas from storytelling have proven to be valuable for this purpose. Figure 15.5 provides a corresponding template, using the "architecture principle" as an example. Once there are defined and agreed business architecture principles, one may also consider the development of some sort of coherent "story" across the whole principles set (again supported by visuals, and using analogies and metaphors from any other fields) as a means to introduce the principles in a way that is memorable and allows for actually reaching the stakeholders.

15.6.2 How to Overcome Stakeholder Objection and Mitigate Risks

As indicated before, a particular problem when introducing business architecture management is getting the buy-in of all major stakeholders. This buy-in is of crucial importance for BAM success. If key players do not commit to and support the change associated with the "new" approach, business architecture management will not become fully effective. In practice, however, it is quite common that certain stakeholders oppose a unified approach to strategic planning. This is most likely the case for the managers of specific business lines, who may favor a silo thinking and tend to keep their business domains separate.

To tackle this, strong top-management support is indispensable. Also, special initiatives to demonstrate the value of business architecture management and to convince these business leaders may be worth the effort (including, e.g., roadshows). To support this, *success stories* should be documented and used for (internal) marketing purposes as soon as first tangible results have been achieved. In addition, shared leadership goals may help counteract silo-thinking tendencies and make architecture "everyone's business."

There may also be concerns that formally documenting the business architecture bears a security risk. This should be taken serious and measures should be implemented to address this issue. After all, disclosing an organization's strategy and business model may represent a considerable security threat. Competitors, for example, may easily clone the business architecture or analyze it for weaknesses and possible points of attack. Therefore, a secure infrastructure for the business architecture model needs to be set up. In addition, and this may need to be pointed out clearly to the top management, access to the business architecture content (at least the business motivation and model parts) may be restricted to a limited audience if considered necessary. The tool set will thus need to bring along differentiated options of role-based access.

A final issue with respect to stakeholder acceptance is the organizational anchoring of business architecture management. Especially organizations that already have an IT architecture management function in place tend to establish business architecture management in the IT unit as well. This may be reasonable given the fact that IT people are more familiar with model-based approaches and may come up with immediate translations into IT. However, it may strongly impede the acceptance "in the business"—the area where BAM practices should actually be effective. If not at least some part of the BAM function is organizationally positioned outside the IT unit, it may become a frustrating exercise and a very long way to gain the required stakeholder acceptance (cf. Hobbs 2012). In addition, BAM may never be able to progress to a state in which it can really act as an accepted partner in shaping the business, going beyond the latter's capturing as a sole context for IT architecture management.

15.6.3 Coping with an IT-Biased Understanding of EA Management

In the past, many organizations set up their EA management functions in an IT-oriented way. This may in fact be reasonable following the concern-oriented approach introduced earlier. If EA management is initially driven by IT concerns, such a focus is valid to start with. However, it is essential to properly communicate right from the beginning that EA management in general goes far beyond the IT and/or to dedicatedly coin the initial setup "enterprise IT architecture management." Otherwise business architecture management, once to be properly established in a further step, will be confronted with an understanding of the term "architecture management" that is completely IT-focused and makes a progression into the business a challenging exercise (see the previous subsection).

In organizations where such an IT-biased understanding has developed, a deliberate decision may be made to "cut off" from the existing function and establish business architecture management in a completely separate way to avoid any affiliation with IT (in consequence, BAM would then be different from EAM). This may also be reflected in the function's title by avoiding the use of the term "architecture." Such a strict separation, however, bears the risk that business and IT architecture will be managed in isolation resulting in a poor alignment of the two. In the end, the two separate functions would still operate on areas that are part of a common enterprise architecture, and it is widely acknowledged that this is all about the relations between different domains or layers. Therefore, special care must then be taken to define interfaces and ensure that an overall architecture community is created.

On the other hand, if business architecture management is to be established as part of an overall enterprise architecture management, it needs to be introduced as such, pointing out that the former will offer additional services that the existing, IT-focused approach was not able to provide. Again, this is unlikely to work if the BAM function is established as part of the IT unit. All constituents of the existing EA management that were labelled as such but actually only represented the IT architecture part will need to be renamed as soon as possible in this case. Training courses and special marketing efforts will be necessary to help rebrand EA management as a whole and point out the particular value proposition of business architecture management.

15.6.4 Making Business Architecture Management a Collaborative Approach

To be successful in the long run, again even more than this is the case for IT architecture management, business architecture management has to become a collaborative effort. Apparently, as already pointed out in Chap. 12, no single individual—not even from a central BAM department, in which many generalists may be assembled—will ever bear enough knowledge about relevant details of different business domains to go at it alone. Therefore, it is crucial that business architects develop a unique network within the enterprise that allows them to act as some sort of "gatekeepers" who can bring together projects working on similar subjects, pass on requests to suitable subject matter experts, catch up and inform about new developments and decisions, moderate in cross-domain initiatives, and so on. Of course, this rather informal part needs to be complemented by the "formal" integration of business architecture management with related processes (as already outlined earlier).

15.7   Conclusion

This final chapter has presented a method for implementing business architecture
management in a given organization. The method broadly follows best practices for
EA management setup and is based on business architecture concepts itself. In
particular, it has been shown how the BAM function may be architected based on
the specific conditions and requirements at hand, thereby ensuring maximum value
creation at minimum costs. Using this book's business architecture framework, it
has been illustrated how the main components of a successful BAM practice may be
developed in a systematic way, covering all aspects from the business motivation
(BAM mission, BAM objectives, BAM principles, etc.) and the business model
(BAM services, BAM service consumers, etc.) down to the business execution
(BAM capabilities, BAM processes, etc.). Beyond that, it has been demonstrated
how BAM practices can be implemented in a stepwise manner, ensuring quick wins
and mitigating implementation risks. Ultimately, the importance of an overarching
change management and skill development has been pointed out and hints have
been provided on how to tackle specific challenges. The proposed method may
serve as a guideline for organizations planning to employ business architecture
management in order to create sustained value for their stakeholders.

References

Aier S, Maletta F, Riege C, Stucki K, Frank A (2008) Aufbau und Einsatz der Geschäftsarchitektur
    bei der AXA Winterthur—Ein minimal invasiver Ansatz. In: Proceedings der DW2008:
    Synergien durch Integration und Informationslogistik
Buckl S, Ernst AM, Lankes J, Matthes F (2008) Enterprise architecture management pattern
    catalogue. TU Munich, Chair for Informatics 19 (sebis), Munich
Greefhorst D, Proper E (2011) Architecture principles: the cornerstones of enterprise architecture.
    Springer, Berlin
Hobbs G (2012) EAM governance and organisation. In: Ahlemann F, Stettiner E,
    Messerschmidt M, Legner C (eds) Strategic enterprise architecture management—challenges,
    best practices, and future developments. Springer, Berlin, pp 35–53
Kurpjuweit S, Winter R (2009) Concern-oriented business architecture engineering. In:
    Proceedings of SAC 2009. ACM Press, New York, pp 265–272
Simon D, Fischbach K, Schoder D (2013) Integrating IT portfolio management with enterprise
    architecture management. Enterp Model Inf Syst Archit 8(2):79–104
Simon D, Fischbach K, Schoder D (2014) Enterprise architecture management and its role in
    corporate strategic management. Inf Syst e-Bus Manag 12(1):5–42
The Open Group (2011) TOGAF® version 9.1. Van Haren Publishing, Zaltbommel
van Gils B (2009) Strategy and architecture—reconciling worldviews. In: Proper E, Harmsen F,
    Dietz J (eds) Advances in enterprise engineering II, first NAF academy working conference on
    practice-driven research on enterprise transformation (PRET 2009), held at CAiSE 2009,
    Amsterdam, The Netherlands, 11 June 2009. Springer, Berlin, pp 181–196

Index

© Springer International Publishing Switzerland 2015
D. Simon, C. Schmidt (eds.), *Business Architecture Management*, Management for Professionals, DOI 10.1007/978-3-319-14571-6